MASTERING SCHOOL REFORM

GEORGE A. GOENS
Wauwatosa Public Schools

SHARON I. R. CLOVER
*New Jersey State Department
of Education*

Allyn and Bacon
Boston London Toronto Sydney Tokyo Singapore

Various quotes throughout the text by John Gardner are from *Excellence* by permission of W. W. Norton & Company, Inc. Copyright © 1984, 1961 by John Gardner.

Copyright © 1991 by Allyn and Bacon
A Division of Simon & Schuster, Inc.
160 Gould Street
Needham Heights, Massachusetts 02194

Library of Congress Cataloging-in-Publication Data
Goens, George A.
    Mastering school reform/George A. Goens, Sharon I. R. Clover.
      p. cm.
    Includes bibliographical references and index.
    ISBN 0-205-12699-5
    1. School management and organization—United States.
2. Leadership. I. Clover, Sharon I. R. II. Title.
LB2805.G538   1991
371.2'00973—dc20   90–43820
                                           CIP

Printed in the United States of America
10 9 8 7 6 5 4 3 2 1   94 93 92 91 90

We are products of our heredity and environment. The environment in which we have chosen to live and work has influenced our perceptions about education and our thinking about the need for transformation of schools. We have also recognized the importance of communication as a vehicle for understanding, so we have attempted to share our visions and dreams with all our professional colleagues—to be genuine, sensitive, and trustworthy in pursuing what is best for future generations. This book, which is the result of our behavior, is proudly dedicated to our parents:

Earl and Stephanie Goens
John and Irene Rozewicz

Their spirit, dedication, perseverance, optimism, and love are interwoven in us, their children. Thank you.

Brief Contents

Contents

Preface

In a world where knowledge is power, our schools are one of this nation's greatest resources. By *power*, we not only mean force in the competitive marketplace and in economics, government, and society, but also in the affairs of citizenship, personal accomplishments, and employment. For a nation like the United States to survive and prosper, it must have effective means to communicate its culture, produce literate citizens and workers, and develop creative thinkers who will generate and apply new ideas, theories, and knowledge.

According to many educational reform proposals, public schools are not meeting the needs of the nation or its children. Change has been proposed by presidents, education secretaries, governors, legislators, and a panoply of others—conservatives, liberals, and moderates. Despite the studies and directives, however, schools remain much the same. Why? And what can be done about it?

Many of the reforms advocate a single solution or tackle only a part of the problem, as if schools were monolithic, rational organizations that respond to isolated strategies. If teachers do not have enough power, empower them and the problems will disappear. If schools are too bureaucratic, decentralize them and they will be more personal and responsive. If the leader is ineffective, change his or her style to match the situation and all the people will follow. If performance is the problem, provide choice and competition and schools will improve instantly.

However, schools are complex socio-technical-political institutions, wrapped in diverse expectations by a broad and demanding public and operated under state and local legislation and policies that are subject to short-term and inconsistent priorities. In many states, school structures were designed at the time of statehood or, in the case of the northeastern and Atlantic states, during the early roots of American history. Times, demands, and society have changed, but most schools have not.

Part of the problem is the segmentalist view of change and the limited way it is proposed. There are no single levers that can be pulled in schools to create an avalanche of change—certainly not permanent or meaningful change. The organization itself, the leadership, and the human resources must be viewed as interconnected components of the change process. A second problem is the bandwagon change efforts that have come and gone, each promising a solution that will make teachers' lives better, cause students to learn more, and create a better society. But the only lasting outcomes these efforts have had are turning teachers into wary cynics of change and leaders into managers because of the pressure for instantaneous results and the lack of true support and training.

Mastering School Reform takes a different approach to the transformation of schools, involving broad-based change in how school organizations, their leaders, and staff perceive, think, and behave. Transforming organizations, leadership, and people for success is the goal of this text. The ultimate criterion for judging the success of an organization is determining how effectively it meets its mission and goals over time and in different contexts.

Success is essential for organizational survival. Successful institutions promote and produce quality and create an internal climate for optimum productivity. These issues, which form the basis for meeting the organization's mission, often go unmeasured. Successful organizations transform themselves and those who work in them. They are self-renewing—rising to challenges, adapting to new conditions, and altering programs to fulfill their values. They have leaders who create conditions for growth and expansion, provide a sense of purpose, and allow people to meet their own needs while fulfilling the goals of the system. Transformation moves beyond the restructuring of roles and the issues of governance and power.

This book is divided into five parts. Part I, the introduction, sets the context for change, explores the importance of perception and thinking, defines transformation, and discusses quality, productivity, and success. Part II reviews organizations in general and schools in particular. The components of transforming organizations are specified and the structures and context that promote change are discussed. Part III focuses on the importance of leadership on perception, thinking, and behavior of organizations and the people who work in them. Various approaches to leadership are considered from an historical perspective and the case for transformational leadership is developed. Part IV explains how people function in organizations. The growth and development of adults is discussed and the needs and roles of professionals are emphasized. Staff development, inservice education, and supervision are presented in the context of transformation. Empowerment, participation, and ethical practice are examined as they relate to educational practitioners. Part V, the final section, summarizes how transforming schools function to meet the quality and productivity requirements for successful programs. Major perceptions and behavior are defined for schools to transform to meet the demands of the future and to ensure posterity for our children.

Interspersed throughout the chapters are Transformations into Practice (TIPs). The purpose of the TIPs is to interject material conceptually related, but not critical, to the text of the various chapters. The ideas are presented to raise questions and even cause perceptual discomfort, to encourage divergent thinking. TIPs may be practical representations of theories or challenging dilemmas for educators to consider.

Having collectively spent nearly 50 years in education, we have concluded that the systems are not working and the structures will not facilitate the innovations necessary for new kinds of learning. We are concerned that time is running out—if educators keep tinkering with insignificant changes and do not attack the big issues, U.S. public education will be doomed. These important issues include, but are not limited to:

- Governance of school districts—school boards, budget votes, and overregulation
- Unionization of professionals
- Students' attitudes toward the value of education
- Rigidity of structures, contracts, and mandates
- Failure to embrace technology as a significant organizational and learning tool
- Outmoded teaching practices
- Stifling, segmented curriculum and programs
- Narrow concepts of accountability and assessment
- Separation of schools from the environment that should enhance learning
- Lack of commitment/recognition from all parts of society as to the importance of a fully educated populace

We want to shake people's perceptions and influence their thinking in broad, new directions, and we believe the concepts in this book can accomplish that purpose. But it is not enough simply to change perceptions and thinking. We cannot just raise issues and ask provocative questions. There is also an obligation to describe possible solutions, create models and examples that translate theory into practice, and suggest behavior that will make transformation a reality.

This book succeeds only if it is useful to readers. The concepts, transformation-into-practice sections, illustrated figures, and detailed descriptions provide realistic and practical translations of the complex, sophisticated material that we are addressing.

Mastering School Reform is a positive and hopeful book. It serves as an initial step in the transformation process, which presents dilemmas, issues, and proposals—but it gives no recipes. There is no way to transform education once and for all and be done with it, because change is dynamic and continuous. Transformation is built on the fundamental principles of assessment, responsiveness to new conditions, adaptable and flexible structures, and open-minded thinking. None of these notions fit into a checklist. We can't give you directions to the nearest transforming school, because each place should feel, look, think, and behave differently, depending on the needs, visions, and missions established.

Instead, we attempt to connect organizations, leadership, and people synergistically through perception, thinking, and behavior to create a vision that will make education a successful, productive enterprise for the twenty-first century. We invite you to join us in this exciting and important work to benefit all the children to come.

We owe a great deal of gratitude to the many audiences who have listened and reacted to our ideas, to colleagues who encouraged us in this venture, to the dedicated reviewers who contributed insight and improved the entire manuscript, and to our competent editors who worked diligently with us to produce the final product. Finally, our deepest appreciation goes to our patient families—Mary, Betsy, Curtis, David, and Adam—who tolerated and supported us once again in our passion for writing.

PART

I INTRODUCTION

Reform movements are complex and sometimes confusing. They are designed by many parties of differing philosophies and occasionally are aimed at contradictory ends. Many proposed changes view schools as organizational structures that operate independently of outside influences and demands. And frequently, the reforms are directed at structures and behavior that do not bring about any lasting change.

The beginning of this section reviews the context of schools, the changes in the private sector, and the influences that will affect the operation and outcome of public schools. The concept of transformation is introduced in Chapter 1 and expanded in Chapter 2. The second chapter is more abstract and filled with definitions of the components of transformational approaches to reform. The reader may want to refer to Chapter 2 while reading the rest of the book. To understand the process of transformation fully, the components of perception and thought must be understood.

The last chapter of this section explores the results of transformational reform. Chapter 3 specifies the concept of the successful school, which moves beyond effectiveness and into the complexities of comprehensive programs. Success is a commonly used concept, but one that is not clearly defined. Successful institutions promote and produce quality and create an internal climate for optimum growth and productivity. Quality and productivity, the values that undergird transformation and should be part and parcel of schools, are also discussed.

1 | Schools: Challenge and Opportunity

Public schools cannot exist as cocoons, isolated from a changing environment and climate. Demands and expectations have increased, creating challenges to the schools' core values, organizational structure, and mission. Although schools have never been at the forefront of innovation, they have been the conduit for the complexities and problems of social change and turmoil. For each issue, whether racism, economic competitiveness, drug and alcohol abuse, or changes in family structure, schools are proposed as the solution by politicians, academicians, and educators themselves.

Groucho Marx said, "It is not so much that hard times are coming; the change observed is mostly soft times going." Groucho's perspective can well be applied to the conditions our school systems are currently facing. The "soft times," when U.S. education was viewed as the best internationally in promoting literacy and creating the great "melting pot," are gone.

Today's world is not as neat and clean as it seemed to be after World War II, when the United States stood as an economic and industrial monolith and the sole nuclear military power. U.S. ingenuity and prosperity were the result of a first-rate system of public education. Now, the view of the world "in which everything worked with clockwork precision has given way to acceptance of a more volatile, chaotic world in which such order does not exist" (Sculley, 1987a, p. 399). The unprecedented prosperity of the 1950s and 1960s gave way to plant shutdowns, loss of market share in critical industries, trade deficits, increased foreign investment in U.S. property and business, and the largest national debt in the history of the world.

3

As people watched the competitiveness of the U.S. economy decline, they began to question the effectiveness of education, debating its very purpose and politicizing its operation. In the last three decades, schools have been pressured to change. They have wrestled with integration, equal opportunity, and educating children from all economic and ethnic groups. Small schools became consolidated ones in suburban and rural areas, and urban schools were faced with larger minority and poor populations. In the 1950s, desegregation focused on human relations, and Sputnik forced science and math initiatives in schools. In the 1960s, civil rights, free speech, and protests from the Viet Nam conflict questioned authority and brought social issues into school hallways. In the 1970s and 1980s, foreign economic and academic competition challenged standards and pressed for curriculum reform. Despite these crises and movements in education, classrooms have remained much the same.

Simply recognizing that schools exist in an era of change is insufficient. We need to understand the causes and conditions for those changes so that we can anticipate their implications for educational practice and create responsive, successful schools for the twenty-first century.

THE LARGER CONTEXT

Charlie Brown, the Peanuts character, stated, "No problem is so big and complicated that it can't be run away from." Today's problems cause frustration and the feeling that they are too convoluted to resolve. But schools cannot run from them; they must respond and adapt if they are to be successful.

Ignoring the problems or clinging to the past will be disastrous to society and schools. Unthinking and strict adherence to the structures that made our country great can spell its very decline. "A society that has reached the heights of excellence may already be caught in the rigidities" that can bring it down (Gardner, 1964, p. xii). The automobile and steel industries are examples of businesses that operated under old assumptions and did not renew their approaches to marketing or production to maintain their competitive edge. As a result, plants closed and workers were displaced, victims of corporate rigidity and failure to invest in the future by making necessary changes. These businesses lost the capacity to compete and thrive in a dynamic environment driven by information, technology, and flexibility.

In 1950, Harvard sociologist Daniel Bell predicted that the most important products in postindustrial society would be information, knowledge, and services (Odiorne, 1987). His prediction proved to be accurate. Drucker (1988) states we have moved away from the "command and control" phase that was prevalent in the 1920s through the 1950s and are moving toward an "information bond" in organizations. Information sharing and availability can alter the structure and responsiveness of institutions in profound ways.

Although more information is available and accessible than ever before, making sense of it all is more difficult. Assessing what decisions or alternatives are best is a larger challenge, as more choices are available because of technology. Technology can define the "horizon of our material world as it shapes the limiting conditions of what is possible and what is barely imaginable" (Zuboff, 1988, p. 387). Successful organizations require technology, inspired and motivated people, adaptable structures that provide information, and leaders with the power to effect change.

Fundamental structural change is not easy to accomplish. The difficulty is compounded because of overspecialization. In theory, specialization is a productive and efficient concept, which emphasizes precise, deep knowledge and skills. Overspecialization, however, impedes an organization's ability to respond creatively because it restricts the broad, divergent thinking necessary to tackle issues and dilemmas, as well as define new approaches to problems.

Changing and renewing a large organization—private or public— is like changing the course of a large ship. The pilot turns the wheel but it takes a long time to see the results (Murrin, in Kilmann & Covin, 1988). A balance between respect for the roots of the past (continuity) and an orientation to the future (change) is essential for renewal. Organizational continuity can be maintained through strong values, tradition, and heritage, which ensure that change does not lead to chaos, loss of purpose, or shallow, bandwagon efforts. Yet investing in the past and valuing permanence and stability can result in organizational stagnation. Such thinking opposes natural adaptation and rebirth. Organizations that look to the future have a vivid sense of what they are becoming, not a preoccupation with what they have been (Gardner, 1964).

Change is the source of strength in the new breed of third-wave companies (Sculley, 1988). Such companies have the ability to transform their products and organization in response to different conditions. The core of strength in second-wave, industrial-based firms is stability, rank, structure, predictability, and institutional needs. The differences in second- and third-wave companies are in perception, thinking, and behavior.

SCHOOLS AND SOCIETAL CHANGES

School organizations also need to become responsive and flexible to address social, economic, and demographic conditions. People in the United States are getting older, and the population is increasing at its lowest rate ever. By the year 2000, one in every three Americans will be nonwhite. In most former immigrant generations, the young tended to do better, economically and educationally, than their parents. This trend may not continue, however. There is a growing sense of pessimism among some people in the United States about their ability to shape the future if economic opportunities decrease for their children (Hodgkinson, 1985).

Hodgkinson (1985) has written extensively about changing demographics and their impact on schools. Table 1–1 specifies the demographic profile of children attending schools today. More minority children and a greater diversity of languages are present in classrooms. A larger proportion of children from families undergoing economic or family stress means that more children with "at-risk" profiles are attending public schools. Hodgkinson warns educators not to lower educational standards but to increase efforts to ensure success for all children. These students need high levels of creativity, effort, and energy so they can find their way into the mainstream of U.S. society. Graham (1984) cautions that historically the curriculum was modified to make it easier for children with academic problems to learn. That tactic needs to

TABLE 1–1   Students: Demographic Profile

Percent	Characteristics
25	Come from families in poverty
14	Children of teenaged mothers
15	Immigrants who speak a language other than English
14	Children of unmarried parents
40	From broken homes before age 18
25–33	Latchkey children

Source: Harold L. Hodgkinson, *All One System* (Washington, DC: Institute for Educational Leadership, 1985).

be changed, and a curriculum that is filled with the subjects that endure and enlighten children should remain. The means of teaching it to all children, however, will vary.

Education is instrumental for success, as it always was, but how it is delivered must be different from that of the past. Ernest Boyer of the Carnegie Foundation indicates that classroom teaching is much the same as it was 25 years ago, but students are different (Danner, 1985). Some students have limited educational support; others are more sophisticated and skeptical, and less willing to be directed without acceptable reasons. Because students have diverse backgrounds and attitudes, making a difference in their education is more difficult. Sometimes, these "demands and expectations force a retreat to traditional methods and 'safe' practices that, ironically, don't work" (Patterson, Purkey, & Parker, 1986, p. viii). The problem is more than just what students are to be taught; it is how to commit and involve them actively in learning.

At a time when students are requiring more varied and comprehensive programs, political support for schools is also undergoing demographic change. Today, only one-fifth of our taxpayers have children in school, leaving the economic and political leverage of parents substantially diminished (Shanker, 1988).

The demographic conditions summarized in Table 1–2 illustrate that as we move into the twenty-first century, the U.S. population is getting older. The aging or "graying" of America in the next 40 years will exacerbate generational politics as competition for tax resources to support services intensifies. Between 1946 and 1964, 70 million people were born—constituting the largest "baby boom" in the country's history. As a result, many citizens had a direct stake in the operation and quality of schools.

TABLE 1–2   Society: Demographic Conditions—The Aging of America

	Year		
	1986	2000	2030
Median age of U.S. population	30	36	40+
Percent of population 65+*	11.6	12.8	21.2

Source: U.S. Census Bureau, Current Population Reports, Series P-25, 1983.
* 1983, for the first time in history the number of Americans over age 65 exceeded the number of teenagers.

In the future, however, the demographic trends indicate that an increasing percentage of citizens will have a vital interest in health, medical, and retirement services, not elementary and secondary education. Couple these data with those in Table 1–1, and the picture emerges of fewer people having a vested stake in the public schools' success at a time when more at-risk students are arriving at the schoolhouse door. Issues of funding and finding more productive ways to meet educational needs become increasingly critical.

SCHOOLS: REFORM AND RESPONSE

Some changes have been made in education since World War II. Schools are different in size and scope, in cost, in population they attempt to serve, in the range and number of objectives they set, and in the role and impact of federal, state, and local governments. These changes, however, have emphasized quantity, not quality (Ravitch, 1983). The fundamental philosophy, processes, procedures, methods, materials, and technology of education are rooted in the past. According to the Rand Corporation, "Reforms that deal with the fundamental stuff of education—teaching and learning—seem to have weak, transitory, and ephemeral effects; while those that expand, solidify, and entrench school bureaucracy seem to have strong, enduring, and concrete effects" (Elmore & McLaughlin, 1988, p. v).

Public education is an extremely conservative social institution and, in many respects, resists innovation more strongly than other segments of society (Perelman, 1987). Looking backward may not be of much assistance, other than to highlight what not to do in the future. "Old assumptions for educational reform have governed our strategies for over forty years with disappointing results. It is time to plan our future from more promising basic beliefs" (Combs, 1988, p. 40).

Demands have been made that education be changed, revitalized, restructured, retooled, and reformed. But fundamental structural change in schools has not happened, in spite of the national school reform studies and reports of the early and mid-1980s. James W. Guthries (1988) writes:

> The current reform strategy is primarily one of intensification. It assumes the conventional mode of schooling is fundamentally correct. States have written their admonitions and aspirations into legislation in the hope that this will return schools to their former state of grace, blithely ignoring the fact that, since those halcyon days, American schools have been bu-

reaucratized, standardized, centralized, homogenized, monopolized, and unionized (p. 515).

In addition, there is skepticism that spending more money on education has failed and that it is not the answer to school reform. Many of these reports use the terms *productivity, cost-effectiveness,* and *efficiency* as indicators of the need to create tangible results for increased fiscal investment and commitment.

Some think that technology will be brought to bear full force on teaching and schools, causing long-lasting change. Perelman (1988) indicates that the technology for learning is already being used in industry and the military, which gives hope that schools will be transformed imminently. Zuboff (1988) agrees, indicating that no sector of the economy will be exempt from the changes technology will bring, as well as the dilemmas it presents.

However, talking about change, even demanding it, will not cause it to happen. Change has been ordered and legislated, but practitioners resist it as they wrestle with the realities of everyday life. It is not enough to tinker with the external trappings of schooling. "A gross disparity seems to exist between the urgency of the crisis situation described in these reports and the comparative mildness, even superficiality of the proposed remedies. If a crisis of such magnitude is indeed upon us, we should be scrutinizing our schools in a more fundamental way" (Danner, 1986, p. 41). Many of these attempts at change have not worked because they were layered on old structures and did not alter perception, thinking, or behavior.

TRANSFORMATION: DEFINITION AND IMPACT

The transformation of organizations requires a paradigm shift—a shift in the perception of reality and how one thinks about it. The metaphor of a photographic lens describes this concept. A paradigm shift is a change of lens—in power or focus—through which one sees reality. Some people see the world through a wide-angle lens, observing the entire landscape and the interrelationships of all of the flora and fauna in the picture. Other individuals view the world through a high-powered lens, emphasizing one shrub and its immediate environment. The lens, or paradigm, through which you view the world, focuses your perception of reality and defines your pattern of thought.

Getting an organization to change its paradigm is very challenging. It is stressful and controversial because reality itself may appear in doubt (Perelman, 1987). Transformation requires a new perspective. "Organizations designed to provide goods and services in yesterday's world are discovering that what made them successful in the past no longer applies" (p. xiii). In transformation, organizations examine what they were, what they are, what they need to be, and how to make the required changes.

Kilmann and Covin (1988) define organizational transformation as "serious, large scale change that demands new ways of perceiving, thinking, and behaving by all members of the organization" (pp. xiii–xiv). Without a change in perception, educators cannot revise their thinking, incorporate different viewpoints, and alter their behavior. Behavior will not change unless people perceive the need to apply new ideas. Combs (1988) agrees that to change behavior effectively, educational reform must concentrate on altering the belief systems of the people who make the decisions and do the work. Emphasizing gadgets or methods will have little long-term impact. The causes of behavior lie in the people's perceptions or personal meanings—especially in the beliefs they hold about them, the situations they are in, and the goals and values they seek to fulfill.

Transformation is not a "fix" but a new way of managing internal and external resources of the system. It is concerned with continuity and discontinuity, juncture and disjuncture, the past and the possible. Transformation implies continuous adaptation to changing circumstances and environment.

Some educational reforms have called for restructuring schools; *restructuring* is not *transformation*. The definitions and antecedents of these words demonstrate some fundamental differences in scope and focus. *Reorganization* and *renewal* are also words that have been used synonymously for *reform* and *change*. Figure 1–1 illustrates the differences and relationships among these terms.

Renewal, restructuring, and transformation are discussed in terms of educational reform, which has three definitional strands: improvement, reorganization, and renovation. Transformation relates to improvement, whereas restructuring and renewal concern reorganization and renovation, respectively. *Transformation* means to change the character or condition of an enterprise completely or essentially. Altering the nature and purpose of education in light of changing conditions and environment is the goal of transformation.

Renewal is a process designed to restore, reestablish, recreate, or rebuild. The focus is on renewing vigor or enthusiasm for established programs or approaches. There is an inherent assumption that the programs being renewed are valuable and necessary. Their viability is not questioned.

FIGURE 1–1   Reform: Renewal, Restructuring, and Transformation

Goal	Focus	Scope

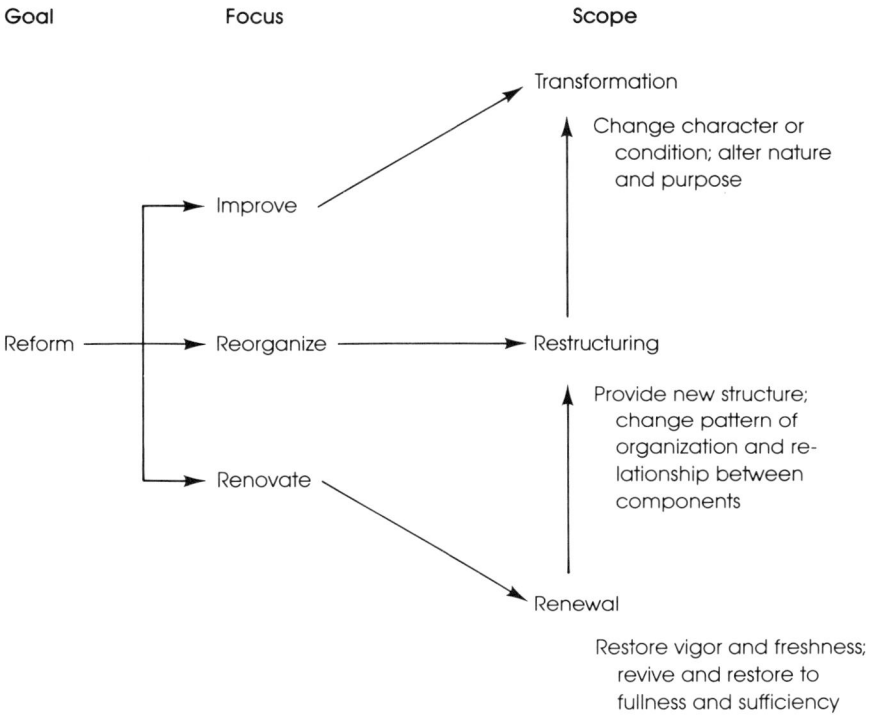

FIGURE 1–1   Reform: Renewal, Restructuring, and Transformation

Transformation

Change character or condition; alter nature and purpose

Improve

Reform ———→ Reorganize ——————→ Restructuring

Provide new structure; change pattern of organization and re- lationship between components

Renovate

Renewal

Restore vigor and freshness; revive and restore to fullness and sufficiency

Restructuring focuses on the patterns of organization or struc- ture—how parts are put together and the relationship between com- ponents. In the contemporary reform movement, restructuring is a buzzword that means "everything and nothing simultaneously," ac- cording to Michael Kirts of Stanford University (Olson, 1988). When restructuring is discussed in the literature or defined in operational projects, emphasis is placed on decentralization, school and student organization, governance, and power. Initially, the goal of restructuring was to broaden change in curriculum, instruction, governance, account- ability, and professionalism. In practice, however, the political ramifi- cations of changing decision-making structures within schools and dis- tricts makes focusing on student needs difficult (Olson, 1989).

Restructuring is a narrower concept than, and therefore a subset of, transformation. The driving question of restructuring is, How can we structure better to do what we are doing? In transformation, the question is more basic and far-reaching: What should we do and how can we organize to do it? Issues of values and purpose are primary, and factors of organization and relationships are secondary. In schools, transformation requires investigating whether basic values and purposes are realized; whether content, courses, or subjects are necessary; whether places and times in which instruction occur are most appropriate; whether methods, training, and professional development enhance student learning; whether the relationships, roles, and responsibilities for delivering education are still relevant; and whether useful or existing organizational patterns are productive and cost-effective.

Transformation is a comprehensive concept, connecting strategic and business aspects of organization with human and psychological issues to create fundamental changes in the way all members and groups *perceive, think,* and *behave* (Kilmann & Covin, 1988). The magnitude, depth, and breadth of change distinguishes transformation from restructuring or renewing. As transformation becomes further defined and expanded throughout the text, the distinctions will become more evident. Essential to building an understanding of the concept of transformation is an explanation of the linkages among perceiving, thinking, and behaving. These operations connect people, organizations, and leaders, and affect their interrelationships.

Perceiving, Thinking, and Behaving

A summary of some of the factors affecting perception, thought, and behavior is included in Figure 1–2. *Perception* is influenced by values, attitudes, experience, education, and environment. Burns (1978) defines *values* as "desirable or preferred *end-states* or collective goals or explicit purposes" (pp. 74–75). Values act as a filter or screen for perceptions, which affect how people react to their world. Perceptions contain judgments, which are based on values. Petty and Cacioppo (1981) define *attitudes* as "general and enduring positive or negative feelings about some person, object or issue" (p. 7). Attitudes are convenient summaries of people's beliefs and help predict behavior. Individuals come to situations with perceptions they obtained through life *experiences* at home, in school, or at work. *Education* also affects perception; a knowledgeable person's viewpoint is different from that of an individual who has little background information or experience.

In addition, the *environment*—the culture, climate, or structure— influences perception. A closed organization, with rigid norms, influences viewpoints differently than an institution that is open, flexible, and free-spirited. Perception has the power either to liberate or constrain thought. For individuals whose perception is based on blind faith, information to the contrary will not affect or alter thinking. Having

FIGURE 1–2   The Transformation Process: Factors Influencing Perceiving, Thinking, and Behaving

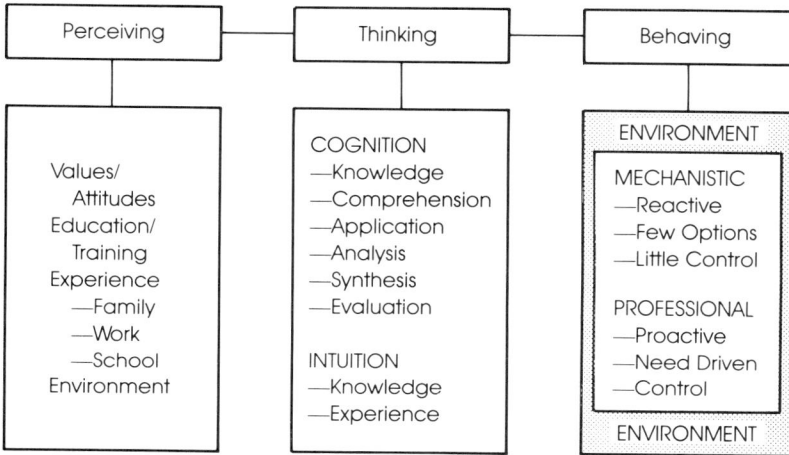

Perceiving	Thinking	Behaving
Values/ Attitudes Education/ Training Experience —Family —Work —School Environment	COGNITION —Knowledge —Comprehension —Application —Analysis —Synthesis —Evaluation INTUITION —Knowledge —Experience	ENVIRONMENT MECHANISTIC —Reactive —Few Options —Little Control PROFESSIONAL —Proactive —Need Driven —Control ENVIRONMENT

a sense of wonder, however, opens minds to ideas and phenomena that are new and previously unexplored.

Thinking has various levels of depth and complexity. It can be based on recall of factual knowledge, or predicated on sophisticated analyses, divergent ideas synthesized into new solutions, or evaluations based on thorough investigation. Thinking can follow a cognitive process from comprehending an issue to evaluating the ramifications of possible solutions. It can also be intuitive, pursuing a less conscious mental process that comes from experience and prior knowledge.

TIP | **TRANSFORMATION INTO PRACTICE**

PERCEPTION AND EXPECTANCY

Do expectancies form perception or does perception mold expectancies? This chicken-or-egg proposition may not be easily resolved, but there is a relationship between perception and expectancies that affect thinking and behavior.

In their landmark book, *Pygmalion in the Classroom*, Rosenthal and Jacobson (1968) discuss how "one person's expectation for another's behavior could come to serve as a self-fulfilling prophecy." Teachers were told that some students who were allegedly academic bloomers were to make significant gains. In actuality, these students were selected at random—the difference being only in the mind of the teacher. The experimental group, the alleged bloomers, made significant gains over the control group. Expectations become major determiners of individual performance.

> Can expectations play a powerful role in the destiny of organizations?
> What impact do expectations have on the transformation of schools?
> How do expectations for teachers affect school success?
> How do expectations for leaders affect school success?
> What are professionals' expectations for their work climate and organizations?
> Will a change of perception affect expectations for schools and their clients?
> Can expectations affect the quality and productivity of schools?

The product of perception and thought is *behavior*, which can be characterized as professional or mechanistic. Professional behavior is proactive to situations, not driven by rules; alternatives, options, and choices are defined based on clients' needs. Mechanistic behavior is more limited and strictly adheres to predetermined guidelines. It is primarily reactive and prescriptive to situations.

A practical illustration of the impact of perception on thinking and the impact of thinking on behavior is included in Figure 1–3. How teachers and others perceive children affects how they they treat them. Research has demonstrated that high expectations on the part of educators and parents produce better outcomes (Rosenthal & Jacobson, 1968). One facet of higher expectations is perceiving students as being able to learn what the schools have to teach. If that belief is held, then the teachers' thinking is not limited; it becomes optimistic and open to alternatives to make the perception a reality. Teachers' behavior is characterized by the use of problem solving to find divergent methods and alternative strategies to help students learn.

On the other hand, if teachers perceive that some children cannot learn because of economic class, prior performance, family situations, or other extraneous factors, then thinking and behavior are significantly different. Thinking becomes pessimistic and constrained, framed by limitations, not possibilities. Reliance on a few standardized methods or programs becomes the norm.

Transformation—changing perception, thinking, and behavior—

FIGURE 1–3   Transformation: Perceiving, Thinking, and Behaving

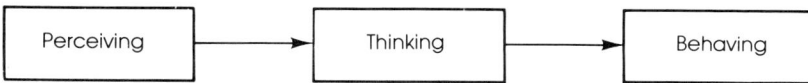

```
┌──────────────┐         ┌──────────────┐         ┌──────────────┐
│  Perceiving  │ ──────▶ │   Thinking   │ ──────▶ │   Behaving   │
└──────────────┘         └──────────────┘         └──────────────┘
```

Example:

```
┌──────────────┐    ┌──────────────┐    ┌──────────────┐
│ All students │ ◀──│ Optimistic   │    │ Professional/│
│  can learn   │ ◀──│ Open-minded  │    │ Alternative  │
│              │    │ Diverse      │ ──│ Strategies   │
└──────────────┘    │ Branched     │    └──────────────┘
                    └──────────────┘
```

```
┌──────────────┐    ┌──────────────┐    ┌──────────────┐
│ All students │ ◀──│ Pessimistic  │    │ Mechanistic/ │
│  can't learn │ ◀──│ Closed-minded│    │ Limited      │
│              │    │ Convergent   │ ──│ Options      │
└──────────────┘    │ Linear       │    └──────────────┘
                    └──────────────┘
```

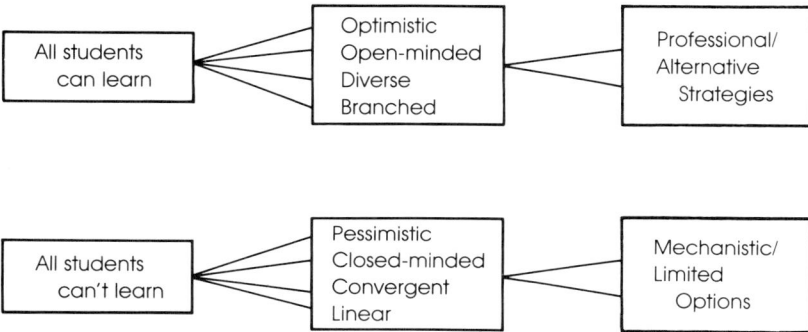

requires strong values, knowledge, intellective skills, and an environment that supports and encourages learning. There must be a commitment by leadership for intellectual development of all staff because information is needed to frame, alter, and expand perceptions and to create effective behavior.

Technology can play an important role in organizational transformation because it generates an incredible amount of information and makes it available quickly to many people throughout the organization. Not only can technology automate but it can "informate" (Zuboff, 1988). To "informate" is to have technology generate information about the administrative and productive processes through which organizations complete their work. Those processes become exposed and more susceptible to scrutiny and change. How and what data are collected and what information they produce are squared against the values and mission of the organization. Technology can also redefine roles and work relationships. In schools, teachers can have access to more information, be given greater authority, and have multiple options, since the opportunity to make choices comes with access to information.

Educational Transformation

Transformation of education is motivated by a concern for serving and influencing the future. Formerly, the future and the past were not drastically different. Over generations, educational change was minimal and slow-paced. The purpose of schooling in relation to what had been and what would be was not questioned. Today, rapid change is stressful and bewildering, but the time for avoiding or tinkering with change is gone. The perception that schools are not working, that they are not meeting the needs of all students, and that they are moribund organizationally due to rule-driven and bureaucratized behavior leads to the conclusion that dramatic steps are necessary to ensure successful schools for the future.

Successful transformation involves several factors (Perelman, 1987). First, the fundamental purpose of transformation cannot be lost; that is, the focus must be tight and fixed on values. Second, the total operation must be considered as a complex entity. The entire socio-technical system, people and systems, must be involved in deciding how structures and purposes should be changed. In addition, attention needs to be given to the concept of how strategies are proposed, evaluated, and adopted. Strategies are essential to create new systems and maintain flexibility. And last, careful planning is needed (too much concentration on planning can be counterproductive, however). Planning cannot be an excuse for not acting. Without action, transformation strategies and structures will not be implemented.

Transformation of organizations and people can occur. After all, education's goal is to transform—taking children and turning them into intelligent, responsible, and cultured citizens. Knowledge transforms passive indifference into active interest. Knowing how to learn turns incapable, dependent people into self-sufficient, effective individuals.

Schools must transform to meet new demands and reach their collective potential. Children will not grow and learn, and teachers will not develop professionally in environments that are staid and sterile and based on unexamined perception and old thought. If schools are dynamic, vibrant places, then the people in them—students, teachers, leaders, and support staff—will transform also.

SUMMARY

Schools exist in an environmental context. That context cannot be ignored because it establishes expectations, requires credibility, and constantly changes. At times in our history, the social, political, economic, and cultural contexts changed dramatically, creating a new era that required the transformation of social and political institutions. The last part of the twentieth century is such a time; technology, economic

FIGURE 1–4　Context, Transformation Process, and Possible Outcomes

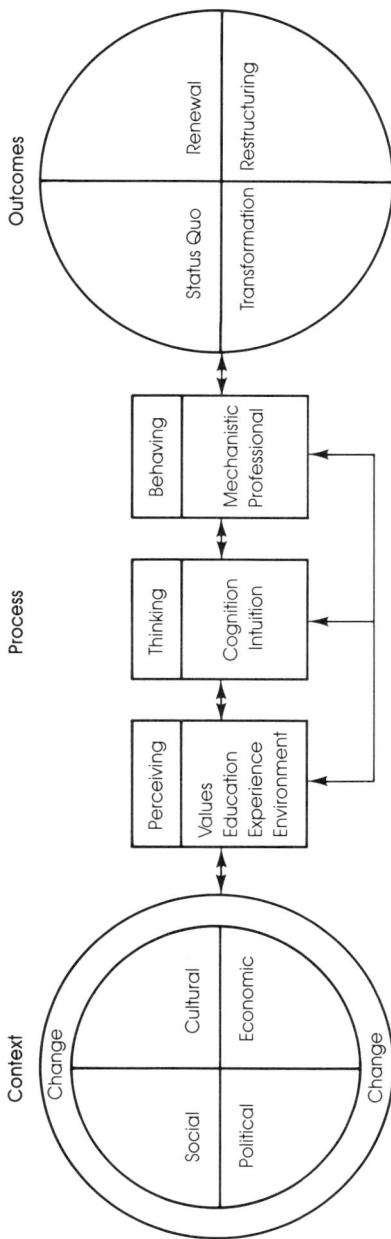

Context

Change

Social

Cultural

Political

Economic

Change

Process

Perceiving

Values
Education
Experience
Environment

Thinking

Cognition
Intuition

Behaving

Mechanistic
Professional

Outcomes

Status Quo

Renewal

Transformation

Restructuring

17

realignment, and new political coalitions demand that countries compete on the basis of knowledge, information, and innovation. The industrial society—based on mechanized labor and raw materials—is not the model for the future.

Schools must review their perceptual frameworks that define issues and problems and begin thinking in new paradigms if they are to respond with action and behavior that will meet the needs of the future. Figure 1–4 simplifies the relationships among the context, the process, and the possible outcomes for transformation.

The transformation process affects schools' organizational structure, leadership, and people. The outcomes either maintain the status quo, renew or restructure present programs, or transform the purpose, mission, and operation of the schools. It is possible to maintain the status quo if the needs of the organization and demands placed on it are congruent. The possibility also exists that renewing programs or restructuring are sufficient. However, broad-based transformation requires new perceptions and paradigms for thinking.

CONCEPTS

1. Public schools are conservative, stable institutions that must be more responsive to the changing world around them.
2. The cycles of reform efforts, whether legislated or introduced by educators, have made little real difference in schooling (how classrooms operate and how children are taught).
3. Demographic conditions and population trends must be understood when planning for the future needs and problems facing education.
4. Schools must recognize that to survive in the twenty-first century, change and adaptability are essential, positive characteristics.
5. Transformation is comprehensive, affecting the total organization. It requires new ways of perceiving, thinking, and behaving.
6. School transformation is more comprehensive than renewing and restructuring because it affects the basic character and purpose of education.
7. The goal of transformation is to change the nature and purpose of education in response to changing contextual and environmental conditions.

2 Transformation: Perception and Thought

Did you ever walk into a school and get the feeling that the people working there think they can take on any challenge and conquer it? In other schools, the atmosphere is different. Problems are viewed cynically—"we've tried that before," "it'll never work," or "don't make waves" are typical attitudes.

Organizations, just like the individuals in them, develop a pattern of thought and a perception of reality that affects how they operate. The way those organizations perceive and think ultimately determines whether behavior and practice change or remain the same. That is why some schools are vibrant and innovative and others are stagnant and dull. Schools are stable, predictable places because educators have not perceived the alterations in society, the new demands from technology, or the changes in economics that should cause them to think and behave differently in their work. Perception frames what is possible; it can liberate or restrict thought.

Neither people nor organizations change unless they perceive the necessity to do so. People make decisions about their behavior based on how they read situations. Sometimes perceived reality and actual circumstances are congruent, resulting in decisions that are effective and productive. In other cases, inappropriate conclusions may be drawn when perceptions and conditions are incongruent. Schools must examine their perceptions and thinking in order to act responsively to the demands of the future.

This chapter focuses on the abstract concepts of perception and thought—what they mean, how they influence organizations, and what implications they have for school transformation.

PERCEPTION

Perception comes from the Latin word *perceptio*, which means receiving, grasping, and gathering together. *Awareness, comprehension, insight,* and *intuition* are words used to define *perception* in Webster's dictionary. *To perceive* is defined as to take hold, feel, comprehend, or grasp mentally; to recognize, observe, and become aware through the senses. These definitions form an important basis for understanding perception and its relation to how thought and action are formed. "Behavior is said to consist of not only overt actions but also internal factors such as thoughts, emotions, perceptions, and needs" (Reitz, 1981, p. 27).

In organizational terms, perception is the way systems interpret and process information from the environment. Feelings, values, impressions, and prior experience of people in the organization are parts of developing perceptions because information is screened and then translated to thought. (Refer to Figures 1–2 and 1–4 in Chapter 1.) For example, political commercials present information by wrapping their appeals in sound, symbolism, and statistics and by establishing an emotional temperature and visual tone for the advertisement. Many senses are used to influence people's perceptions of the candidates and subsequently their decisions in voting. Emotion and affect are powerful influences that color impressions, govern meaning, and guide behavior. In organizations, people use both cognitive and affective sources for processing information and drawing conclusions.

How Perception Works

How frequently have you heard the following phrases?

"You don't see the whole picture . . ."
"I can't imagine . . ."
"You have to broaden your outlook . . ."
"I can't understand your viewpoint . . ."
"From your standpoint . . ."

All of these phrases concern perception. Terms like *picture, outlook,* and *viewpoint* involve sight, and perception deals with insight. "Seeing is believing" is a piece of conventional wisdom that implies if people viewed the same thing, they would perceive it in the same manner. We know that perception is not that simple. The camera lens metaphor in

Chapter 1 illustrated how there can be different perceptions and perspectives of the same scene.

The perceptual process has four components: sensation, selection, organization, and translation. In addition, the process is affected by the environment, the intensity of the event, and the characteristics and personality of the individual. Figure 2–1 summarizes this complex process. In the first stage, objects, events, information, symbols, language, and images are recognized as *sensations*. Our minds are constantly being bombarded with sensations, and to make sense of them we must have some screening device or filter. Each person's filter is unique because it is based on one's personality, motives, values, beliefs, ethos, and experience. In behavior theory, these sensations are referred to as *stimuli*.

After a person has filtered all of these sensations, or stimuli, the mind organizes them and chooses some for further processing, which is called *selection*. This selection step is influenced by certain factors that draw and hold our attention to some sensations rather than others. These factors are potency, contrast, frequency, intensity, number, and novelty.

Potency refers to a sensation that draws attention because it relates to one's motives or personality characteristics. For example, if your motive is to ensure that boys and girls have equal opportunity for academic success, you would notice and react to the fact that advanced science and math classes are predominantly filled with boys.

Contrast suggests that a sensation is stronger when it stands out rather than blending in with the rest of the environment. One person

FIGURE 2–1   The Perceptual Process

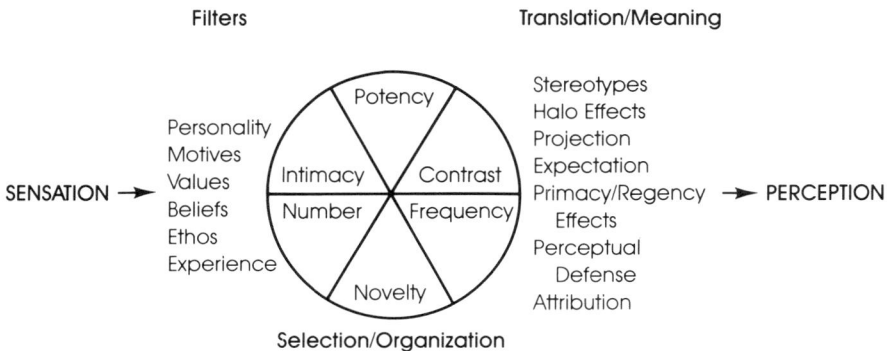

talking to another during a formal presentation will get noticed and generally command some response, because the behavior is in such contrast to what everyone else is doing.

Frequency refers to the fact that the more often a sensation occurs the more likely it is to be selected. A student who squirms around repeatedly throughout the lesson will eventually catch the attention of the teacher.

Intensity of a sensation is the severity, shocking, or crisis nature of an event that demands notice. Although an administrator may be busy with a number of disciplinary activities, a fight in the hall reorders the priorities immediately.

Number refers to how many sensations are occurring at the same time. The more bombarded we are with many different stimuli, the less likely we are able to select a specific one and react to it. When we are overburdened with running from one issue to another, we can more easily miss something important.

Novelty is simply that the unusual draws our attention quickly. That is why some advertisements catch on better than others. We are exposed to so many commercials that, when one is very different, we usually pay attention and remember it.

After selection of the sensation has taken place, influenced by one or more of the preceding factors, perceptual *organization* occurs. This step happens almost concurrently with selection, as we categorize and arrange events by similarity, continuity, or proximity in time or space. After sensations have been selected and organized, they need to be *translated* into some meaningful constructs for us to use them.

One cautionary note is important at this time. As we seek to explain this abstract process, it begins to sound like an organized, linear set of events. However, perception is subtle, complicated, nonrational, and highly interactive with the environment. These factors can positively or negatively affect the translation and result in accurate interpretations or distortions of reality. Distortions work like optical illusions that alter visual impressions (Dunham, 1984). In perceptual terms, translation activities include stereotypes, halo effects, projection, expectancy, primacy/regency effects, perceptual defense, and attribution.

Translation: Positives and Negatives

Stereotypes provide shorthand impressions. Perceptions of individuals or ideas come from general conclusions and beliefs we develop about groups. When we use stereotypes to translate meaning, we may draw conclusions without direct information. *Halo effects* are similar to stereotypes in that they are based on a specific characteristic that is generalized to a whole group. For example, all students in the orchestra are perceived to be self-motivated because many are very good students. Teachers may not consider other reasons for participation. *Projections* cause people to see their own characteristics in other people or circumstances. Motivated people see others as motivated.

Expectancy suggests that we perceive an object or event consistent with the expectations we generate for it. The Pygmalion studies in classrooms have been mentioned as a good example of this factor. If we expect the staff or students to behave in a certain way, they usually meet those expectations.

Primacy/regency effects concern first and last impressions. People often rate first impressions highly (*primacy*) and weigh the last piece of information they receive (*regency*) with greater strength than earlier information. An example of this influence can be seen in interviewing. People often advise that the best position to be in when a number of people are being interviewed is either first or last, since the interviewer will be more likely to remember those candidates.

When translating sensations into meaning, *perceptual defense* can also color the process. If the defense mechanism is working, a person is likely to support existing perceptions and react against recent impressions. New information that does not agree with the established perception is generally denied. A teacher who has negative perceptions about mainstreaming special education children will consider a child who does well in the situation as an exception to the rule. Regardless of new facts, the prior perception remains intact.

The final factor that influences perception is *attribution*, which is making judgments about people or events based on whether internal or external causes are operating. If a person acts in a strange way, but that behavior is attributed to conditions not in his or her control, others' perceptions about the person will not be altered. A teacher who temporarily performs poorly in the classroom because of an impending divorce will not be viewed as a poor teacher, as long as the situation does not affect the internal motives, traits, or abilities of the person over time.

These seven influencing factors apply to perceptions of people, programs, ideas, processes, organizations, and events. Perceptions may appear distorted and out of touch with reality to some people, but they are the reality that forms the basis for thought and behavior for others. Since perception is a mental structure through which we visualize, analyze, and interact with our environment, it is important that we try to fend off perceptual errors by taking into account the following:

- Acknowledge the susceptibility to errors of stereotypes, halo effects, and other similar factors.
- Focus on relevant facts and ideas and establish a system for consciously processing and evaluating information.
- Test reality and accuracy by checking perceptions with outside sources.
- Guard against becoming self-satisfied because of the comfort of familiar perceptions.

The perceptual process—filtering, selecting, and translating events, information, symbols, and images—establishes the framework for interpreting individual and organizational reality.

Perception, Mindscapes, and Image Theory

Perceptual frameworks are described as "mindscapes" by Sergiovanni (1987b), who defines them as "a person's mental image, view, theory and set of beliefs that orient a person to problems, help sort out the important from the unimportant, and provide a rationale for guiding one's action and decisions" (p. 339). Mindscapes program thinking so that responses become automatic. Since Sergiovanni is writing about school principals, he explains, "Mindscapes are implicit mental images and frameworks through which administrative and schooling reality and one's place within these realities is envisioned. They are intellectual and psychological images of the real world of schooling and the boundaries and parameters of rationality that help us make sense of this world" (p. xi).

Sims and Gioia (1986) indicate that people come to organizations with preconceived notions and expectations, which they use to make sense of their new surroundings. They match new experiences and communication with their old mental structures to formulate perceptions, to aid in thinking, and to create meaning.

Perceptual frameworks and mindscapes provide security by guiding behavior to help us get where we want to be, despite the uncertainty of circumstances. Just as people have self-images and perceptions, so do organizations; image theory affects both. It suggests four interrelated concepts—self-image, trajectory image, projected image, and action image—which can be simply translated into who and where we are, where we want to be, and how we can get there.

Self-images of people and organizations involve the beliefs and values that guide behavior. For organizations, formal charters and philosophies reflect their self-images, as well as the values they espouse. A trajectory image suggests what the organization hopes to become or wants to achieve. It includes the vision of the leader, the ideal future, and the goals set to reach this image. Projected image is provided by a reality test. Future events and roles are assessed in the present environmental conditions to determine the probability of success. Finally, the action image defines what needs to happen to make the vision a reality. It involves eliminating the incongruities among the earlier images and strategically planning to fulfill the mission.

Image theory has been used in very practical senses. Skiers and other athletes in competitions are prime examples. They imagine themselves shooting down the ski course at record speed or implementing a game strategy to improve performance. This imaging has also formed the basis of management training seminars, where executives are directed to create positive affirmations (words), visualizations (pictures), and imprinting (feelings) to change their self-image and behavior (Tice, 1980).

Such techniques are successful because they carefully incorporate perceiving, thinking, and behaving into the change process. People begin to perceive themselves as successes and establish positive mindscapes through self- and trajectory images tied to an action plan. What they envision in their mindscapes affects their thought patterns, decisions, and behavior. Organizations with strong self- and trajectory images do not question their goals and motives, but instead focus on action and strategies designed to meet their missions.

Perceptions and Schools

People who work in schools have varied perceptions of their roles and mindscapes that influence how they view themselves and the organization. Schools and classrooms are different in approaches, in content and methods, in goals and objectives, in culture and climate, and in outcomes and accountability. Many of these differences can be attributed to the perceptions professionals have that influence practice and possibilities for schools.

Perception affects our disposition toward change and the status quo. In order for transformation to take place, we need to establish perceptual frameworks and mindscapes that are open to new information and conditions. It is also necessary to guard against the barriers to change erected by stereotypes, halo effects, and other distortions. Transformation must produce a paradigm shift—a change in the perception of reality—so that thinking can be altered. The perceptions held by professionals and organizations control what kind of thinking occurs in schools. How organizations think—how they process information and perceptions—determines the nature of behavior.

TIP | TRANSFORMATION INTO PRACTICE

PERCEPTIONS, MINDSCAPES, AND THE TWENTY-FIRST CENTURY

In the face of change, management strategies depend on perception to determine the future. When institutions did not adapt in periods of fast-paced change, they failed. Making the best buggy whips was no consolation at a time when the automobile was catching the imagination of the public, and gas stations were replacing stables. Our country has seen a scientific technological revolution in the last 75 years, and the future holds more of the same. What will schools look like in the next 20 to 50 years?

Schools are not separated from the environment and the future that is shaping it. What they will become and what they will teach will be defined by the perceptions of educational leaders. Noted futurist, Marvin J. Cetron, identified long-term trends that will affect the United States, which certainly includes the nature and role of schools.

General:
There will be a rise of knowledge industries and a knowledge-dependent society.

- Computers will provide access to the card catalogs of the world's libraries by the end of the 1990s.
- Videodiscs will enhance books, providing audio and visual information.
- About half of the service workers will be involved in collecting, synthesizing, storing, and retrieving information by the year 2000.
- Occupational and job mobility will increase as people retrain for new careers and change location.

Technological:
Many advances will directly affect the way people live and work.

- By 2001, artificial intelligence will be used by companies and the government to help collect and analyze data and to solve problems.
- Growth of an international economy will occur, with an emphasis on the quality of goods and services.
- Research and development will grow as a factor in the economy.
- Telecommunications will remove geographical barriers—satellite-transmitted data will be sent via computer anywhere in the world and beyond.

Educational:
Education and training will be expanded throughout society.

- There will be fewer and fewer well-paying jobs that do not require advanced training.
- Schools will be used to educate and train both children and adults.
- New technologies, such as simulations, computer models, and tele-communications systems, will facilitate training.
- Education will be more individualized through interactive computers and videodiscs.
- Education costs will rise, along with heavy pressure to control them.
- Schools will be concerned with assessing outcomes and effectiveness.
- The learning environment will not be as important in the future as people will learn more on their own.

Management:
- The typical business of 2010 will have half the levels of management that firms of today have and about one-third of the managers.
- The command-control model of management will be a relic of the past.

Family:
- The birth rate will continue to decline.
- Leisure time will increase and people will have a shorter work week.
- Improved nutrition and wellness will increase life expectancy.

How do those trends affect our perceptions of schools—their role, purpose, mission, structure, and practice? Their potential impact depends on whether our perception is global or provincial, generalized or specialized.

Source: Marvin J. Cetron, World Future Society, Bethesda, Maryland, 1988. Adapted by permission of World Future Society.

THINKING

Organizations are products of the thoughts and actions of the people in them (Sims & Gioia, 1986). Successful organizations are composed of people who perceive, think, and act, not people who respond like mechanized devices programmed for task completion. Issues of empowerment, decentralization, and participation are based on the notion that professionals have the ability to make intelligent decisions when given the opportunity. Professionals use cognitive systems in this process, which enable them to give meaning to new thoughts, form attitudes, generate emotional and rational responses, and provide motivation for behavior (Reitz, 1981).

When individuals think collectively, organizations think. Since people comprise organizations, their perceptions, thinking, and behavior influence the character of that organization. Organizational thought is based on the assumption that a collective intelligence exists—that a rational ability to reason and solve problems is present in the institution. Organizational intelligence means that the organization as a whole can perceive, think, reason, and translate information into behavior. This description closely parallels the cognitive action of individuals just described.

Organizational intelligence affects collective thought and the action emanating from it. Schools, like other organizations, should take action based on common purposes and shared values so that the strategies that are designed to meet their particular objectives and needs fit with the mission. This concerted action is the reason that organizations were created in the first place.

Organizational, or collective, intelligence is affected by a number of circumstances. First, the structure of the system needs to be considered. An isolated environment with little shared information restricts perception, imagination, and motivation. Schools are often criticized for their isolated structures of individual classrooms, which inhibit teachers' collegial dialogue, exchange, and reflection.

A second circumstance that can influence collective intelligence both positively and negatively is the degree of the organization's cooperation and agreement on how things should get done. In the positive vein, if everyone in the organization is in agreement about what direction should be taken, action is facilitated. However, this very consensus can retard change. In order for change to succeed, old patterns of thought and action may have to be sacrificed, and the new cognitive patterns may create dissonance, not agreement.

A third influence on the collective intelligence of an organization is a phenomenon called *endemic administrative feudality*. This phrase conjures images of systemic disease, but in simple terms, Dimock (Netzer et al., 1970) indicated bureaucracy's stereotyped procedures can stifle people's energy and vitality. Working without thinking, by habit or routine, may provide security and stability for some people, but it ultimately becomes stifling, dull, and uncreative. Organizations suffering from this condition become inner-directed, insulated from the environment, and they rely on established thought and behavior patterns. They are closed systems, impervious to scrutiny, which constrict new thought and patterns of action.

Awareness of these potential inhibitors of productive organizational thought can assist leaders in moving systems forward and in ensuring they are responsive to changing environmental conditions and client expectations. Organizations have to think continuously in order to improve.

How Organizations Think

Cognition, or the thinking process, derives from the Greek "cognos," to think. Before action is taken, information needs to be processed. Cognitive structures order and define knowledge and interrelationships so that we can make sense of them in some systematic way. This process may be automatic and unconsciously executed, or it may be highly structured and complex. These cognitive structures are called *schemas* by Sims and Gioia (1986), who suggest they are a "network of expectations learned from experiences and stored in memory" (p. 55), without which people would have difficulty in figuring out what is going on around them. They propose three types of schemas—prototypes, scripts, and symbols—which have both benefits and costs associated with them.

For example, *prototypes* are mental abstractions that capture the defining characteristics of people and situations. As such, they provide generalizations that can be used to make decisions. As a benefit, they save people the time of researching each individual case, but as a negative, they can suggest stereotypes that may be misleading and prejudicial.

Scripts supply knowledge about expected consequences of events and provide a guide to behavior so that it is appropriate to the situation. Scripts fill in the gaps when information is missing. People know how to behave and what to say in most social situations, even though the specific circumstances of the occasion are unknown. In schools, the behavior of the teaching staff and administration can be anticipated when contract negotiations are at impasse. Scripts can be helpful, but they provide a false sense of security if they are used constantly, instead of attempting to gather important information that could more accurately guide decision making and behavior.

Finally, *symbols* stand for their objects or concepts and are used to convey meaning and understanding. They can be visual (logos), verbal (slogans), material (medals, pins), or abstract (viewpoints, ideology). An obvious example of a symbol is the American flag. Symbols are powerful in relating values and ideas; the danger is when the symbol becomes more important than the value or idea it represents.

In summary, schemas provide a structure for organizational experiences, allow for interpretation of ambiguous situations, and supply missing information in circumstances where incomplete data exist. On the negative side, schemas persevere, even in the face of contrary information, and they are resistant to change. Schemas can work against change by pushing organizational thought into regularized and predictable patterns. If schemas can be created for change, people will begin to accept the fact that the only certainty is change. Schemas are structures of expectation, and when people can learn to accept change and even welcome it, then they will be able to manage their own responses to it (Sims & Gioia, 1986).

Thinking, Decisions, and Intuition

The cognitive structures—schemas of prototypes, scripts, and symbols—set the framework for how organizations think collectively and apply thinking skills to problem solving. The schemas either expand or contract thought, causing broad-minded or narrow-minded approaches. They direct how people think and behave in institutions.

When thinking is discussed in most contexts, the scientific process for problem solving is stressed. Chester Barnard (1938) identified two types of processes in executives' thinking: logical and nonlogical. Logical processes, which involve analytical thinking, apply to situations when goals and objectives are clear and alternatives are explicit. The consequences of alternatives can be defined and calculated with respect to attaining the goals. Nonlogical processes are those that cannot be expressed or easily defined. Barnard believed that executives depend on intuition or judgmental responses in some types of decision-making situations.

Barnard's descriptions closely parallel Simon's (1987) proposal that there are two types of decisions: logical and judgmental. Logical decisions relate to goals with alternatives that can be defined in terms of specific consequences, and those consequences can be evaluated for success. The decision maker identifies the targets, defines the strategies, implements the plans, and assesses the outcomes. On the other hand, judgmental decisions are too rapid for orderly analysis because the need for a decision is imminent. The decision maker cannot give detailed accounts or describe processes or data used for determining the correctness of the decision. Such decisions are loosely structured, qualitative, and affected by intuition.

Costa (1985) also mentions intuition in his description of four complex thinking processes. Three involve analytical skills—problem solving, decision making, and critical thinking. Such processes were referred to by Barnard as the *logical thinking*. The fourth, creative thinking, uses both analysis and intuition. Intuition as a factor of informed judgment was not taken seriously by scientific management thinkers who emphasized quantifiable, observable information and data applied in a systematic manner. But we now know that thinking is not always based on scientifically defined processes or validated data. Simon (1987) indicates that separating intuition and analysis too distinctly is a mistake. "It is a fallacy to contrast 'analytical' and 'intuitive' styles of management. Intuition and judgment . . . are simply analyses frozen into habit and into the capacity for rapid response through recognition" (p. 63).

Freezing analyses into habit comes with years of experience and training. Experts appear to take giant leaps in reasoning and judgment, whereas novices take minute steps. "The experienced manager . . . has in his or her memory large amounts of knowledge, gained from training and experience and organized in terms of recognizable chunks and associated information" (Simon, 1987, p. 61). Experts can quickly identify the main components and patterns of issues and problems and often arrive at decisions without being able to specify how they got there.

Wagner (1969) agrees, stating that those who trust science do not necessarily abandon hunches or intuition, because many scientific breakthroughs came as a result of hunch, serendipity, and dreams. When discussing the creative process, Arthur Koestler talks of an "intuitive leap" that connects two unrelated facts or ideas into a new one (Waterman, 1987). To act on hunches requires a high level of knowledge and understanding about a particular area. The founder of Electronic Data Systems, H. Ross Perot, calls intuition "knowing your business. It means being able to bring to bear on a situation everything you've seen, felt, tasted and experienced in an industry" (Waterman, 1987, p. 43). In education, Sergiovanni (1987b) indicated that professionals rely on intuition as they "create knowledge in use. Intuition is formed by theoretical knowledge on one hand and by interacting with the context of practice on the other. When teachers use informed intuition, they are engaging in reflective practice" (p. xiv). Reflective practice—what one does and how one thinks about it—provides for growth and change because it involves thinking about what one does on the job.

Knowing how to combine analytical thinking and intuitive thought effectively is congruent with the concept of schemas and their use. Cognitive structures help process information through both formal analysis and reflective practice. Waterman (1987) also states that information comes from two sources: left-brain analysis and right-brain intuition. Both affect individual thought and judgment about available opportunities, when and what decisions should be made, and when action should be taken.

TIP | **TRANSFORMATION INTO PRACTICE**

APPROACHES TO DECISION MAKING

Leaders and professionals make decisions in complex, ambiguous environments. In an article entitled "Humble Decision Making," Amatai Etzioni (1989) identifies a number of approaches to making decisions.

Rational:
Rationalists argue that all alternatives should be explored, information on each should be collected, and the impact of each should be compared. They optimistically think that the best choice can be found because all the information will be available. Therefore, a decision can be made objectively, without emotional or political influence.

Muddling Through:
Also called *incrementalism,* muddling through is a very conservative approach to making decisions because it chooses a direction close to the prevailing one. However, it eliminates the need for volumes of new information and avoids grand policy changes. Enormous departures do not occur, as issues are subdivided into increments and decisions are made accordingly.

Go-for-It Approach:
This approach is opposed to reflection and analysis; it encourages leaders to remake the world rather than understand it. A "don't sit back and wait" approach to predict what will happen is not advocated because it recognizes the ambiguity and uncertainty of the world. Committing to a course of action based on experience, intuition, and available information is advocated.

Rational Ritualism:
This approach is seldom discussed, but it is evident when leaders and their staffs collect information of questionable validity, analyze it, then ignore it in making choices. Ritualistic projections are made, and everyone plays the game, without challenging the process.

Mixed Scanning:
Etzioni advocates mixed scanning, also called *adaptive decision making,* as an approach that allows shallow and deep examination of information. Two basic judgments must be made: first, the broad choice of fundamental

policy, and second, incremental decisions that pave the way for new basic judgments. He indicates that mixed scanning is the way physicians make decisions. They do not have all the information but know what they want to achieve and move incrementally, collecting more data, modifying decisions until they reach their goal. This approach adapts to conditions, with opportunities for revision and not "burning bridges."

School leaders, particularly those engaged in reform, do not have all the data and information because educational policy and the conditions of schools are not always clear and certain.

What, if any, one model is best for educational professionals?

Is there a place for intuition and collective experience in the process?

Is there a place for "go-for-it" approaches in schools?

Are schools too conservative in making decisions?

What are school board and community expectations for leaders' decision-making approaches?

Source: A. Etzioni, "Humble Decision Making," *Harvard Business Review,* 67, no. 4 (July–August, 1989): 122–126.

SUMMARY

To have an impact on changing school structures, educational leadership, and professional staff, we need an understanding of the role that perception and thought will play. How educators perceive their roles and think about the operation of schools affect professional practice for millions of children each day.

Figure 2-2 illustrates how perception and thought relate to transformation. Every organization interacts with two environments—internal and external. Those environments create possibilities and raise issues that will define whether the organization will survive and succeed. More will be said about the environment in Part II.

Those possibilities and issues require actions that, hopefully, are predicated on thought. Schemas are helpful in providing a knowledge base for interpreting data, turning the data into useful information, and developing expectations and actions. These sense-making cognitive structures affect decisions—analytically or intuitively—that lead to organizational action. This action will guide organizations and the individual professionals in meeting goals and objectives.

Perception and thought are critical components in school reform and change. When schools were studied in the past, they were perceived as segmented organizations: Leadership was thought about in isolation

FIGURE 2–2   Perception and Thought: Paths to Transformation

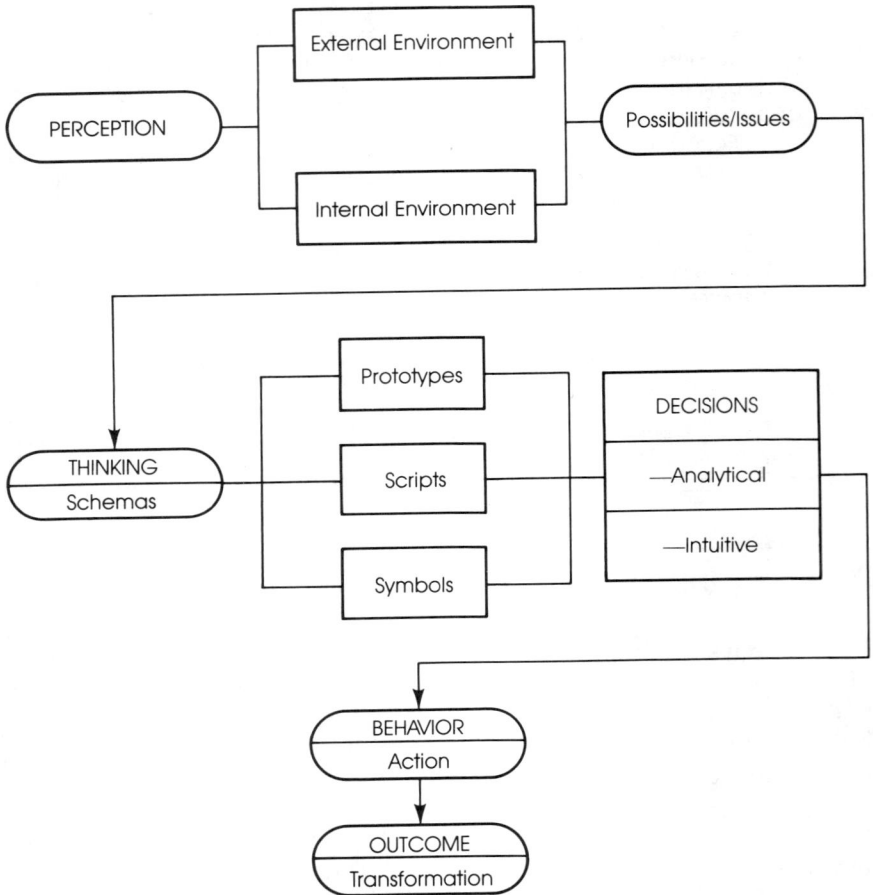

of organizational development, professional behavior was reviewed without regard for the dynamics of leadership, and structures were separated from outcomes and people. Our view is that reality interrelates theory on organizations, leadership, and professional practice. This concept is necessary in order to lead and change schools as total organizations because schools are not antiseptic, theoretical places. They are complex institutions composed of people, ideas, pressures, and conflicts. Schools will only become successful and productive by perceiving, thinking, and behaving in new ways.

Transforming schools raise questions that challenge perception and thinking, which will guide transformation efforts and affect the framing of visions, issues, problems, strategies, and solutions.

What is your perception of school organizations? Are they social systems or sociotechnical systems? Can and should school structures be changed? What is the role of teacher organizations in this process? Are schools service organizations or government agencies? Who holds power and who should have power in schools? Is it desirable to have schools decentralized, and, if so, how and for what functions? Do the systems of schools promote or inhibit change and reform? Should schools be more entrepreneurial or more cooperative in nature? Are some organizations more creative than others, and why?

There are perceptions on leadership that affect behavior. What is the role of leaders? Can leaders be made or leadership skills be taught? Do leaders have common traits or behave in similar ways? Is leadership in the form of a principal necessary in contemporary schools? How do leaders and the organization interact? Do some organizations restrict leadership? How do values influence leadership? Do leaders form school culture? What kind of leadership do professionals need?

Finally, what is your perception of teachers? Are they professionals, technicians, craftspersons, or laborers? Do collective bargaining agreements promote professional perspectives and behavior? If teachers are professionals, can they be charged with malpractice? Do organizational structures promote the self-perception of teachers as professionals?

CONCEPTS

1. Transformation is dependent on changing the perceptions and thinking of the people in the organization.
2. Perception is a mental process by which an individual uses cognition and affect—knowledge, insight, feelings, and intuition—to assess information, organize it, and create meaning.
3. Sensation, selection, organization, and translation are the four steps in the perception process.
4. A mindscape is a mental framework made up of psychological and intellectual images that help us organize and make sense of our world.

5. When people in organizations think collectively, organizations think.

6. Organizational intelligence is based on its ability to put together collective perceptions, establish common purposes, and take concerted action.

7. Schemas are cognitive structures used by organizations to explain experiences, interpret information, make decisions, and predict outcomes.

8. Thinking should combine both left-brain analysis and right-brain intuition to form judgments and make decisions.

9. Intuition is a nonlogical thinking process, based on informed professional judgment, hunches, serendipity, and experiences collected and processed over time for rapid recall.

10. Perceptions control thinking, and thought influences action and behavior.

11. A new perception on the interconnectedness of organizations, leaders, and people is necessary for school transformation to take place.

3

Quality and Productivity in Successful Schools: The Case for Transformation

School histories are littered with failed efforts at meaningful and lasting change. Many of the proposals and pilot programs that were to improve education are discussed in faculty lounges as former "bandwagon" efforts that did not work. Schools have not only been resistant to reform, but they appear to be immune to long-term, significant change. How, then, should parents, educators, and others engage in the difficult task of bringing about broad-based change in schools? Why do schools need to transform?

The obvious answer is to improve schools' quality, productivity, and outcomes to make them more successful. But what are quality schools? How can productivity be gauged in education? How can success be measured when schools serve different students from a variety of family, socioeconomic, and cultural backgrounds?

The objective of this chapter is to present a design for successful schools that includes the concepts of quality and productivity, as well as other components. Because schools exist in a greater context or environment, quality, productivity, and success are discussed generally and then related specifically to education. All three concepts are influenced by standards and attitudes; these connections are also explored.

QUALITY

Quality is an elusive concept, open to varied criteria and perceptions. For private sector firms, quality is the driving force behind building a strong business culture and positive climate. Customer service is

37

emphasized, and success is measured in profits and competitiveness. In the marketplace, consumer preferences place quality above price, appearance, and availability (Kilmann & Covin, 1988). U.S. corporations are recognizing that value systems have changed and that quality plays a greater role in product marketing today than it has in the past. People want quality in goods and services as well as in education for their children.

In simple terms, *quality* is the degree of excellence or superiority present in an act, product, service, or institution. Quality is a value, and achieving it depends on the organization's commitment. Tuchman (1980) defined quality as "the investment of the best skill and effort possible to produce the finest and most admirable result possible" (p. 38). According to this definition, quality must pervade the entire organization. It becomes everyone's job.

Although schools have been criticized for poor quality, that charge is not reserved for education alone. Questions about quality have been raised with respect to many facets of U.S. life. In business, tolerance for defects based on what was affordable became a standard in many companies. Quality and profit were seen as competing values, and quality lost. The world of government and politics has been altered drastically by modern technology and media, but the quality of the dialogue has been trivialized. Style has overcome substance. In the automobile industry, quality was the victim of volume—making more faster. Work lost meaning, pride dissipated, and negative worker attitude toward the product and the company resulted. Managers appealed to pride of workmanship through symbolic slogans like "Quality is Job One" to raise standards.

Quality also depends on standards. *Standards* are guideposts for comparison in measuring quality, value, or achievement. Gardner (1984) stated:

> Because of the leveling influences that are inevitable in popular government, a democracy must, more than any other form of society, maintain what Ralph Barton Perry called "an express insistence upon quality and distinction." When it does not do so, the consequences are all too familiar. Standards are contagious. They spread throughout an organization or society. If an organization or group cherishes high standards, the behavior of individuals who enter it is inevitably influenced. Similarly, if slovenliness infects a society, it is not easy for any member of that society to remain uninfluenced in his own behavior (p. 110).

Table 3–1 identifies the characteristics of organizations with high standards. Striving for excellence through high standards has a corollary feature. Even if a society or organization does not meet the stan-

TABLE 3–1   What Does an Organization with High
Standards Have?

• Dedication to the purposes of the system
• Strong value system and sense of mission
• Visionary leadership
• Accountability
• Motivated and committed workers
• Pride in achievement
• Expectations for success
• Commitment to quality services and outcomes
• Effective channels of communication
• Realistic expectations for clients

dards, it is better for having tried. Settling for less does not enrich, but effort does. Everyone who works toward excellence benefits from the attempt.

Without appropriate standards, organizations can suffer from the dry rot of complacency that eats away at quality and achievement. High standards motivate. The perception that human nature is lazy and apathetic is false; the truth is most people gravitate toward enterprises that involve not only effort but purposefulness (Gardner, 1978).

High standards must also be the driving force and the prime motivator in education for school boards, administrators, teachers, and students. Standards are exemplars. Wiggins (1989) believes that standards refer to qualities, not quantities. He identifies students with high standards as having habits of the mind—qualities of being diligent, thoughtful, persistent, engaged, and thorough. Carrying standards to the organizational level, Wiggins indicates that standards are prevalent and revealed through everyday behavior and policies of each person or school.

Commitment to quality, properly communicated and modeled, enhances identification with the organization and its goals. Pride follows identification, and people with pride go above and beyond the minimum to produce quality. "As long as people exist, some will always strive for the best; some will attain it" (Tuchman, 1980, p. 104).

Quality: Attitude and Motivation

Attitudes are strongly linked to motivation. They are based on perception—how people think about their role, the organization's mission, and their commitment to that mission. Attitudes come from a person's set of interrelated beliefs that affect individual behavior and response to circumstances (Rokeach, 1968). Influencing or shaping attitudes is difficult because they are formulated over time by knowledge, values, experience, and upbringing.

Attitudes are also affected by leadership. W. Edwards Deming, a private sector expert who consulted with many Japanese firms on quality and quality control, stated that "94% of quality failures are not caused by workers but by the system—that is, management" (Main, 1984, p. 114). Contrary to conventional wisdom and practice, quotas, close monitoring, and mass inspections do not produce or enhance quality. In fact, those management techniques place ceilings on productivity, creativity, divergent thought, and standards. Processes and techniques can be controlled and improved, but attitudes toward quality cannot be monitored into employees. Glasser (1990) believes we need to replace the way we manage now with a method of management that emphasizes quality. Quality should be an organizational goal, modeled by leaders and shared with employees. More attention to attitude and perception is needed for quality service to be provided and for workers to be motivated.

Employees who identify with and are knowledgeable about the organization's mission, and who have opportunities for participation in decision making, become motivated to achieve quality. The following issues must be addressed to obtain quality in organizations:

- Fear of failure must be eliminated because it acts as an anesthetic, deadening the nerve to grow and paralyzing the pursuit of quality through new ideas, processes, and methods.
- Two-way communication and dialogue must be present. Dialogue on key issues removes unnecessary filters to perception and enhances thinking. Communication implies an organizational attitude of tolerance, openness, and room for divergent viewpoints.
- Invisible walls to communication must be destroyed and a unity of purpose constructed, so that organizational structure and processes can be regularly reviewed for flexibility and effectiveness.
- Professional and supportive staff must be recognized and their contributions celebrated to increase motivation and understanding of purpose. Abstract goals like quality must be made real through symbols of achievement.

Individuals need to know they can make significant contributions to the organization, no matter what their role. Providing information to workers, seeking their opinions, and engaging them in problem solving create greater openness and increase their sense of self-worth. It is motivating to have input into the process that creates the product and to know that the work being done is worth the effort.

Attitude, commitment, and input affect not only quality but also productivity. Murrin (Kilmann & Covin, 1988) stipulates that programs that were initially aimed at improving quality had a reciprocal effect on productivity. Quality and productivity go hand in hand, with quality driving productivity—not the other way around. Instead of "more is better," better produces more. Schools are no different from other organizations in respect to quality. Steps can be taken to transform them into institutions with the purpose, effort, and intent to produce quality educational services.

TIP | TRANSFORMATION INTO PRACTICE

EQUALITY AND QUALITY

John Gardner's book, *Excellence* (1984), poses the question, "Can we be equal and excellent too?" Does egalitarianism foster mediocrity and deter quality? Everyone is equal in terms of legal and political rights and privileges, and all people should have equal opportunity. But in achievement, differences exist because not everyone is equal in motivation or talent.

Gardner states that egalitarianism "wrongly conceived—which ignores differences in native capacity and achievement and eliminates incentives to individual performance—has not served democracy well. Carried far enough, it means the end of striving for excellence that has produced history's greatest achievements" (p. 30). Tuchman (1980), in "The Decline of Quality," agrees with Gardner in her contention that a "flat philosophy" of equality of everything is detrimental when quality is "castigated as elitism." Difference in capacity exists and must be recognized.

Concerning standards of labor, Tuchman postulates that the decline in quality is directly related to the increase in worker security. "No one likes to admit this, because it is depressing and because it does not fit into the sentimental conviction that all's well that is meant well, that good things have good results" (p. 41). According to this position, bureaucratic procedures and union rules reduce incentive, stymie quality, and promote mediocrity.

School boards, administrators, teachers, and unions need to examine some pertinent questions:

How can quality be fostered when organizational structures may work against them?

Can quality be guaranteed if hiring and promotion practices rest on seniority?

Can transformation of schools take place in a union-management, rule-driven, and norm-governed environment?

What are the antidotes to the diseases of complacency, cynicism, and narrow labor-management perception and thinking?

Quality and Schools

The level of quality in education is an important issue, but it cannot be measured in simplistic terms or solely by tests that stress the accumulation of facts. Assessing the quality of schools is a complicated task and it needs to encompass the broad mission of values, academics, attitudes, behavior, and organizational structure. Key factors influencing school quality are the disposition of the organization as a whole, leadership, and the staff's attitude. Quality schools stress high student achievement in academics; expect purposeful, ethical, and responsible behavior; and provide a structure that promotes caring, achievement, and equity. These schools emphasize multiple outcomes and believe that all students can learn.

If schools do not appreciate teaching and learning, then children will not work hard or take education seriously. To some, learning must be fun, work is to be avoided, and students should study what they like (Tuchman, 1980). Schools cannot afford to leave work only to those who are highly motivated and to expect very little from the rest. The gulf between the motivated and unmotivated will broaden, further dividing students into categories carrying destructive labels.

Quality school programs ensure equity. They define and uphold appropriate standards for every student. All students must be exposed to quality in order to value it. Challenging programs are designed for all levels of ability, and school goals are applicable to the entire student population. Personnel must care about children of every economic class and ability level, and not create favored categories.

In many schools, there is a tendency to underestimate pupils who are not perceived to be college bound. These students should not be given "soft" courses or ill-conceived experiences that will have no long-term benefit. Providing job-specific training, for instance, instead of academic education is short-sighted and reinforces the categorization of students and the deterioration of expectations.

Improving school quality must also consider organizational structure. The alienation caused by structure on the assembly line, in mass production, and impersonal offices contributes to the loss of quality. Malaise and complacency, found in a "don't knock yourself out" attitude and an untiring quest for diversion, affect both private and public sectors. Scientific management's dysfunctional consequences are wrapped in the dehumanizing and isolated structures it created. People who deal only with the minute parts of a system cannot feel committed or responsible for the final outcome.

Schools need to be cognizant of the impact of bureaucratization on quality. Isolation of classroom teachers, overregulation of teachers' roles, inflexibility of teachers' assignments to grades and subjects, limited opportunities for designing and implementing new programs, and a lack of understanding of the values and mission of the school lead to alienation.

Finally, schools, like other institutions, must constantly assess their outcomes and upgrade goals and practices for effectiveness. Quality in programs must be evaluated because organizations should assess what they value. Specific data must be collected to determine whether outcome quality is congruent with school values. Table 3–2 summarizes the dimensions and factors of school quality.

Quality: Effectiveness and Excellence

Quality is a larger concept than excellence and effectiveness, but both are necessary for quality to exist. Confusion occurs when these

TABLE 3–2   School Quality: Summary

Dimension	Factors
Mission	Multiple Goals
	High Achievement
	Teaching/Learning Valued
Client	Equity
	All Students Can Learn
	Focus on Expectations
Structure	Limited Bureaucracy
	Build Commitment
	Eliminate Isolation
Assessment	Encourage Collaboration
	Goal Oriented; Outcome-Based
	Specific; Data-Based
	Multiple Measures

terms are used interchangeably, as they have been in the literature on school and organizational reform. *Excellence* means that exceptional merit is present. *Effectiveness* requires producing a desired result efficiently. Effectiveness, however, can be devoid of quality or excellence. We can do mindless things effectively or we can do an excellent job pursuing frivolity.

Excellence in private sector companies has been studied intently since global competition threatened the U.S. economic standing. Excellent companies continuously innovate to perform to higher standards. These companies "keep things simple in a complex world. They persist. They insist on top quality. They fawn on their customers. They listen to their employees and treat them like adults. They allow their innovative product and service 'champions' long tethers. They allow some chaos in return for quick action and regular experimentation" (Peters & Waterman, 1982, p. 13). Characteristics of companies that have achieved excellence include:

1. A bias for action
2. Staying close to the customer
3. Autonomy and entrepreneurship
4. Productivity through people
5. Value-driven culture
6. Sticking to the knitting
7. Simple form and lean staff
8. Simultaneous loose-tight perspectives (centralized and decentralized) (Peters & Waterman, 1982).

These characteristics have not been applied to schools; however, they should be considered when standards are set for excellence. Everyone in an organization with high standards expects a lot from themselves and others. When organizations fail to inspire excellence in performance, they begin to decline.

Excellent organizations also need high morale and vitality. *Vitality* is the desire and ability to perform effectively and vigorously, which produces personal and professional growth (Miller, 1977). Developing high morale and vitality requires that individuals have a sense of significance and power. Professionals say that they "usually have a sense of authority about what they do, and they are recognized as experts in their field. They feel good about themselves and are respected by others" (Maeroff, 1988, p. 475). Significance kindles ambition and effort; people pursue their work because it is important and because they feel they can make a difference. Power, in turn, breeds a sense of identity and control.

Feelings of powerlessness are common in bureaucracies, where power and authority are dispersed in a hierarchical structure. Empowering people increases responsibility, ownership, and commitment, which have an impact on productivity. Morale and vitality come from doing important things and influencing positive outcomes.

PRODUCTIVITY

The concept of productivity has not been viewed positively by many educators because it sounds too mechanistic, simplistic, and assembly-line oriented. Arguments against measuring productivity include the perception that teaching is an art or craft, that the outcomes of education are too intangible to be measured, that the effort and potential of students cannot be evaluated uniformly, and that cause-and-effect relationships cannot be discerned.

How do you measure the productivity of attorneys? Or psychologists? Or teachers? All are knowledge workers—they possess, create, and transmit knowledge. In that respect, work product is not always produced at a consistent rate; thus, tangible results are not readily available.

Productivity: Definition and Influence

Productivity concerns the ratio of quality of results (output) to the resource (input) invested to obtain them (Patten, 1980). Effectiveness and efficiency are inherent in this ratio. *Effectiveness* is the way programs achieve their desired results, and *efficiency* is the management of resources to implement programs at minimum cost. Simply, efficiency is doing things right, and effectiveness is doing the right things.

In measuring school productivity, profit margin is not available as a guidepost as it is in the private sector, and competitive marketplace criteria do not apply. Schools are financed by tax dollars, and those dollars are spent on objectives set by elected public bodies. Objectives and spending are susceptible to change with each election, making continuity of goals a problem in consistently measuring productivity.

Productivity in schools is defined as achieving more effective educational results while using resources more efficiently (Perelman, 1987). Perelman points out that if learning is the goal, then productivity is a function of the performance of not only teachers and principals but of students—the learners—as well. Since productivity is partly dependent on the consumers (students), then schools and their staffs must target service to the consumers and understand their needs and environment. According to Kanter (1984), nonmechanical productivity is the capacity of an organization to "satisfy customer needs most fully with whatever resources it has at its disposal" (p. 22). She indicates that satisfying customers or clients requires innovation at every level of the organization.

Schools are labor intensive. The chances to become more productive by replacing people with machines or technology are more remote than in the private sector. Therefore, productivity relies on the better utilization of the talents of people—teachers, administrators, and students—their minute-by-minute decisions, motivation, ambition, and commitment.

As in quality, attitudes influence productivity. Studies with professional engineers concluded that improving the quality of work life increased productivity. The same factors concerning people that affect excellence and effectiveness have an impact on productivity. A sense of mission or purpose, commitment, lack of routinization, discretion and autonomy, positive self-concept, and openness are important ingredients to a productive work climate and environment. A knowledge worker's productivity is complex because the value of the output is usually determinable over a long period of time (Miller, 1977, p. 74).

In a quality, productive work climate, people value learning, encourage greater self-understanding, find valid measures to evaluate outcomes, use research, share information, trust each other, eliminate blaming, encourage risk taking, and personalize the organization through face-to-face interaction.

Perelman (1987) indicates that the next wave of educational reform will concern productivity because improvement in education is going to have to take place without additional finances. The present fiscal and human resources will have to be applied more productively. Walberg (1984) agrees that research on educational productivity is a high priority. Many industries have found ways to increase the value of their output and still reduce costs, which results in raising human welfare. He cautions educators that, like in business, cost and values must be assessed and the effects of educational inputs and outputs must be estimated.

Productivity as Cost-Effectiveness

There are two major concepts of productivity: cost-benefit and cost-effectiveness. Determining cost-benefit requires an analysis of the value of the outcomes resulting from different alternatives. Cost-benefit is difficult to apply to education generally because the alternative of no education is not viable. The basic assumption behind public schools is that they benefit society in the form of an enlightened and capable citizenry. Ignorance as an option is unacceptable. The cost-benefit of acquiring an education, however, has been measured in terms of increases in personal income.

Cost-effectiveness, on the other hand, is applicable to schools because the expense of alternatives and outcomes can be assessed and compared. One can measure the cost of achieving specific outcomes, which are reached through different methods, approaches, or processes, and over various spans of time. Cost-effectiveness is important for schools because fiscal resources are finite and the decisions about the allocation of dollars for outcome gained have to be made (Levin, 1988). The expense of the processes and the time spent, compared to the outcomes, will determine which method is more cost-effective—the same or better results at less cost or the same or better results in less time at the same or lower cost. *Costs* refer to the value of resources applied to effect the alternative or intervention, and *achievement* is frequently expressed in the gains each student or group of students make in learning skills, content, or concepts. Lower ratios of cost to outcomes reflect the highest cost-effectiveness. Figure 3–1 illustrates the factors involved in school productivity.

FIGURE 3–1   Organizational Factors in School Productivity

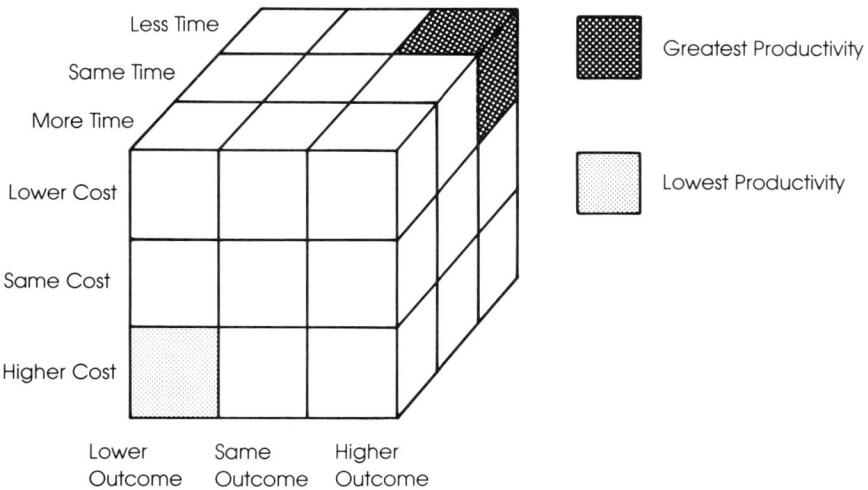

Cost-effectiveness in schools can be gained in four ways: (1) reduce costs and maintain outcomes, (2) fix costs and increase outcomes, (3) reduce costs and increase outcomes, or (4) increase costs and significantly increase outcomes. Cost-effectiveness is a factor of the ratio of costs to outcome. Increased costs can be desirable if the level of achievement outcomes is significantly higher than the cost-achievement ratio of less expensive options.

Outcomes should not be restricted to cognitive achievement measured on standardized tests. They can be more complex than that, encompassing higher-order thinking, as well as behavioral, affective, and psychomotor outcomes. Time is also an important part of the equation. If students learn the same amount or more in less time for the same or less cost, then productivity increases.

Outcomes also can relate to the number of students learning. If more students achieve the instructional objectives in the same amount of time and at the same cost, then the strategy is more productive. Another example might be that the costs are lowered as enrollment declines to produce the same or higher outcomes.

Applying these factors to an example may clarify the dynamics among them. The productivity of a teaching-learning strategy involves cost, time, and outcomes. If a school district invested in technology with a teaching-learning approach that allows a teacher and a group of students to make greater learning gains in a shorter period of time in remedial reading than the traditional approach, it may be cost-effective even if it requires an initial investment. If the gains the class makes are three grade levels in 100 hours of instruction for the investment in hardware and software, then it may be more cost-effective than the year and a half gain made in 180 hours of instruction using traditional methods. The cost per outcome gain over the long term may justify the added expense of the technology.

In examining cost-effectiveness, there are many permutations of the three variables of outcomes, time, and cost. Maximum productivity involves higher outcomes in less time for less cost. To measure maximum productivity, the highest level of outcome must be determined beforehand, and the cost and time limitations must be defined realistically. A totally nonproductive strategy would cost the district more, take more time, and produce lower outcomes than what currently happens. Before cost-effectiveness is determined, the appropriate level of outcomes should be defined.

Cost-effectiveness in education is not easy to measure. Teacher and administrative salaries, cost of specialized programs, and ranges of student abilities are all potential components of a productivity measure. The cost-effectiveness of a program may have to be assessed over a period of time so that a larger representative number of students can be included in the sample. Transforming schools search for ways to determine and assess productivity.

Productivity: Schools and Classrooms

The crisis in education, in part, concerns productivity. People perceive that today's students know less than students in the past, after spending the same amount of time in school but with a greater expenditure of tax dollars per student. Whether or not educators want to recognize productivity issues in teaching and learning, politicians, citizens, school board members, parents, and students are asking for more productivity—better results in more diverse objectives after 13 years of public education.

Some educators indicate that they are as productive as in the past, but the students have changed. Pupils come to school with greater needs and with less support than before; thus, educators should not be blamed for children's lack of performance. This explanation is dangerous. At worst, it suggests that it is futile to teach because teaching and learning are victims of forces beyond the control of schools. At best, it assumes that objectives will be harder to achieve due to the impediments to success of student social, economic, and family situations.

The factors of time, cost, and outcomes do not consider the students or their unique needs. With some students, where educational deprivation and disability may be great, more time and money may have to be given and the objectives modified to achieve success. Costs in these circumstances must be reviewed and evaluated in terms of the gains made.

At the school and classroom levels, teachers and principals can take steps to increase their own productivity relating to practices, behavior, environment, and attitudes. For example, if teachers do not measure what students already know, before setting objectives, they may spend time teaching previously learned material—wasting valuable time, energy, and resources.

In one school district, an evaluation of the mathematics program found that students performed well on computation skills but needed improvement on problem solving. A teacher realized that instructors at the seventh-grade level were teaching 10 weeks of computational skills that tests demonstrated were known by the vast proportion of students. Yet, teachers were concerned with finding more time for problem solving. In this instance, time was spent on the repetition of skills students knew, to the detriment of problem-solving applications in which they were deficient. Careful assessment and lesson planning can increase productivity by keeping on task and ensuring that all subjects and concepts get appropriate attention.

Another issue in productivity is curriculum overlap—having students learn the same content or objectives in different content areas. If this is occurring, learning time is squandered. Curriculum structure also can affect teachers' productivity and needs evaluation to eliminate redundancy.

The characteristics of productive schools and classrooms have been identified in a meta-analysis conducted by Georgiades, Fuentes, and Snyder (no date). They define them in the cognitive, affective, and behavioral areas:

Behavioral
- Flexibility in instructional approaches
- Cooperative work environment
- High task orientation; no time wasted
- Visible, fair leadership
- Expectations related to outcomes
- Fluid grouping
- Teacher-principal interactions related to instruction
- Supportive environment—students ask for help and receive it

Cognitive
- Continuous staff development/inservice related to instruction
- Application of research-based principles to teaching
- Teachers knowledgeable about instruction, curriculum, and content
- Principals knowledgeable about instruction

Affective
- Discipline in a supportive climate
- Positive rapport with students
- Teachers demonstrate high control and satisfaction
- Staff has high interpersonal skills
- Teachers show ownership of the curriculum
- Teachers perceive parents as supportive and students as desiring to learn
- High student and staff morale
- Rapport between teachers and parents high
- High levels of parent-initiated involvement
- Staff attitudes positive and commitment high*

* Adapted from William Georgiades, Ernestina Fuentes, and Karolyn Snyder, A Meta-Analysis of Productive School Cultures. Pedamorphosis, Inc., no date.

Ignoring productivity issues and not making the effort to determine cost-effectiveness leaves educators in the uncomfortable position of not being able to evaluate what works best. Productivity measures must be applied to schools for greater accountability and success in the future.

SUCCESS

In general terms, success means achieving favorable, quality outcomes in a productive way. Defining success necessitates delving into purpose, values, and goals. Some people define success in concrete symbols, such as material rewards or high personal position or status. In a different sense, success can be viewed as self-fulfillment and satisfaction. Yankelovich (1982) found that the struggle for self-fulfillment is on the edge of a cultural revolution, moving away from competitive success and the accumulation of money and power. Even in some businesses, success now has less to do with competition than with enlarging the playing field (Sculley, 1987) for everyone, thereby making the total industry stronger for more people. Enlarging the market, in a more competitive environment, is becoming the goal.

Organizational success depends on several factors, including flexibility, creativity, innovation, information, and expertise. Flexibility is a key to organizational survival. Structures should not be permanent; they should be adaptable to changes in internal and external demands, expectations, and challenges. Systems that do not have the ability to adapt become anachronistic remnants. Reorganizing and restructuring should be viewed positively because technology, changing demographics, economic structure, and knowledge explosion demand responsiveness to change.

Information-age organizations also need *creativity* and *innovation* to remain successful. The traditional bureaucracy makes creativity and innovation difficult because each layer or department in the organization acts as a filter with the ability to reject but seldom with the right to approve change. Ideas move slowly through the bureaucracy, seldom making it to the top. Bureaucracy often strangles itself in its own structure, with ideas and change becoming the victims.

Change must be a positive value. Survival depends on eliminating processes and procedures that no longer work. The most difficult change, however, is the willingness to abandon what was once successful. Commitment, security, and tradition make this modification difficult, even though times and conditions may have changed. Schools are classic examples of traditional, secure institutions, which hold tenaciously to rituals, procedures, and methods of the past.

Creative organizations, in contrast, perceive usual problems in unusual ways (Sims & Gioia, 1986). They define change as an opportunity, not a problem. Although schools frequently perceive the change process as problematic, not one of positive redefinition, creative organizations accept the paradoxes, ambiguities, dilemmas, and uncertainties in change.

Success also depends on *information* and how it is perceived, interpreted, and used. Data can be confounding and contradictory; there is an inundation of facts, statistics, and numbers, but sometimes not much useful information. Successful organizations have people who construct a workable world from available information by forging an understanding from it and then taking action. They do not wait for complete clarity and total unambiguous information before making decisions.

Successful organizations use information to become learning organizations (Miller, 1977) that:

- Build feedback processes with means to measure growth
- Relate each department's objectives to the mission of the entire organization
- Provide departments with autonomy for process implementation, education, and learning
- Develop open relationships between people to assist with the exchange of information

Access to information also contributes to the level of success. The perceived power structure determines who has access to what information and when. Information should not be used as a chip in organizational power games. It should be widely available to all who need it and accurately dispersed in a timely fashion.

Finally, skilled and knowledgeable professionals who demonstrate their *expertise* are essential for organizations to function successfully. Adaptive structures, organizational flexibility, and good information are useless if there are not competent people in critical positions with the experience, knowledge, and skills to orchestrate success. Table 3–3 summarizes the factors that contribute to organizational success.

Successful Schools

Can schools use the same criteria as other organizations to determine if they are successful? The literature on effective and excellent

TABLE 3–3   Successful Organizations

Dimension	Factors
Structure	Objectives related to mission
	Flexibility
	Responsibility
	Adaptability
	Competent workers
Values	Innovation
	Change is positive
	Creativity
Information	Developing understanding
	Learning
	Open communication
	channels
	Expertise
	Shared power

schools begins to measure school quality, but success goes farther than these characteristics. The differences between effective, excellent, and successful schools are presented in Figure 3–2, and relate to perspective, mission, and scope of goals. Successful schools speak to a broader mission than effective or excellent ones, and they include the outcomes of these two movements.

The effective schools' movement focuses on basic skills development as measured by standardized tests. This limited educational goal is not sufficient for children to work, compete, and succeed in the complex, technological society of tomorrow. Reform to achieve excellence emphasizes academic achievement, a more extensive purpose than simply basic skills. However, only norm- and criterion-referenced tests were used to evaluate the level of excellence.

Successful schools attend to basic skills and academic achievement, but character, citizenship, interpersonal, social, physical, and cultural aspects of education are also given priority. The successful school concept views education more comprehensively and measures outcomes in more diverse ways—tests, goal attainment, standards, projects, and behavior. The outcomes have significantly greater breadth and depth.

Schools cannot be accused of being shining examples of adaptiveness, flexibility, or continuous improvement. They need these characteristics for the future, however, if they are to contend with changes in

FIGURE 3–2   School Success, Excellence, and Effectiveness

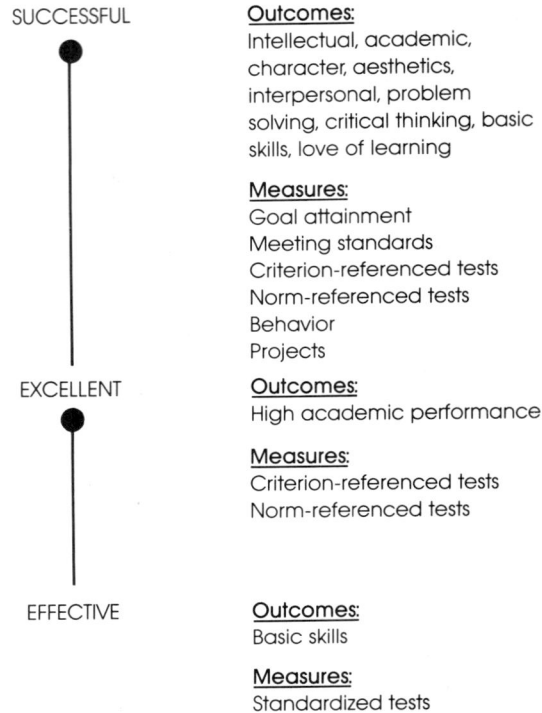

SUCCESSFUL ●	**Outcomes:** Intellectual, academic, character, aesthetics, interpersonal, problem solving, critical thinking, basic skills, love of learning **Measures:** Goal attainment Meeting standards Criterion-referenced tests Norm-referenced tests Behavior Projects
EXCELLENT ●	**Outcomes:** High academic performance **Measures:** Criterion-referenced tests Norm-referenced tests
EFFECTIVE	**Outcomes:** Basic skills **Measures:** Standardized tests

Adapted from Thomas J. Sergiovanni, *The Principalship* (Boston: Allyn and Bacon, 1987).

society, expectations, and goals, as well as the challenge of alternatives and the choices technology will afford.

The definition and characteristics of successful schools are consistent with those of private sector organizations. Schools, after all, are service organizations that have to maintain the confidence and support of citizens—both parents and nonparents—and clients. Credibility with the public cannot be obtained and maintained without demonstrated or perceived success. Sergiovanni (1987b) states that in successful schools everything "hangs together" and that there is a sense of purpose and mission that rally teachers and other staff to a common cause. The meaning of the school's work is clear to students and staff, and accomplishments are recognized. The spirit of cooperation is obvious between students and teachers.

The components of successful schools are defined in Figure 3–3.

They include school culture, outcomes, leadership, climate, quality, and productivity. Quality and productivity have been discussed in detail. Cultural, outcome, leadership, and climate components, although touched on here, are treated in other sections of the book.

Successful schools have strong organizational cultures with clear values that are used as a unifying, cohesive force. The mission is based on a distinct vision of what the school is and what it can become. It ties people together with a strong bond of purpose or collective ideology. The culture and values make sense only if they are linked and welded to outcomes. Positive attitudes, with no significant outcomes, will erode into disillusionment because one's work will have little meaning.

FIGURE 3–3   Components of Successful Schools

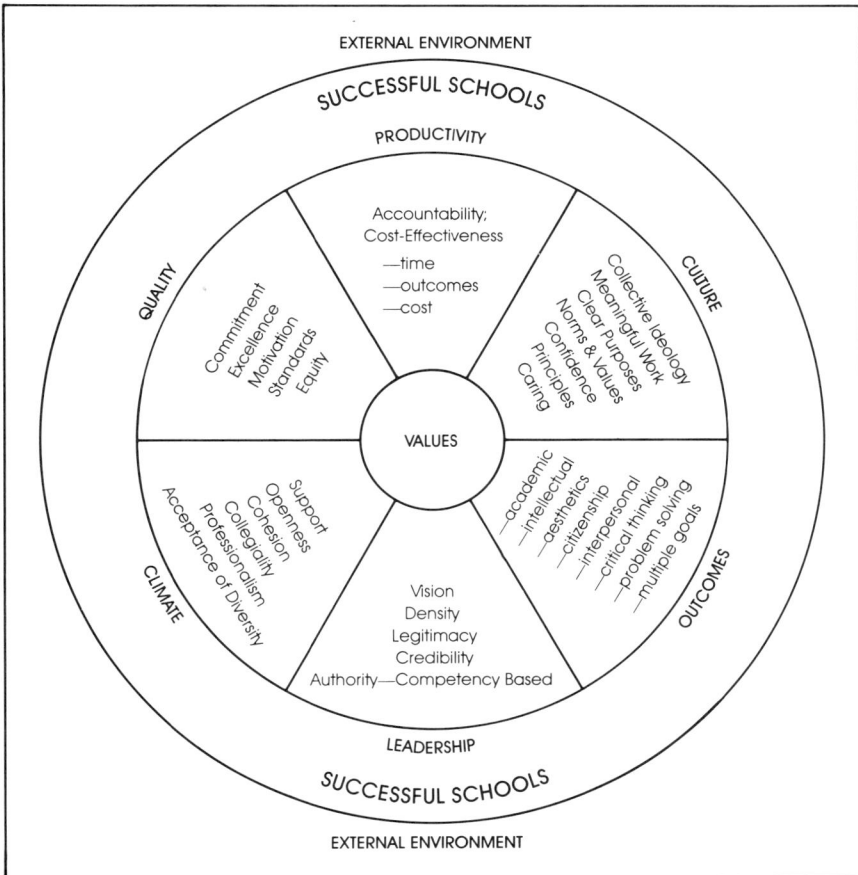

An open climate allows teachers and other professionals to have the autonomy to fulfill their responsibilities but with high accountability expectations. They are empowered, and they have a sense of control over their roles and professional destinies. The principles of cooperation, empowerment, responsibility, accountability, and meaningfulness exist and thrive. Teachers have authority, and the gap between their ability and authority is narrowed.

In successful schools, teaching is viewed as a professional decision-making process and not as a mechanical task dictated by the organization, textbook companies, or teacher unions. Teaching promotes critical thinking, intellectual inquiry, an appreciation of knowledge, the joy and satisfaction of learning, and the development of strong self-images for students. These practices reflect the core values and standards of the organization and produce the desired outcomes.

Principals of successful schools are less concerned with being bosses than with seeing their schools succeed. Maeroff (1988) indicated that they are more like symphony conductors who blend the skills of artists rather than train conductors who efficiently manage comings and goings. Leadership must be perceived as legitimate, with authority based on competence. School principals who share leadership with faculty create greater leadership density (Sergiovanni, 1987b).

Schools as organizational structures can be bureaucratic in nature with all their dysfunctional, inertia-producing characteristics. Sergiovanni (1987b) suggests that a "cooperative" bureaucracy be established that allows staff discretion but not complete autonomy in meeting the purposes of the school. Cooperative bureaucracies define the nonnegotiable imperatives that must be met, and they rely on teamwork among and between principals, teachers, and support staff.

Peters and Waterman (1982) state that successful schools have a "loose-tight" relationship that occurs in successful private sector companies—tight around values and mission but loose in the means and methods professionals select to reach them. There is a very strong link between mission and teacher and administrative decisions concerning curriculum, instruction, teaching, supervision, and evaluation. The loose-tight condition can exist when climate is collegial, supportive, and professional.

SUMMARY

To achieve successful schools, organizations, people, and leadership must be transformed. Reaching success cannot be accomplished in structures that prohibit it, by people who do not perceive the need or value it, or by leaders who behave transactionally instead of transformationally.

CONCEPTS

1. Standards in organizations are contagious. They formulate the expectations for quality, productivity, and success.
2. Quality is the product of effort, purpose, and intent. It is a value that requires commitment from everyone in the organization.
3. Emphasis on quality has a reciprocal effect on productivity. Quotas, close monitoring, and mass inspections do not improve quality.
4. School climate and the disposition, posture, and structure of the organization are key factors in school quality.
5. School productivity rests on people's motivation, ambition, decisions, and commitment. It also rests on students' efforts and commitment.
6. There are two major concepts of productivity: cost-benefit and cost-effectiveness. Cost-effectiveness in schools can be measured by outcomes, cost of methods and approaches, and time required to learn. It refers to achieving more effective educational results while using resources more efficiently.
7. The effective schools' movement focuses on limited outcomes, whereas successful schools view education more comprehensively and use multiple measures for evaluation.
8. Attitude of teachers is an important factor in school success. Attitudes toward quality are shaped by an individual's background experience, but also by management and leadership.
9. Motivated teachers identify with and are knowledgeable about the mission of schools, have input into decision making, and contribute to the achievement of quality.
10. Quality, excellence, and effectiveness are not synonymous. Quality encompasses effectiveness and excellence.
11. Quality school programs stress equity for all types of students.
12. Organizational success requires flexibility, creativity, innovation, information, and expertise. Traditional bureaucracies pose severe impediments to these factors.
13. The model for successful schools consists of six dimensions: culture, outcomes, leadership, climate, quality, and productivity.

PART II | TRANSFORMING ORGANIZATIONS

Successful organizations transform themselves and those who work in them. They are self-renewing; changing, growing, and rising to challenges. Transforming organizations create conditions for growth and expansion, provide a sense of purpose, and allow people to meet their own needs while helping the organization achieve its mission. These organizations, as social systems, operate synergistically—the sum of the parts being greater than the whole. Understanding the evolution of organizational operations is necessary for assessing behavior within these complex structures, for analyzing purposes and policies, for developing creative and effective systems, and for relating these activities to the transforming process.

The context and structural dimensions of organizations are reviewed in Chapter 4, along with the life cycles they experience. Chapter 5 emphasizes culture and the process of change and innovation. Organizations are designed to make decisions. That process is linked with and dependent on information, which is critical to assessing perception, thinking, and behavior.

4 Organizations: Context and Dimensions

Organizations provide services and products that are crucial to our standard of living. Without them, society would be less affluent and more primitive. In the private and public sector, an understanding of organizations is necessary for critically analyzing how they can continue to function effectively in a changing environment and to determine if they will be useful structures for the future.

An organization "is a human instrument created for some purpose" which is "distinguished from other social units . . . by its design and objectives" (Reitz, 1981, p. 14). Because organizations must have members to exist, they develop mechanisms to divide, coordinate, and control member activities. Membership changes throughout the life of most organizations, so they tend to develop an identity independent of individual members. This unique social unit—the organization—has been a valuable tool for our world. Yet, the term *organization* produces images of red tape, regimentation, bureaucracy, and mindless conformity. Bureaucratic organizations seem to be antithetical to creative achievement and growth, and contrary to the value of individualism associated with the United States.

In any "large, elaborately organized technological society," the threat to individuality is part of the problem (Gardner, 1978). Organizational life can reduce people's sense of belonging and cause them to lose their relationship to the whole enterprise. Often, members of an organization end up feeling anonymous. An irony of human society is "that individual human beings, acting together, build great institutional structures . . . that tend to devalue individual human beings" (pp. 70–71), resulting in depersonalization and lack of communication.

TABLE 4–1   Organizations: Purpose and Goals

Organizations	Purpose	Outcome
Corporation	Profits	Products
Hospital	Medical Care	Healthy Community
Army	Protection	Secure Nation
School	Instruction	Educated Citizenry
Church	Instill Religion	Saved Sinners
Symphony	Cultural Entertainment	Cultured Community
Political Party	Democratic Choices	Community Power

Source: Joseph H. Reitz, Behavior in Organizations (Homewood, IL: Richard D. Irwin, 1981), p. 13.

One's perception of organizations determines whether one sees them as vehicles for creativity and growth or as a means for control and power. There are organizations that create opportunities and those that suppress progress—some are successful and others fail. Schools are no different; they may be creative, dynamic places or stiflingly restrictive to students and teachers. To create productive institutions in which structures and procedures promote, not handicap, obtaining their mission, it is important to conceptualize what organizations are and how they operate. Examples of different types of organizations in our society are defined in Table 4–1.

Do schools have anything in common with AT&T or General Motors? There are obvious differences in motive and development between corporations and school districts. Are all school systems the same? Vast differences exist in the size, scope, and structure of schools in rural areas compared to urban or metropolitan districts, and there are many variations between these extremes. Despite the differences among school systems, and between schools and private sector organizations, there are common characteristics.

ORGANIZATIONS

All organizations are "social entities that are goal directed, deliberatively structured activity systems with an identifiable boundary" (Daft, 1989, p. 9). Social entities are composed of groups of people who interact and engage in a common endeavor or purpose. They attempt to achieve desired goals through a deliberatively structured set of work activities or tasks. The identifiable boundaries specify what is inside or outside the confines of the formal organization. Davis (1982) simplifies the components of organizations as culture, structure, systems, and people.

Both of these definitions use the concept of system. A *system* is a "set of interacting elements that acquires inputs from the environment, transforms them, and discharges outputs to the external environments" (Daft, 1989, p. 11). Interacting with the external environment is a characteristic of an open system, which adapts to and changes with the environment. Closed systems, on the other hand, do not depend on the environment; they are autonomous and cocooned from its effects.

According to Schein (1985), organizations "are themselves open systems in constant interaction with their many environments, and they consist of many subgroups, occupational units, hierarchical layers, and geographically dispersed segments" (p. 7). These systems depend on the environment for their survival—in the private sector it may be resources, in the public sector it may be credibility and tax support.

Schools are open social systems in which alterations in the external environment have consequences and implications for the design and structure of the internal organization. Many decisions can be traced to the external environment. For example, the change to a global economy with strong international competition led to pressure from parents, businesses, and government for schools to produce students with appropriate skills to enter that environment.

Open social systems are complex and political, because they are comprised of many factors operating simultaneously to affect how they function. Human interactions and role relationships are major components of organizational life. These change continuously, influenced by norms and values of both the organization and the people within it, as well as by the external environment. Social systems function through communication and action, which may be formal and easy to observe, or informal and intangible (such as using symbols and specialized jargon).

The perception of organizations as open, social systems differs dramatically from the view that organizations are closed, rational systems. The social-systems view assumes that organizations, at times, are somewhat chaotic, disorderly, and nonrational. It recognizes the influence of the environment and the impact of power and political decisions, where disagreements and conflict are evident. Leaders in these circumstances must help the organization adapt to external situations, while understanding the needs of people inside the system. The rational perception, however, assumes a stable predictability in organizations. Logic and order dominate, and the leader's responsibility is to establish efficient work relationships. This perspective is oriented to closed systems, which can be protected from external influences, where certainty and predictability are typical.

The constructs of open and closed systems help in understanding how systems can function, but they do not present a complete picture for contemporary organizations. The emergence of technology and its influence on systems demands a broader perspective, which introduces *sociotechnical systems* theory. Sociotechnical systems theory combines the needs of people in organizations with the implications of technology and the enhancement it can bring. Thoreau stated that we become tools of our tools. The machines we invent reinvent us to the extent that they change our perception, our interactions, and our potential.

In schools, the tools have long been paper, chalkboards, books, and visual and auditory aids like tape recorders, film projectors, and record players. These tools place very different demands and possibilities on the system and people than networked computers, interactive television, and satellite transmissions. Technology in education presents new challenges and may lead to different behavior in teaching and learning. It affects how teachers work, defines the information they have available, suggests dramatic alterations in teaching-learning strategies, and influences school management and productivity.

The principles of sociotechnical systems evolved in the 1950s and 1960s at the Travistock Institute in England. Merging structure and technology to meet people's needs to become more productive and improve quality was the goal. Sociotechnical systems link people and technology because "an organization will function best only if the socio and technical systems are designed to fit the needs of one another. Designing the structure to meet human needs while ignoring the technical system, or changing technology to improve efficiency while ignoring human needs, may inadvertently cause performance problems" (Daft, 1989, p. 159).

Organizations are usually viewed as systems, but Morgan (1986) introduces some other images of organizations. These include organizations as

> *Machines:* The organization is a tool, with interlocking parts, which works to achieve service or product outcomes.
>
> *Brains:* Organizations are mechanisms for learning and intelligence. Creativity and information are valued and are circulated to workers who need a similar body of data.
>
> *Cultures:* Organizations are designed for shared meaning and purpose. Norms, values, rituals, and traditions provide meaning and guide organizational life.

Psychic Prisons: People working within the organization become imprisoned by the rigid structure and activities of the organization.

Instruments of Domination: Organizations use host communities and employees for the selfish pursuit of profits, often to the detriment of society.

The perception of organizations—as closed or open systems, as rational or political bodies, as machines or instruments of domination—affects how one approaches their administration.

Perspectives on Organizational Administration

Four views of organizational administration have developed over the course of this century. The first, *scientific management*, was established by Fredrick Taylor in 1911 and emphasized efficiency. The keys were a rational orientation to work, one best way of doing things, and tasks specialized to promote efficiency. Scientific management assumed the presence of a rational, self-correcting system with "consensus around goals, coordination of the dissemination of information, and the predictability of problems and the responses to them" (Sergiovanni & Corbally, 1984, p. 4). While emphasizing efficiency, scientific management short-changed and underestimated the human side of organizational life.

In contrast, human relations or *human resources theory*, promoted by the Hawthorne studies by Roethlisberger, examined people's roles, commitment, and motivation in organizations. Loyalty and the meaning of work are important concepts to individuals. Participative decision making, joint planning, common goals, shared responsibility, and increased accountability are the main tenets of human relations approaches to administration.

The third approach—a *political perspective*—views organizations as open systems with inputs and outputs to the external environment. In this milieu, issues are raised, pressure groups are active, and bargains are struck. Policy development is emphasized and goals are negotiated in order to satisfy a variety of needs. Conflict is considered natural and necessary, with debates over values, goals, and strategies.

Finally, the *cultural perspective* considers organizations as "artificial entities subject to the whims of human conventions and predispositions" (Sergiovanni & Corbally, 1984, p. 7). Concepts of community and shared values and meanings underlie this perception. Leadership becomes important because the leader's purpose and communication are key to establishing meaning and stimulating people's conscious-ness. Symbols, values, and beliefs are the main ingredients in the cul-tural cement that holds the organization together. A summary of the relationships between systems and administrative perspectives is de-fined in Table 4–2.

These administrative perspectives produce contrasting view-points about organizational life. Traditional perspectives follow ra-tional, efficiency designs—organizations containing groups united in some common goal, with little attention to individual needs or as-pirations. A more contemporary viewpoint sees organizations as non-rational places with leaders who create vision and develop com-mitment. This approach focuses on patterns of interactions between individuals and their roles and purposes.

Whether organizations are viewed as open or closed, rational or nonrational, all organizations have two dimensions in common—structure and context. The *structural* dimension describes the internal characteristics of organizations, whereas the *contextual* dimension con-cerns the external settings that affect the structural dimension.

Contextual Dimension: Organizational Environment

A simple definition of *environment* is "all elements that exist outside the boundary of the organization and have the potential to affect all or part of the organization" (Daft, 1989, p. 45). The complexity, change, and uncertainty of the external environment can influence orga-nizational success; thus, information is needed to understand and adapt to its conditions.

Organizations exist in a context that "creates a reality, and the

TABLE 4–2   Systems, Organizational Perceptions, and Administrative Perspectives

System	Organizational Perception	Administrative Perspective
Open	Social Systems Sociotechnical Systems	Human Relations Cultural Political
Closed	Rational	Scientific Management

reality it creates is the content. Most managers manage the content, and only during a major strategic shift is the context brought into question'' (Davis, 1982, p. 65). Davis believes that managers should spend as much time framing questions as trying to answer them. Asking the right question is important because it determines the boundaries of the inquiry and thinking that is to follow. The questions raised affect which elements in the external environment get the attention of the organization.

The external environment can be categorized into sectors, which affect organizations to different degrees. Leaders must understand the dynamics between and among these sectors, their relevance to the organization's mission, and their potency at any given time. These sectors are defined in Table 4–3.

Environmental complexity simply means that a large number of elements interact with and influence the organization. Simple environments have only three or four factors of influence; complex ones feel pressure from many. In addition, complexity can be coupled with stability, which adds another degree of complexity. A stable environment

TABLE 4–3   Environment: Sectors

Sector	Components
Human Resources	Labor market, unionization, training
Financial Resources	Tax structure, loans, banks
Technology	Research, automation, techniques to produce services
Market	Clients, needs, demands
Economic Conditions	Recession, unemployment, inflation, economic growth
Government	Laws, regulations, services, mandates, court cases, political processes
Sociocultural	Demographic characteristics, values, beliefs, work ethic, urban/rural
Professional	Competitors, size, characteristics of related support services
Materials	Real estate, manufacturers, suppliers

Source: Adapted from Richard L. Daft, *Organizational Theory and Design* (St. Paul: West, 1989).

is more easily predictable and known, whereas unstable ones have abrupt shifts and turnabouts.

The relationship between organization and environmental complexity is shown in Table 4–4. How does this concept of environmental conditions apply to schools? Schools are complex, open systems that must interact with increasingly unstable environments. They are not as simple and stable as they used to be. Often schools have only looked inward without regard to the pressures, expectations, and changes in the external environment. As a result, the massive number of reports in the early and mid-1980s primarily came from external sources— government, business, and private foundations. These sectors demanded schools to be responsive and to examine their programs and structures, which led to a discourse on the purpose of education and the strategies needed for change.

The major environmental factors affecting schools include four areas: governmental, human resources, financial/economic, and sociocultural (see Figure 4–1). In many cases, schools have little direct influence or control over the sectors affecting them.

Sociocultural Factors.   Community expectations determine the standards that local schools are supposed to meet. These expectations can translate into support for schools, cries for reform, or loss of credibility. But they are factors to which local school board members need to be receptive and responsive because they represent and serve the community.

Support for schools is affected by who has a vested interest in

TABLE 4–4   Environmental Complexity

Organization	Stability	Characteristics
Simple	Stable	Few external sectors
		Sectors remain same
Simple	Unstable	Few external sectors
		Sectors change frequently
Complex	Stable	Many dissimilar sectors
		Sectors remain same or change slowly
Complex	Unstable	Many dissimilar sectors
		Sectors change frequently and unpredictably

Source: Adapted from Richard L. Daft, *Organizational Theory and Design* (St. Paul: West, 1989), pp. 46–50.

FIGURE 4–1   Environment and School Organizations

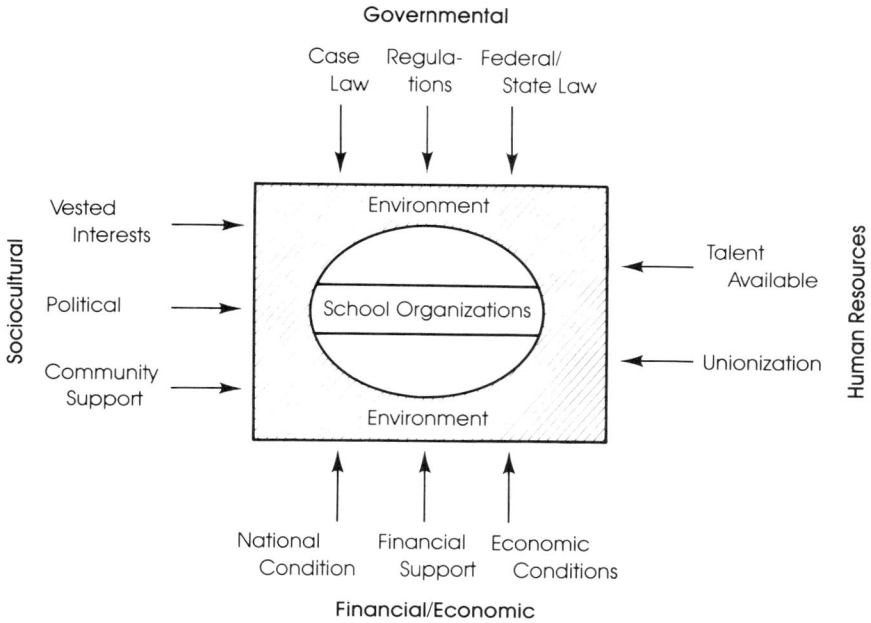

them. Vested interests are created by people who have a stake in the operation and success of the schools. The number of private and parochial children and parents in the district affect support, as does the number of senior citizens. The level of vested support can be affected by the schools and their programs; schools can expand the vested interest in programs by responding to all segments of their population.

Demographics influence vested interest because the ethnic and age makeup of our society enters into expectations and the level of support for schools. Large numbers of preschool children translate into the need for more classrooms and teachers. Having more people over age 65 than there are teenagers affects the fiscal and moral support for schools. Some parts of the nation grow and other sections shrink because of the transitory nature of society and economy. The impact of age, immigration, and social mobility pressures schools to expand or contract programs. Frequently, these pressures are contradictory and inconsistent in content and intent.

At the local level, school board politics, single-issue interest groups, and cooperation between units of government can establish the climate in which school policy and other matters are considered. Local political issues may also affect schools' operation and programs. Single-interest power groups may pressure school boards and teachers to implement or remove programs from the course of study. Some communities are known to be liberal or conservative, which may influence the nature of the issues that are politically sensitive. At times, school programs and spending become issues in partisan elections for mayor or governor, which place educators and programs in the limelight of controversy and review.

Fiscal/Economic Factors.   Both national and local economic conditions influence educational policy. If a major plant closes in a community and unemployment soars, then the local school board will have more difficulty with its budget and fiscal support than in times of economic prosperity. A national or regional recession also affects school policy at all levels of government, sometimes imposing cost controls on local districts or establishing greater competition among local units of government for tax dollars.

The national condition is reflected in the morale, competitiveness, and esteem of the country. A troubled nation may turn to education for relief or it may blame the schools for its plight. A loss of economic competitiveness can get translated into the failure of public schools to prepare students adequately. Sputnik and the loss of U.S. electronic and auto market share are obvious examples. National agendas and circumstances are influenced by and affect the economy and expectations for schools.

Governmental Factors.   State and federal law, case law, and regulations can increase or decrease bureaucracy as well as programs and expectations. They affect policy and procedures, determine how students and staff are treated, and designate the nature of programs offered and the level of opportunity for pupils. In fact, these governmental factors have a profound influence on local school expenditures and taxes.

Human Resource Factors.   Schools do not control the flow of human resources available for their talent pool. The depth and breadth of available talent in colleges aspiring to become teachers are determined by market forces, societal status conferred on teachers, and collegiate demands and programs. Schools can draw only from the available talent pool, and the competition for talent will become a more pressing problem for schools and corporations in the future. Another issue is the degree of unionization prevalent in the state and region of the school. Unions can greatly influence funding, programs, and flexibility.

Environmental factors also have an impact on schools' structure. "Organizations structure themselves in response to their internal and external environments. By accepting certain structural and figurative imperatives from these environments (such as goals, formal hierarchy, rational norms), organizations become legitimate" (Sergiovanni & Corbally, 1984, p. 115). Movements to decentralize schools, institute site-based management, and instill more participative decision making relate directly to environmental pressures on schools from business and industry.

Structural Dimension: Organizational Operation

When people think of organizations, structured hierarchies usually come to mind. Structure is specified in the line and staff organizational chart, which spells out the formal reporting relationships between and among positions. The different levels in the organization are established and the span of control (the number of people reporting to a particular position) is defined. Structure determines the dispersal and location of power. "Formal organizations are based on certain principles such as 'task specialization,' 'chain of command,' 'unity of direction' and 'rationality.' These are the basic 'genes' that are supported by, and at times modified in varying degrees by, the technology, the kinds of managerial controls, and the patterns of leadership used in the organization" (Argyris, 1964, p. 14).

Congruent with Argyris's notion of genes, Daft (1989, pp. 17–20) identifies the dimensions of organizational structure as formalization, specialization, standardization, hierarchy of authority, complexity, centralization, and professionalism. These components, which are summarized in Table 4–5, are highly interrelated. For example, formalization of organizations affects the behavior and activities of people. The greater the formalization, the less flexible the system. More written documentation increases the standardization. Specialization affects interaction because it narrows the range of tasks people are responsible for completing. It also affects perception, as indicated in Chapter 2. Highly specialized organizations are more complex because they have more departments, activities, and levels.

The hierarchy of authority is an important dimension because it determines the shape of the organization. Wide span of control results in flat organizations, whereas a narrow span of control creates a pyramidal-shaped one. Reducing the number of people who report to another

TABLE 4–5   Structure: Dimensions

Dimension	Components
Formalization	Written procedures
	Job descriptions
	Policy manuals
Specialization	Division of labor
	Task separation
Standardization	Similar tasks performed in similar manner
Hierarchy of authority	Position reporting patterns
	Span of control
Complexity	Number of subsystems
	Number of levels
	Number of geographical locations
Centralization	Hierarchical level that has decision-making authority
Professionalism	Level of training/education required of staff

Source: Adapted from Richard L. Daft, Organizational Theory and Design (St. Paul: West, 1989), p. 54.

creates high structures and increases the levels of bureaucracy. Centralization is determined by the location of decision-making authority. In highly centralized organizations, decision-making authority rests at the top of the structure. Decentralized systems give authority for making decisions to positions closest to the level that is affected most by them. Professional workers, with high degrees of training and expertise, expect to be involved meaningfully in decisions. Much of the restructuring movement in education is designed to flatten school structure so more decisions are made by the teacher.

Mintzberg (1979) views organizational structure as having top management, middle management, a technical core, administrative support services (in the form of clerical and maintenance resources), and technical support staff. In schools, top management relates to central office administrative positions, and middle management is analagous to the role of principals. The technical core is the professional staff, which has diverse skills and is divided among the various grade levels and departments. Technical support staff is composed of guidance counselors, curriculum supervisors, psychologists, social workers, exceptional education specialists, and others.

Some organizations function well and meet their goals and others do not. Structural deficiencies can cause dysfunction, by affecting decision making, environmental responsiveness, and internal conflict (Daft, 1989). Delays in decision making, inertia, or the poor quality of decisions can be related to structure. If the organization is highly central-ized, decision makers at the top may be overloaded, creating a logjam of problems needing resolution or stopping strategies from being imple-mented. Decisions are delayed when delegation of authority is lax or insufficient. The quality of decisions can be poor if timely information does not reach the people who determine options or strategies.

A second area where structure can cause deficiency is in the han-dling of conflict, which is always a part of organizational life. Some conflict is healthy, but too much can be counterproductive to goal achievement. If organizational goals and departmental or school goals are incongruent, conflict will result. Turmoil in determining priorities and allocating resources between competing goals is a serious problem.

How the subsystems in organizations interact with the external environment is another structural concern. Proficiency in scanning the environment for problems and opportunities is necessary for effective-ness. Environmental awareness can be lost in an organization unless it is specified as a priority. In many cases, schools are not very sophisticated in environmental scanning or in identifying influences and trends.

Structure and the Environment

Some structures are better suited to stable environments, whereas others respond well to unstable conditions. Unstable environments are those with a great deal of uncertainty (see Table 4–4). Four different structures can be identified—functional, product, hybrid, and matrix—each of which can be effective in meeting the demands of certain envi-ronmental conditions (Daft, 1989, pp. 227–243). The matching of struc-ture with condition determines how well the organization will work.

Functional structures perform well in stable environments with low uncertainty where internal efficiency is valued. Although this structure is suited for small- or medium-sized organizations and pro-vides for in-depth skill development of employees, it does not respond rapidly to environmental change because many decisions are central-ized at the top. Functional organizations may develop good products or services, but they are not designed for innovation. Many schools are structured in this manner. In the past, when school environments were stable and certain, this structure may have been effective.

Product-oriented structures are effective in environments of mod-erate or high uncertainty. External effectiveness and adaptation are important because the organization must be responsive to clients or customers. Responsiveness to fast changes is possible through decen-tralized decision making, allowing units to adapt to local conditions.

High coordination is evident across all of the organizational functions. Standardization, however, is not a strength because of the decentralized, responsive decision-making operation. The movement to restructure schools is modeled after a decentralized system that emphasizes site-based management and participatory decisions at the level closest to their effect.

The *hybrid* structure combines the characteristics of the product and functional structures, valuing efficiency and effectiveness in meeting external changes and demands. Alignment between central office (corporate) and building (division) goals is tight. Efficiency is attained through centralization, but adaptation is possible at the local level. Hybrid structures are conservative in that they have both centralized and decentralized characteristics that may be effective in environments with moderate degrees of uncertainty.

The *matrix* structure is designed for highly innovative and research-based organizations. This structure is suited to making complex decisions in an unstable environment. Because individuals may report to a number of people at the same time, confusion and frustration can occur. Good communication is necessary and frequent meetings are required.

Structure and Control

Organizations must respond to the environment, and their structure determines their responsiveness. Loose structures, described as *organic*, allow discretion and decision making throughout. Tight structures, described as *mechanistic*, centralize control and authority.

According to Weick and McDaniel (Sergiovanni & Moore, 1989) organic organizations are free-flowing, "restless organizations where there is a continuous search for definition, information, and meaning. If everyone is slightly uncertain most of the time, then attentiveness and discussion increase, which means more is known" (p. 347). Organic organizations are highly complex and specialized, with a low degree of centralization. Interaction and horizontal communication are necessary to reduce uncertainty. More interaction, less isolation, and greater networking of departments and roles are required. Organic organizations are less hierarchical and are governed by fewer rules than mechanistic ones. They function well in uncertain environments and emphasize effectiveness. Product-oriented or matrix structures exemplify organic control.

Mechanistic organizations have high formalization of roles, with tasks specifically defined in detail. Communication is primarily vertical, and knowledge and control are centralized at the top of the hierarchy. Mechanistic control is synonymous with hierarchy. "Most people cannot even imagine what an organization would look like without layers of management and support staff to provide counsel and, at times, direction to that hierarchy" (Lawler, 1988, p. 5). Most schools follow a mechanistic, functional bureaucratic model. In fact, many educators cannot perceive of organizations that are not hierarchical and bureaucratic in nature.

ORGANIZATIONS AS BUREAUCRACIES

Bureaucracies are generally perceived negatively; however, virtually all complex organizations are bureaucracies (Perrow, 1972), and they were not intended to be associated with bloated, inefficient systems. Actually, bureaucracies formed over centuries, growing from the Middle Ages and reaching their full potential in the twentieth century. Before 1850, most organizations were family-run enterprises with simple administrative structures because the systems to run and manage large organizations were not available. Organizations had to remain small to be effective and efficient.

German sociologist, Max Weber, developed the administrative framework to make large organizations both rational and efficient (Daft, 1989). Rational control was the central idea, and, to achieve that, several characteristics had to be present. First, rules and standard operating procedures were needed to enable work to be performed in a predictable manner. Second, expertise and competence were the bases for getting work completed, not dependence on politics and favoritism. Competence established the standard for hiring and promotion, and all employees were treated equally with rules and regulations binding both managers and workers. Third, a hierarchical structure, with lower offices under the direct supervision of higher ones, was established. Professional administrators, separated from owners, were hired to provide impartial management. Fourth, record keeping was necessary to create a formal organizational memory.

Despite the positive intentions of bureaucracy—a reliance on expertise, an end to favoritism, and an emphasis on rationality—it is criticized for being unresponsive, inflexible, and inefficient. In addition, it is perceived to stifle spontaneity, freedom, and the self-actualization of employees. Finally, the power in bureaucracies is a concern because of concentrated influence in the hands of a few leaders (Perrow, 1972).

Ideally, bureaucracies are supposed to be rational, but that ideal can never be reached. For example, it is impossible to remove extraorganizational influences from people's behavior. People are not always rational, and the problems in their individual lives affect their performance at work. In times of rapid change and in a complex environment, bureaucracies fall short because they are designed to deal with routine tasks in a stable environment.

Two areas of great concern in schools are bureaucratic rules and the hierarchical structure they create and perpetuate. The changes proposed in schools have been aimed at altering their bureaucratic nature. Too much bureaucracy can be dysfunctional, particularly when organizations are small, when employees are highly professional, when the environment is unstable, and when technology is nonroutine (Daft, 1989).

In small organizations, control should be through face-to-face personal interaction. Since individual schools are small, they can be less bureaucratic. Teachers think of themselves as professionals with specialized training, which helps to organize and regularize standards of performance. Bureaucratic rules and hierarchy work against the size, professionalism, and environmental issues with which schools contend.

Rules and Hierarchy

Bureaucratic rules (often called red tape) have drawn the scorn of scholars as well as workers. Rules are needed in every organization, but the general feeling is that there are too many of them. Rules "do a lot of things in organizations: they protect as well as restrict; coordinate as well as block; channel effort as well as limit it; permit universalism as well as promote a sanctuary for the inept; maintain stability as well as retard change; permit diversity as well as restrict it. They constitute the organizational memory and the means for change" (Perrow, 1972, p. 32).

One problem with bureaucratic rules concerns organizations and their environment, which may change faster than the rules are able to be modified. Rules are derived from past organizational practice, bargains, agreements, and payoffs, and they can be changed only in small increments because they are a part of the social fabric of the institution. Most rules are good, but as times change, the situation they were to address may no longer exist.

Rules can also result from power struggles. For example, collective bargaining between school boards and teachers' unions creates rules as part of the jockeying for power, control, or security. These rules act to enhance the control of boards or unions and frequently decrease professional discretion and flexibility. At the local school level, such controls make it more difficult to meet the challenges of the neighborhood or community, the possibilities of technology, the alterations in demography, and the unique needs of students and parents.

In the private sector, rules can be minimized by mechanizing, sealing off the organization from the environment, developing uniform work standards, or producing very simple products. However, schools must interact with their environment; they cannot have technology replace personnel, and they cannot simplify the complex service of teaching.

Rules are prominent in the life of schools. People cannot be free to "do as they please" when the public trust is involved. Professionals have some rules already built into them in the form of standards of ethical practice. If the standards or codes of practice are not clear, then institutional rules may need to be specified. Teachers' codes of professional practice are either unstated, very general, or not uniform across schools or training institutions, nor are they tested at the time of certification.

Working with teachers in defining professional practice and binding them tightly around a core of values and principles may reduce the need for levels of bureaucratic rules. Control should come intrinsically from the commitment to the core values. It cannot be monitored into professionals. These concepts will be expanded in Part IV of this book.

Hierarchical control is enforced through rules. In a study of urban schools, Chubb (1988) states, "If urban public schools are to be given more autonomy yet held meaningfully accountable, there is little alternative but to reorganize school systems along the lines that rely less on top-down controls of bureaucracy and more on market controls of school competition and parent choice" (p. 31). Hierarchy is perceived as an enemy by parents because of its unresponsiveness and by teachers who see it restricting their autonomy, creativity, and independence (Perrow, 1972). The functions of hierarchy were not only to control but also to coordinate work, motivate employees through sanctions, enhance communication, channel expertise through designated positions, and maintain records.

Lawler (1988) identifies substitutes to hierarchy, summarized in Table 4–6, that can meet the functions it was designed to achieve. These substitutes do not stand alone—installing one will not make a difference. They require an integrated impact, moving away from a control-oriented organization to a commitment-based one.

TABLE 4–6   Substitutes for Hierarchy

Substitute	Components
Values	Core of beliefs that guides organizational behavior
Information systems	Technological networks to share and gain access to information
Work design	Work constructed around whole services
Client contact	Input and feedback from client group
Training and development	Increase skills, create common perspective
Reward systems	Skill-based pay, incentives, psychic rewards
Emergent leadership	Informal leadership from staff, empowerment

Values provide a sense of direction and guide behavior. Goals and performance should be geared to those values, because core values motivate, attract, and retain talented people. Information is the lifeblood of organizations, and sharing it can substitute for hierarchical direction. People who have access to information become more self-managing. Information about progress on attaining objectives can have an impact on motivation and can help people identify and solve problems.

The research on work design indicates that when "work is designed around whole products or services, much of the need for supervisors to coordinate work and motivate workers disappears" (Lawler, 1988, p. 8). Work becomes intrinsically interesting and challenging because the individual is involved in the whole process.

Client contact—staying close to the needs of students and parents—provides feedback on the quality of the educational service. Feedback is a necessary ingredient in intrinsic motivation; it also improves self-monitoring, coordination, and goal identification and attainment.

Training and skill development allow individuals to be more self-reliant in pursuing their roles. It enhances problem solving and improves decision making and planning. Training increases individual skills and confidence and can be related to reward systems. Professional development offers increased prestige, expertise, and respect, which are translated into psychic rewards. Skill-based pay is becoming more popular in the private sector. It motivates people to learn a number of different skills; the more skills they have, the more value they bring to the organization.

Finally, leadership, as a substitute for hierarchy, does not have to be designated in one formal role; it can emerge throughout the entire organization. Increasing leadership density can enhance goal attainment, increase commitment, and empower professionals. In addition, emergent leadership rises from expertise and gains its authority from competence, which in turn elicits a more potent impact.

ORGANIZATIONAL LIFE CYCLES

Some organizations continue to grow, while others suffer from stagnation. An organization as a social system "is a living, changing thing, liable to decay and distintegration as well as revitalizing and reinforcement" (Gardner, 1964, p. 157). Schools are not immune from this principle simply because they are public sector, tax-based institutions. Perpetuation does not ensure growth or success. Private sector companies can die and disappear, whereas public sector institutions may endure but not operate effectively or productively.

As organizations get older, they can operate more bureaucratically and suffer from entropy. Excess staff and cumbersome and complex rules and procedures choke off coordination and reduce communication. Schools are among the oldest of public sector organizations. They have been called to restructure professional roles and empower participants because they have been too bureaucratized and structurally sluggish. When successful organizations begin to take their success for granted and lose their dynamic edge and enthusiasm, they "die of sophistication" (Gardner, 1984, p. 146).

Daft (1989) suggests that organizations have life cycles or four sequential stages: entrepreneurial, collectivity, formalization, and elaboration. These stages can also be applied to schools. The *entrepreneurial* stage is exciting because the organization is nonbureaucratic and informal, requiring strong leadership. Staff time and effort is spent on technical activities—program, curriculum, and instruction—and the development of processes. People are enthusiastic and vigorous, stemming from the belief in the organization and its success. After this initial stage, the organization goes through a period of *collectivity* when department and authority relationships become more formally established. Job descriptions are defined and new formal systems appear. Through strong leadership, clear goals and direction are formulated. Employees identify with the mission and commit time and talent to the cause. The need for delegation with control is necessary as initiatives need coordination.

After the period of collectivity, standard control and information systems are *formalized* through the development of a significant middle-management corps. Top management is concerned primarily with strategy and planning. A critical need at the formalization stage is reducing red tape and overbureaucratization. Many public schools are at this stage. The final stage, *elaboration*, leads to the recognition that the organization needs revitalization and renewal. Rule-driven behavior is questioned and calls for teamwork emerge. Managers review bureaucracy and try not to add to it, as well as begin to problem solve and get people to work together again.

Schools can avoid the pitfalls of formalizaton if they continue to learn, which is defined as "the process by which organizations develop knowledge about organizational actions and environment outcomes" (Daft, 1989 p. 549). The transformation of schools requires a changed perception of how they operate structurally and contextually. They cannot simply look inward at their internal needs and operation; they must get more information about the environment. They must collect data about their effectiveness and their environment, interpret those data, and then respond to the information they have gained. Quantitative and perceptual data are necessary if new structures or responses are to be considered and implemented. An influx of diverse ideas is needed, with a balance between efficiency and innovation. *Efficiency* is the careful use of resources, frequently requiring bureaucratic structures, whereas *innovation* pushes the organization to the leading edge of new ideas and services. Since efficiency and innovation are at odds, they require different skills of leaders.

Miller (1977) found that in an organization where growth is valued, new responsibilities and assignments are inherent. Change in the mission of the organization means alterations in roles and staff development. It could also require job redesign and rotation. Learning becomes the responsibility of all individuals, who need information and feedback to make better decisions, to adjust their performance, and to meet clients' needs and system objectives.

Organizational Success

Successful schools learn and grow. Peters and Waterman (1982) identified factors associated with corporate success: they correspond to environmental, managerial, structural, and personnel needs and issues. Schools, as service organizations, are subject to these factors because they are generic to both private and public sectors. Table 4–7 summarizes the dimensions and factors associated with organizational success.

TABLE 4–7   Organizational Success: Dimensions and Factors

Dimension	Factor
Environment	Close to the customer
	Proactive
	Clear focus
Management	Leadership and vision
	Bias toward action
	Rationality and intuition
Structure	Simple form and lean staff
	Autonomy
	Loose-tight properties
Personnel	Trusting climate
	Productivity through consensus
	Long-term view

Schools must understand their local communities and the needs of parents and students. Treating students as preferred customers, maintaining good communication, instituting a service orientation, customizing programs, and getting feedback are required to identify needs and assess service performance. Schools also need to be proactive in the environment to the demands placed on them from outside. Turning data into information and examining trends are a part of proactive behavior. Schools can be the victims of crises from outside if they do not monitor the environment and establish a clear organizational focus and goals.

Good leadership has a bias for action—taking a risk—to achieve goals. "Nothing ventured, nothing gained" should be an operational strategy. Action should be taken, however, on the basis of a vision of what the organization can be. Vision and leadership are synonymous with successful enterprises. Vision motivates, and rational and intuitive thought processes enable leaders to move forward with proposals and programs.

Structure must be simple, with good coordination, communication, and flexibility. Autonomy of professionals can instill commitment and energy. A loose organizational structure, with autonomy and flexibility, tightened around a core of uncompromised values and principles, produces motivated people.

Finally, people need to feel trusted to do their work if a positive climate is to be created. With consensus around the vision and values of the organization, productivity can increase. Looking to long-term success and not settling for short-term achievements will use finite fiscal and knowledge resources more potently.

SUMMARY

Investigating the evolution of organizations and their complex dynamics is necessary for understanding transformation. Some types of organizations have become obsolete because they were unable to change to meet new needs and conditions. Educational organizations cannot fail; our country's future depends on an educated populace. Schools must transform to ensure their survival and continued growth to be successful in their mission.

CONCEPTS

1. Organizations are necessary systems that accomplish various purposes in contemporary society.
2. Organizations have both positive and negative connotations, depending on the perception of what they can and do accomplish.
3. Organizations are social entities that are goal directed, deliberatively structured activity systems with an identifiable boundary.
4. Organizations may be either open or closed systems.
5. Open systems are responsive and adaptable to the environment, whereas closed systems are autonomous and protected from environmental influences.
6. Organizations are either social systems that are people and communication oriented, with flexible configurations and loosely connected parts—or they are rational systems in which order and control dominate, and predictability and certainty are valued.
7. Sociotechnical systems theory affords a broader perspective from which to view contemporary organizations. It integrates people, the organization, and technology to attain more productivity and better quality.
8. Four theories of organizational administration influence our perceptions or definitions of the purposes of these institutions—scientific management, human relations, political, and cultural.

9. Two dimensions common to all types of organizations are structure (internal characteristics) and context (external environment).

10. The external environment affects organizations based on how simple or complex and how stable or unstable conditions are at any given time.

11. Schools operate in a context of complex, unstable environmental conditions.

12. The structure of an organization includes all systems for authority, decision making, communication, and task accomplishment.

13. Organizational structures have been defined and described by many theorists to explain how structures relate to functions and outcomes.

14. Nearly all organizations have characteristics of bureaucracies, which can facilitate or impede the process of the systems.

15. Organizations pass through stages, or life cycles, in their development.

16. Organizational success depends on the environmental, management, structural, and personnel factors combined and working in consort with one another.

5 | Organizations: Systems, Transformation, and Innovation

Bureaucracy was planned to filter out any irrational aspects from organizations to make them operate efficiently. However, organizations are not that tidy. They are subject to internal and external forces that create uncertainty and conflict.

People in schools must change how they think about what they do and adopt new assumptions about organizations (Kanter, 1984). One major assumption is that schools are open systems, subject to and dependent on people for their operation and sometimes constrained by the decisions of others. This chapter focuses on the internal aspects of schools—culture and informal organization—and explores decision making, change, and innovation. The context and structural components from the last chapter should be coupled with these internal ones to analyze and evaluate the issues facing professionals and communities in transforming schools.

CULTURE AND THE INFORMAL ORGANIZATION

The culture of organizations has received attention, in part due to the rise of innovative, entrepreneurial companies that operate differently from traditional ones. These new high-tech companies accentuate the dynamic and sometimes informal culture, whose people behave differently and seem to have a strong, deep commitment to the company's goals.

Culture affects how people work—their interactions, decisions, attitudes, and commitment. It goes to the heart of values and norms and is more than a friendly climate or atmosphere. It may be innovative or staid, supportive or divisive, integrated or segmented, dynamic or predictable, and synergistic or disconnected. Webster defines *culture* as the integrated pattern of human behavior that includes thought, speech, action, and artifacts, and depends on people's capacity for learning and transmitting knowledge to future generations. Concerning corporations, Deal and Kennedy (1982) define *culture* as "a cohesion of values, myths, heroes, and symbols" that help communicate the purpose and goals of the organization (p. 4). They point out that in a strong culture, there is "a system of informal rules that spells out how people are to behave most of the time" and it "enables people to feel better about what they do, so they are more likely to work harder" (pp. 15–16).

The shared values, behavior patterns, mores, symbols, attitudes, and norms for doing business make each culture distinct. The idea of culture is expanded by Feldman (1988) as a set of meanings created within the organization but influenced by broader social and historical processes. Schein (1985) relates culture to the greater context of organizations and defines it as "a pattern of basic assumptions—invented, discovered, or developed by a given group as it learns to cope with its problems of external adaptation and internal integration—that worked well enough to be considered valid and, therefore, to be taught to new members as the correct way to perceive, think, and feel in relation to those problems" (p. 9). He also raises the issue that organizations may have more than one culture within them—a managerial culture, workers' culture, department culture, or overall culture if there is a significant shared history.

Culture is a product of learned experience, which is quickly defined for new staff members so they know how things are done around the organization. Schein (1985) believes that because culture is learned and evolves with new experiences, it can be changed. However, to do so requires understanding the dynamics of the learning process.

Culture provides stability, certainty, and predictability. It "imbues life with meaning and through symbols creates a sense of efficacy and control" (Deal & Kennedy, 1982, p. 7). Kanter (1984) speaks in more global terms but agrees that culture gives some sense of security for people within an organization. She concludes that culture provides "a sense that there is a whole and that there are clear principles guiding it" (p. 34).

In summary, culture defines organizational values and communicates to new members how they should think and act. It defines how things are to be done and represents the unwritten part of the organization. Culture is in evidence through people, not paper. It generates commitment to values greater than each individual's needs, as well as provides stability so people can make sense of organizational events and activities.

Elements of Culture

Decisions in a strong culture are influenced by the organization's self-image and projected image. Strong cultures have cohesion and consensus around specific, articulated values and beliefs, shared knowledge of symbolic models and patterns, and social processes—leadership and language—that maintain the integrity of the group (Sims & Gioia, 1986). The elements of culture listed in Table 5–1 are present in public and private sector organizations. These elements define social interaction and norms. "Norms are social glue. They hold things together" (Yankelovich, 1982, p. 84). Cultural norms help interpret everyday occurrences and assist people with sorting out the confusion, uncertainty, and ambiguity of work life.

Schein (1985) categorizes culture as basic assumptions, values, artifacts, and creations. Basic assumptions are invisible and taken for granted; they are implicit, nondebatable, nonconfrontable theories-in-use that guide behavior. They are woven into the fabric of a system's operation and reflect the relationship of the organization to the environment; the nature of reality, time, and space; and the nature of human relationships.

TABLE 5–1   Elements of Organizational Culture

Element	Description
Environment	Determines what the organization must do to be successful
Values	Basic beliefs and concepts defining the organization's ideology and philosophy
Heroes	People who personify the organization's culture
Rites and Rituals	Routines of day-to-day organizational life are used as behavioral models
Cultural Network	The primary and informal means of communication in an organization

Source: Terrence E. Deal and Allan A. Kennedy, *Corporate Cultures* (Reading, MA: Addison-Wesley, 1982), pp. 13–15.

Values, on the other hand, are the consequence of basic assumptions. They pull a group together and bind it. There is greater awareness of values because they provide a sense of "what ought to be." They serve a normative function, guiding behavior and establishing standards. Values that are congruent with basic assumptions are powerful; those that are not are simply aspirations or rationalizations.

The most evident elements of culture are its artifacts and creations, and its constructed physical and social environments. These elements are visible through technology, art, and written and spoken behavior patterns, and they deal with overt behavior. Although observable, their meaning and interrelations are not easy to determine (Schein, 1985). Each day teachers, students, parents, and others have contact with the elements of culture. For school leaders, culture is an important consideration in moving the organization toward its mission.

Culture and Leaders

Leaders deal with symbols and images; consequently, they affect culture. Many leaders use metaphorical language, express values, define visions, and manage labels and symbols. Some leaders themselves become legends and a part of an organization's mythology. Their language affects the discourse of the entire organization because it expresses ideas, values, and perceptions of reality.

Leaders are intertwined with the culture's creation and management, and possibly its destruction.

> Culture is created in the first instance by the actions of leaders; culture is also embedded and strengthened by leaders. When culture becomes dysfunctional, leadership is needed to help the group unlearn some of its cultural assumptions and learn new ones. Such transformations require what amounts to conscious and deliberate destruction of cultural elements, and it is this aspect of cultural dynamics that makes leadership important and difficult to define (Schein, 1985, pp. 313–337).

Under this premise, an organization would be hard pressed to adapt to changing circumstances and conditions without strong leadership.

Changing culture is important but difficult because culture creates "patterns of perception, thought, and feeling of every new generation in the organization" (Schein, 1985, p. 313). An organization may be predisposed to certain kinds of leadership for different phases of its life. The leadership types for the creation, midlife, and mature phases of organization life are illustrated in Table 5–2. These phases closely parallel the four life cycles of organizations defined in the previous chapter.

TABLE 5–2   Leadership, Culture, and Organizational Phases

Phase	Culture and Leadership
Organizational Creation	Leaders create vision
	Communication in clear, consistent messages
	Persistence and patience to curb anxiety and promote stability and emotional reassurance
Organizational Midlife	Culture is more cause than effect—influences strategy, structure, and processes
	Culture affects perception, thinking, and feeling
	Leaders need insight into effects of culture on organization's mission
Organizational Maturity	Culture affects what is defined as leadership
	Leaders need:
	—to detect cultural dysfunctions
	—motivation and skill to unfreeze culture
	—strength to absorb anxiety change brings
	—depth of vision to step outside culture to review the validity of assumptions

In the private sector, an entrepreneurial company may change leaders after the first flush of success because different skills are called for at the next stage of organizational evolution. Apple Computer was a prime example of leadership change as the corporation matured and faced different challenges.

Trice and Beyer (Daft, 1989, pp. 505–506) concur in their unpublished working paper that there are different kinds of cultural leaders. They identify four types rather than three, but their focus is similar to Schein's. The first category of leaders is the "cultural creators," who have vision, identify values, and have impact when the organization is new. "Cultural embodiers" preserve and protect prevailing values; they manage and defend the culture, but they do not change it. "Culture integrators" create harmony and consensus; they listen well and are good at working through people—many are perceived as politicians. Finally, the "culture changers" emerge when fundamental value change is required—in periods of organizational transformation. They inspire through vision and revitalize the organization through transformational leadership.

Chapters 6 and 7 have a more detailed discussion of leadership in all its aspects relating to transforming schools. Superintendents, principals, teachers, and other school leaders need to understand the importance of culture because it affects performance and change.

Culture: Importance and Innovation

A strong culture is a powerful lever for guiding people in their behavior at work, and it helps them do a better job in two ways. First, since culture is a system of informal rules defining how people are to behave most of the time, less time is wasted and productivity increases when people know the system. Second, it enables people to feel better about what they do—the pursuit of values, mission, and purpose—so they work harder (Deal & Kennedy, 1982).

Culture is potent and its patterns can be seen in collective behavior, but Schein (1985) cautions:

- Culture and climate are not the same.
- Culture cannot be manipulated because it controls people more than they control it.
- There is no correct or better culture.
- Culture affects more than the human side of organizations; it also involves the mission of the organization.
- Not all aspects of culture are relevant to organizational effectiveness; leaders should focus on important components and not get bogged down with the rest (p. 314).

Not all cultures are functional—some are dysfunctional and influence ideas, actions, and productivity in negative ways. A troubled culture has conflicting or ill-defined beliefs. Some schools have no beliefs about how to succeed or they cannot agree on what they stand for. In other schools, departments or grade levels may have conflicting beliefs and so they do not work toward unified ends. In these situations, schools will not succeed because the culture is disruptive and does not build common understanding or cohesion.

Troubled cultures can also occur when schools take an inward focus and become isolated from the external environment. They are short-sighted, planning for the short term and accepting immediate gain without a long-term perspective. Organizations with troubled cultures have morale problems, experience chronic unhappiness, and suffer high staff turnover. In conjunction with these morale problems are emotional outbursts and displays of anger because the culture is not strong enough to provide security; instead, it is fragmented and inconsistent, resulting in confusion and frustration (Deal & Kennedy, 1982).

Change can threaten culture. That is why change is so difficult to implement. It can strip teachers of their daily rituals, ceremonies, and symbols, which causes anxiety. Changing behavior means changing culture. Deal and Kennedy (1982) state, "The stronger the culture, the harder it is to change. Culture causes organizational inertia; it's the brake that resists change because that's precisely what culture should do—protect the organization from willy-nilly responses to fads and short-term fluctuation" (p. 158). Fundamental cultural change takes time because people must identify with new heroes, tell different stories, and adopt different patterns of interaction.

Kanter (1984) indicates, however, that the highest proportion of innovative accomplishments are found in companies "that are least segmented and segmentalist"; those "that have integrative structures and cultures emphasizing pride, commitment, collaboration, and teamwork" (p. 178). A strong peer culture can be a positive force for innovation because pride, commitment, and success are intangibles that create an emotional commitment between the individual and the organization. These cultures are people-centered, emphasizing an esprit de corps between workmates and mutual respect and expectation (Kanter, 1984, pp. 149–151).

To Sculley (1987), however, the concept of culture is a "feel-good" tool that puts blinders on the organization and makes it comfortable with its habits. He thinks the concept of culture is akin to a closed system, looking inward and devoid of action or change. Sculley proposes dropping the idea of culture for the metaphor of genetic change, believing that culture is tribal—looking backward to myths, rituals, stories, and traditions. The genetic metaphor looks forward to the future through the passing of a "genetic" code that includes identity, direction, and values (pp. 319–322).

With genetic change, cells grow and divide. The genetic code is always present even though the code's message may be expressed diversely in different organisms. Genetic coding imprints the notions of identity and values as culture does, but in so doing, it suggests a sense that everything done today is an investment in the future, not an expression of the past. The code is constant over a lifetime, but cells can change. Metaphorically, this becomes a forward-looking model because as an organization changes its genetic code remains the same.

The contrasts between genetic coding and culture are:

Vision vs. goals: Vision is the direction and push for reaching for the future, whereas goals are tangible expressions of the near future based on the past.

Metaphors vs. myths: Metaphors mean movement and focus on ideas and images. They create tension from the collision of ideas and do not rest on the achievements and stories of past victories and successes.

Directions vs. rituals: Clear direction is based on values and vision, with no baggage from the past. Rituals are activities and events that had meaning in the past that are carried into the future.

Whether culture or genetic code metaphors are used, values, norms, beliefs, and informal relationships and routines become critical issues in school transformation. They relate to the concept of the informal organization, which is also concerned with norms, expectations, and behavior.

Informal Organization

The informal organization is viewed as both a nemesis to and an advocate for the success of the formal organization. There are three perceptions of the informal organization: (1) subversive to the formal structure, (2) a healthy supplement to it, and (3) a means to meet the psychological welfare of the group (Iannaccone, 1964, pp. 223–224).

The group is the basis for the informal organization. Blau and Scott (1962, p. 6) state that informal groups have their own practices, values, norms, and relationships. There are friendship groups, hobby groups, workgroups, self-protective groups, and convenience groups. They have regular interactions, a perception on each individual's part that a group exists, has common objectives, and maintains a set of values and norms that influence members' behavior. The nature and the number of groups in operation depend on the interactions and needs of the people involved. Informal groups meet the social needs of their members and provide emotional support. The psychological concerns of the group are significant because people have a need to belong.

The relationships of people within groups provide a "sense of belongingness, of amounting to something, the sense of mutual obligation and support" (Sherif & Sherif, 1964, p. 54). Individuals are influenced by the norms the group holds and considers important. These norms direct individual behavior and regulate what is acceptable or unacceptable. They are the product of the "give and take" that transpires during the interactions of the group. Norms are not intended to bring about blind conformity but are products of the goals and motives that created the group.

Other properties of informal groups include a sanction system that rewards or punishes individuals who live within or outside of the expectations held by the members (Reeves, 1970). The informal organization also has leaders, an instinct for self-preservation, and the capability for concerted action.

"Informal relationships are vital for the effective functioning of the organization. Frequently, groups develop spontaneously an informal means for dealing with important activities which contribute to the overall performance. . . . The informal organization may be adaptive and serve innovative functions which may not be met by the formal organization" (Kast & Rosenzweig, 1970, p. 172). An organization's work culture is the product of both formal and informal influences. Many of the characteristics of the informal organization—like norms and standards—are also cultural aspects. They affect and contribute to the culture, as do the values and norms expressed by the formal organization.

Organizations are structured to make decisions, the quality of which determines the effectiveness of the enterprise. The formal organization, the informal organization, and the culture of the entire system affect the decision making.

TIP | TRANSFORMATION INTO PRACTICE

ORGANIZATIONS: A SENSE OF HUMOR IS NOTHING TO LAUGH AT

Despite the enjoyment it brings, humor in the workplace is seldom discussed in professional literature. We all enjoy a good laugh, and people with a good sense of humor and wit are fun to be around. In fact, presidents have found humor to be an asset to deflect difficult issues, make light of personal foibles, or humanize press conferences and interviews. But what about organizational humor? Are laughing employees wasting time, making fun of the boss, or not committed to the organization's goals? In *Anatomy of an Illness,* Norman Cousins found that laughter had therapeutic value in recovering from an illness. But is humor good medicine in transforming organizations?

According to Duncan and Feisal (1989), "Humor is any type of communication that intentionally creates incongruent meanings and thereby causes laughter. Puns can produce the desired effect; so can cartoons. But in workgroups, humor most often assumes the form of jokes" (pp. 21–29). This rather technical definition produces a heavier tone than what Steve Allen (1988) stated about humor: "Even if laughter were nothing more than sheer silliness, it would be a precious boon" (pp. 2–5). Although humor is perceived as important, it must be perceived sensitively and must consider the cultural, historical, and demographic composition of workgroups, where most humor takes place.

Duncan and Feisal (1989) indicate that leaders and managers should perceive humor in workgroups as more than idle behavior, because the joking relationships can specify patterns of group interaction, such as "friendship and leadership patterns." Patterns of humor can identify the isolates, who is respected, and the extent of work integration. For managers, being the butt of jokes is not always negative because "trust, respect, and friendship determine a group member's position in the pattern of joking behavior far more than official status does."

Duncan and Feisal (1989) identified four types of stereotypes at work that affect humor:

Arrogant Executives:
    Formal authority and socially isolated
    Least often joked with or butt of jokes
    Jokes told about them when they're absent
    Lost right to joke; found offensive by workers
Benign Bureaucrats:
    Perceived as powerless
    Jokes told to and the butt of jokes
    Joking by them resented because they are not respected as productive members
Solid Citizens:
    Power from expertise; preferred leaders
    Joking privileges; can tell jokes and be the butt of them
    Good sense of humor is essential
Novices:
    Powerless, no authority, nonthreatening
    Making the butt of jokes considered tasteless
    Rarely joke about others: not part of the group

What value does organizational humor have, besides creating laughter? Allen (1988) and Duncan and Feisal (1989) cite that humor and laughter are essential to emotional health. They dispel tension and relieve frustrations. Allen states, "Laughter is also remarkably useful in the context of the process of human communication. It can be an aid to the expression of other emotions and to the transmission of important messages of a spiritual, political, educational, or commercial nature. It is a crucial component of psychological well-being, and of sanity itself." Duncan and Feisal also see the benefit of humor in the transfer of information, particularly if it is risky. Gallows humor can reduce anxiety.

Srivastva (1988, p. 299) and Duncan and Feisal (1989) identify the bonding nature of humor. Humor is the "great equalizer" because when people laugh together, status differentials disappear. Humor heals and bonds people in common survival pursuits. Duncan and Feisal find that "lubricant humor" is not abrasive, reduces tensions, and makes people feel as if they belong. People do not joke with people they disdain. Humor has an indirect influence on productivity because cohesive groups are more productive, and if the group norm is high performance it has a positive influence on individuals.

What is the role of humor in schools?
What does it say about school values?
Can schools transform without a collective sense of humor?
What role does humor play in the commitment, pride, and productivity of professionals?
How does humor affect school leaders?

ORGANIZATION: DECISIONS AND INFORMATION

There are two perspectives of organizations that influence how people perceive the decision-making process (Daft, 1989). As stated earlier, one perspective is that organizations are rational places, characterized by clear goals and a logical decision-making process. In this model, goals are defined, alternatives are listed, and choices are made on the prospect of the highest probability of success, with information flowing from reliable systems. Behavior is not random or accidental, and there is little conflict.

The second perspective is the political model, which assumes that organizations are not clean and tidy, as under the rational notion. Disagreement is an integral part of the political perspective because coalitions with different interests disagree about goals. Complete, unambiguous information is not always available, or, when it is, it may be disputed. In a political system, decisions are not always orderly and they are subject to influence. Bargaining and negotiating are the norm.

Politics are internal and external. Daft (1989) defines *politics* as the process of bargaining and negotiating to overcome conflicts and make decisions. He states, "Politics is simply the activity through which power is exercised in the resolution of conflicts and uncertainty. Politics is neutral, and is not necessarily harmful to the organization" (pp. 406–417).

Schools are political organizations. Negotiations from labor groups are an obvious political process that incorporates shared decision making and vested interest. At the community level, school boards are involved in political decisions about school goals, finances, curriculum, and programs. In the last decade, education has been the prime focus at the gubernatorial and national levels, in addition to private sector corporations trying to influence and define expectations for schools. All of this political endeavor does not always lead to clear goals and direction—in many cases, the desired outcomes and expectations for schools are philosophically incompatible.

There are some rational decisions made by teachers and administrators that are based on clear goals and quality information. Selecting an appropriate teaching method is rational, as is defining an evaluation strategy for a lesson. But the context of the larger school organization is political, uncertain, and complex. Schools are mixed models, composed of both rational and political characteristics.

Uncertainty—the absence of complete information—determines whether decisions are rational or political. When goals, objectives, conditions, alternatives, or environments are uncertain, decisions become political because that process helps reach consensus and agreement. Debate does not take place when the alternatives and circumstances are clear, but in social organizations, these conditions are rare.

Many organizational decisions are political and affect power. *Power* is the ability to influence in order to achieve goals (Daft, 1989, p. 399). It is distributed through the designated structure of the organization; is vested in positions, not people; and moves vertically and horizontally in the structure. *Vertical* power moves up and down the hierarchy and comes from a formal position—the ability to allocate resources and control information. Being at the center of the organization's network of roles and information is a powerful position. *Horizontal* power concerns the relationships of people across departments, which are not always defined in the organizational chart. If a department controls resources or information, it has power. It can gain power by taking up the slack in uncertain times and filling voids, or it can lose power if it is dependent on others to accomplish its purpose.

Power is important in innovation. "The degree to which the opportunity to use power effectively is granted to or withheld from individuals is one operative difference between those companies which stagnate and those which innovate" (Kanter, 1984, p. 18). People can gain power through their expertise or their persuasive ability. Individuals can build coalitions, expand their personal networks, and create alliances, which are helpful when decisions have to be made.

Information, resources, and support are power tools. Kanter (1984) likens these tools to markets: Information is the marketplace of ideas, resources involve the economic market, and support—backing, approval, endorsements—encompasses the political market. Power must be balanced. It cannot be dispersed throughout organizations in an atomized manner. Balance is the issue, "never to disperse power fully but merely to temporarily loosen it, to allow units autonomy and single-minded focus when they need it while preventing segmentalism" (p. 172).

Information was cited as a central issue in power, innovation, and decision making because it is essential in knowledge-based organizations like schools. Professional decisions are only as good as the information available.

Information: Organizational Lifeblood

The most important resource an organization has is valid information because it feeds decisions and is essential to control and to quality outcomes. It helps leaders to gain cohesion and hold the organization on course. *Information* is "data endowed with relevance and purpose. Converting data into information thus requires knowledge" (Drucker, 1988, p. 46). Professionals want and need information.

There are two types of information with which professionals deal. *Routine* information comes in clear and consistent patterns, changes slowly, and is easy to understand and quantify. It can be classified and is simple to process. *Nonroutine* information is less clear. It is susceptible to continuous change with unclear patterns, and is difficult to understand, classify, or quantify (Sergiovanni & Moore, 1989, p. 336).

Access to information is a concern for leaders because they rely on information gathered by others from many segments of the organization. Gathering information, however, does not guarantee accurate perceptions. Gardner (1964) calls this the *filtered experience* because many leaders at the top of the organization "depend less and less on first-hand experience, more and more on heavily processed data. Before reaching them, the raw data—what actually goes on 'out there'—have been sampled, screened, condensed, compiled, coded, expressed in statistical form, spun into generalizations, and crystallized into recommendations" (p. 97). The emotion, feeling, mood, and sentiment are filtered out, particularly in large organizations.

Getting information that is congruent with accepted interpretation is another issue. Weick and McDaniel (Sergiovanni & Moore, 1989) indicate that people make sense of their environment through interpretation if there is insufficient information, and "interpretation is strengthened by learning, because people tend to learn those things that are congruent with interpretations rather than those things that challenge interpretations. . . . They see what they expect to see and, to a large measure, what the organization lets them see" (p. 331). Access to information is important if people are to analyze it in line with reality, not standard interpretation.

Information-based organizations rely on knowledge and require feedback. These organizations are structurally flatter, with less middle management, more ad hoc teams based on contemporary needs, and a direct link to the top to eliminate some of the filtering (Drucker, 1988, pp. 45–50). The requirements for an information-based organization are defined in Table 5–3.

People in information-based organizations need to consider what information is necessary for them to determine what they are doing, to decide what they should do, and to appraise how they are doing it (Drucker, 1988, p. 50). Schools are information-based organizations, not because students and teachers deal with knowledge but because they require quality information to provide professional service and make decisions.

Zuboff (1988) has studied work and the transformation it has taken over the centuries. She states that in the transformation process, organizations need an "informating strategy" because knowledge is a critical component. Knowledge requires intellective skills and learning. Informating demands a redistribution of authority and a commitment to

TABLE 5–3   Information-Based Organizations

Dimension	Description
Goals	Clear, simple goals that translate into actions
	Concentrate on one or a few objectives
Leadership	Focus people's skills and knowledge on the mission and goals
Structure	Based around goals and performance expectations
Information	Regular feedback to employees so everyone can exercise control and can self-manage
	Everyone takes information responsibility—people get information they need
	No data overload

intellectual skill development, which is impaired by the division of labor evident in bureaucracies. An informated work environment is different from a traditional one. Learning is at the heart of productive behavior—it becomes the new form of labor (Zuboff, 1988, pp. 394–395). The metaphor is not command, but learning. Team orientation is the rule, and power rests and roves on the basis of need and function. Colleagueship, not superordinate relationships, is emphasized as people become co-learners. However, an informated work environment can create some insecurities, because some find sustenance in organizational norms and the protection of bureaucratic and union relationships.

In organizations that are directed toward change and innovation, informated work environments are necessary. Transformation requires knowledge, information, and the open flow of communication.

TRANSFORMATION, RENEWAL, AND INNOVATION

Organizations need to adapt and innovate to keep pace with external changes and internal demands. There are times in history, so-called transformation eras, when more than adaptation and minor changes are required. Kuhn (1962) defines *transformation eras* as "when circumstances change sufficiently to warrant a major shift of assumptions." Paradigm shifts are required in these times to alter existing assumptions and replace them with a more appropriate set.

To break out of a paradigm, organizations must use a new one. "In many ways, therefore, it is useful to work within a very foreign paradigm if you want to make fundamental contributions to your field" (Davis, 1982, p. 80). Davis relates transformation as a shift in context, whereas change is a shift of content. Beer (Kilmann & Covin, 1988) agrees with the necessity for context to be altered. "Only a change in the context— structure, systems, staffing patterns, and management process—in which employees function can stimulate and sustain new management approaches" (p. 35). Organizational arrangements that demand or enable new behavior must lead the transformation process.

Renz (Kilmann & Covin, 1988, p. 476) identifies six major subsystems that are involved in the transformation of a public sector bureaucracy: organizational processes, formal organizations, political subsystems, sociocultural subsystems, people, and production systems. Table 5–4 defines the components of these subsystems for transformation.

TABLE 5–4   Transformation of Public Bureaucracies: Subsystems and Focus

Subsystem	Focus
Organization Process	Interactions: manage dynamic interactions with environment
Formal Organization	Structures/Systems: manage systems that channel support and reinforce behavior
Political	Power/Authority: manage influence processes re: choices, resource allocation, and reward behavior
Sociocultural	Meaning and Climate: manage norms, values, experiences, and meaning that support effective behavior
People	Motivation/Energy/Ability: focus people's attention on mission and goals
Production	Purpose of Organization: manage technologies, tasks, and methods to get work done

The environment that provides resources may pose constraints on a public sector bureaucracy like school districts. Organizational process must scan the environment for external events, trends, or dynamics that may be crucial to the school's success (Kilmann & Covin, 1988). Critical information about the changing economic, legal, social, political, technical, and demographic conditions is necessary in today's schools if there is going to be a chance at transforming them. Decision makers' perceptions and actions must be attuned to the forces and resources in the world outside the organization—its context. Kanter (1984) states that successful organizations are ones "with more 'surface' exposed to the environment and with a whole host of sensing mechanisms for recognizing emerging changes and their implications. In such an organization, more people with greater skills than ever before will link the organization to its environment" (p. 142).

Transformation cannot take place without leaders because they are needed to translate external demands into a commitment to change. Leaders provide information to employees so they can see the realities of the organization (Beer, in Kilmann & Covin, 1988, pp. 28–29) and where it must go. They must also develop trust so that clear messages can be communicated. Trustworthy information and high performance standards need to be detailed for departments and individuals, and leaders must model appropriate behavior and find innovative models to manage people.

School transformation must also consider unions. Many teachers are unionized and have collective bargaining rights designed to provide protection and influence in the decision-making process. The old adversarial nature of union-management relationships needs to change to reflect "creative partnerships" (Kilmann & Covin 1988, p. 534). Because of new technologies and changes in external dynamics, there is the danger that collective bargaining language may become obsolete and constrain effective professional service. For example, as technology changed, railroads' union contracts required hiring unnecessary firemen to man deisel trains that did not need them, creating a new term, *featherbedding*, and a less productive and efficient transportation system.

Transformation must take place on a broad front, across the entire organization, and involve all subsystems and units of schools. Transformation should be synergystic—its impact greater than the sum of the changes in the various subunits or subsystems (Beer, in Kilmann & Covin, 1988, p. 22).

TIP | TRANSFORMATION INTO PRACTICE

ORGANIZATIONAL RENEWAL AND CREATIVITY

People who change jobs often feel a sense of excitement and energy. Tasks and problems become challenges, and there is a sense that odds can be overcome and progress made. The spirit soars because possibilities exist. The same is true of organizations. The concept of renewal has been discussed in the literature for over 20 years.

Gardner (1964) stated, "A social institution is created out of human ardor and conviction. As its assets expand, the ardor wanes. The buildings grow bigger and the spirit wanes" (p. 20). Renewal, according to Gardner, is more than change and innovation. It concerns bringing the results of change into line with our purposes. Organizations and individuals needing renewal are victims of past success.

The artist can become a prisoner of his style. The civilization becomes trapped by its greatest achievements. Established individuals become less adventurous because they have reputations to preserve. People cannot break new paths because they have prior commitments and obligations. Possessions possess. All the comfortable, known things that make for emotional security stand between us and the hazards of the unknown. The human being, greatest of all generalists, moves toward a specialization that limits growth (Gardner, 1978, p. 146).

Organizations in this state are not creative nor do they pursue change.

The president of Apple Computer, John Sculley (1987), states "Traditional management gospel only thwarts us in trying to understand creativity. Management and creativity might even be antithetical states. While management demands consensus, control, certainty, and the status quo, creativity thrives on the opposite: instinct, uncertainty, freedom and iconoclasm" (p. 184). Robert Waterman (1987) discusses management practices and renewal and adds the concept of empowerment and politics. He states that organizations must renew to compete and avoid stagnation. He thinks that everyone is a source of creativity and that information in contemporary organizations is a crucial factor in testing reality and getting in the habit of breaking habits.

If renewal was a goal in school organizations:

What role would values and norms play in the renewal process?

What vertical and horizontal communication practices might be instituted to stop stagnation?

Would specialization be encouraged or discouraged?

Would a staff rotation plan across functions and levels be productive and revitalizing?

Does commitment to purpose keep organizations renewing?

How do internal politics affect renewal? Do "we-they" attitudes build in antagonism that works against creativity?

Do union-management relationships and contracts emphasize status quo commitment to the past practices and successes?

Do "vested interests" produce rigidity and diminish the prospect for change?

Organizational Change

For people to change, there must be trust. Dowling (1978, p. 76) defines trust as a person's ability to take risks in front of another individual. In organizations, change and transformation require a great deal of risk taking by a large number of people. They must change their assumptions and perceptions before they can transform structures and designs.

Dealing with perception has been emphasized in this book as a prerequisite for changing thinking and behavior. Kanter (1984, p. 281) states, "Organizational change consists in part of a series of emerging constructions of reality, including revision of the past to correspond to the requisites of new players and new demands" (p. 287). Change requires the crystallization of new action based on "reconceptualized patterns in organization. The architecture of change involves the design and construction of new patterns, or the reconceptualization of old ones, to make new, and hopefully more productive actions possible" (p. 279).

What are the signs that change is necessary? Deal and Kennedy (1982, pp. 159–161) identify four circumstances when organizational change is required:

- When the environment undergoes fundamental change
- When competition is fierce and the environment is unstable
- When the organization is mediocre or worse
- When the organization is on the threshold of growing into a larger one

To bring about change, Deal and Kennedy indicate that leadership is a requisite. Leaders must envision a new reality and communicate it to people in the organization, to help them convert new conceptions into behavior. They need to provide tangible symbols of the new direction and create security for people to take risks. Change needs momentum; more and more people have to demonstrate new attitudes and behavior so that it becomes unacceptable not to change.

Change can be terrifying to some, particularly if it is unexpected and sudden. However, "Change can be either friend or foe, depending on the resources available to cope with it and master it by innovating. It is disturbing when it is done to us, exhilarating when it is done by us. It is considered positive when we are active contributors to bringing about something that we desire" (Kanter, 1984, p. 64). Change that results in altering perceptions to create new ideas can transform behavior and structures.

Innovation and Organizations

Innovation must affect the organization intimately.

[It needs to take place] not merely in the traditional sense of new products and services, but in the very ways that organizations operate, in their view of themselves and in the mechanisms that can develop and engage their resources to the maximum extent possible. Most important, organizations need innovation to shift from the present tendency to deal with their tasks in a relatively single-minded, top-directed way and to a capacity to respond innovatively, locally, and promptly to a whole variety of organizational contingencies—to change shape, so to speak (Kanter, 1984, p. 41).

These organizations have the right people (with ideas beyond the established practice) in the right places (in integrative, coalition-building environments) at the right time (when reality can be reconstructed).

Innovative organizations are flexible; they provide people with the freedom to act. Many organizations, however, are not inclined to innovation or giving people opportunity for autonomy. Their structures are geared to protect against change and deviation and are concerned primarily with ensuring conformity.

> The contrasting style of thought is anti-change-oriented and prevents innovation. I call it "segmentalism" because it is concerned with compartmentalizing actions, events, and problems and keeping each piece isolated from the others. Segmentalist approaches see problems as narrowly as possible, independently of their context, independently of their connections to any other problems (Kanter, 1984, p. 28).

This is the image of the bureaucratic structure: departments, levels, and roles, with problems cut into segments and assigned to specialists. Isolation and little communication occurs in segmentalist structures, and change threatens and challenges the order of these organizations.

Kanter (1984) identifies several reasons for segmentalist organizations inhibiting innovation:

- People fail to see problems and lack the motivation to solve them because problem identification is a sign of failure.
- Segmentalism keeps people in their jobs and does not encourage them to communicate and try ideas.
- Precedent is important, limiting choices and causing the organization to repeat old solutions and do what it knows.
- Specialists' perceptions constrain to solutions because of their biases. Increased specialization can lead to internal political problems.

Segmented organizations think about the world in a rational way and break problems into subproblems. The entire problem is dispersed. In these environments, there is less chance that people will strike out and try new ideas or go against the "grain" or structure. And if innovation does occur in one place, it is difficult for it to be transferred to other parts of the organization because the links and networks between departments are not fluid and open.

The other approach is an integrated one, with different characteristics from segmentalism. Integrative action is the "willingness to move beyond perceived wisdom, to combine ideas from unconnected sources, to embrace change as an opportunity to test limits. To see problems integratively is to see them as wholes, related to larger wholes, and thus challenging established practices" (Kanter, 1984, p. 27). This approach decreases isolation, increases the exchange of information, and provides multiple perspectives on issues. Interdependence and cooperative teamwork can expand relationships and engage more resources in an integrative and participative approach to creativity. Aggregate wholes can release more creative alternatives.

Kanter thinks that networking (ensuring supportive peers) is also important for innovation. It comes from three conditions: (1) mobility, which circulates people across a variety of jobs; (2) employment security, which encourages risk taking; and (3) team structure, which allows information to be exchanged with people within departments or across disciplines so coalitions are formed and segmentalism is eliminated.

Strategies for Innovation

Innovation does not just happen. People and conditions must exist to foster it. Setting the stage for innovation requires stability, havens for ideas, and champions.

Although it sounds like a paradox, change requires some stability. Innovation cannot take place in an environment where there is high turnover. When people come and go, too much time is spent on relearning old lessons, thus new learning does not occur. Learning requires time for thought and reflection on new ways and ideas, which will sustain communication, establish coalitions, and build trust. People need stability to take risks and innovate, but innovation creates uncertainty. People dealing with uncertainty require some security to move through the change.

Galbraith (1982) recommends that organizations establish reservations that are totally devoted to new ideas. These reservations are havens for learning, where differentiation is the standard and divergent thinking is encouraged. Perelman (1987) defines this behavior as "imagineering," where people creatively imagine reaching goals. He also recommends that a "gap analysis" be completed to measure current conditions against potential alternatives.

Ideas need champions who are committed to an idea and can communicate it forcefully. These people are empowered to pursue ideas and push the organization to take productive action. They set up a culture of change. Encouraging innovation is not easy because there are forces at work that discourage it. That is why most organizations are operational, not innovative. Change produces conflict, and conflict encourages defensive reasoning. Leaders must work with managing conflict as well as agreement.

Innovation, Agreement, and Defensive Reasoning

A principal was once heard to say, "If you stand still long enough, you'll be at the head of the line." This attitude is reflective of a "if it's not broken, don't fix it" mentality. Changing things that were once successful is very difficult, even though times are different. Success can cause complacency because it encourages doing things according to the way they have always been done.

TIP	**TRANSFORMATION INTO PRACTICE**

CAN AGREEMENT CAUSE ORGANIZATIONAL CONFLICT?

Managing conflict is a common theme in workshops on leadership in organizations. But not much is stated about organizational agreement. Can it cause conflict? Does it need management? The "Abilene Paradox" concerns the management of agreement and the conflict it can create.

Picture a hot Sunday morning in Texas, the summer wind blowing stifling, dust-infested air through the house. According to Jerry Harvey in "The Abilene Paradox: The Management of Agreement" (1988, pp. 17–43), that is when he learned firsthand of the repression of agreement. He was at an uncle's house that Sunday in the mid-1950s with his family, when someone suggested that they go to a diner in Abilene, Texas, an hour and a half away, to have dinner. His mother replied, "If that's what you'd like to do, O.K." His aunt said, "It sounds good to me." And his grandmother stated, "I haven't been there in a long time." So, they all jumped into the non-air-conditioned Packard, drove the distance over the baked, suffocating landscape, ate bad food at the diner, and drove another one and a half hours back to the farmhouse—worn out and exhausted. When they returned, his uncle, after collapsing in a heap on the couch, said, "Who's idea was it to go to Abilene anyway?" "Not mine," his wife said, "I thought you wanted to go." "Well, I didn't want to go," his mother said, "I thought it was a dumb idea, with the heat and all."

Everyone thought that going to Abilene was a bad idea, but no one protested when the suggestion came up. Everyone went along with the idea even though they knew better. The "Abilene Paradox" occurs when organizations "take actions in contradiction to what they really want to do and therefore defeat many of the purposes they are trying to achieve" (p. 19).

Harvey believes that the inability to manage agreement is a source of organizational dysfunction. He states that there are two types of conflict: real, when people have real differences; and phony, when people agree on actions they want to take but then do the opposite. The resulting anger, frustration, and blaming—conflict—are not based on real conflict or disagreement; they stem from protective reactions.

The "Abilene Paradox" is about group tyranny and its resulting individual conformity—group-think. People become unwilling to speak up for what they believe because they perceive agreement on a course of action they think is incorrect. According to Harvey, "Each person in a self-defeating, Abilene-bound organization *colludes* with others, including peers, superiors, and subordinates, sometimes consciously and sometimes subconsciously, to create the dilemma in which the organization finds itself" (p. 27). The antidotes to the "Abilene Paradox" are: establishing debates, assigning gadflies and devil's advocates, developing a culture of pride, and creating empowering structures. It must be safe to express opinions, dissent with facts, and change one's mind when new facts arise.

> Are schools heading for Abilene in some of their curricular offerings or instructional practices?
> Do schools' structures encourage dissent or group-think?
> Do teachers' unions promote group-think or encourage a culture of professional pride?
> When does second-guessing become unprofessional and dysfunctional?

Used by permission of publisher, from *Organizational Dynamics*, Summer, 1974. © 1974. American Management Association, New York. All rights reserved.

Attitude, which relates to an organization's self-concept, can also get in the way of change. A "culture of inferiority" exists when people feel that anyone inside the organization is less able than those outside the organization. The ability of people from inside the system to think of or implement new ideas is questioned, causing heavy reliance on outsiders and reinforcing the negative self-concept.

How people think in organizations and their conduct toward ideas and proposals for change either deters or facilitates change. The items in Table 5–5 reflect thought processes or attitudes.

Many innovations are tried in organizations. As one teacher said, "I've lived through four cycles of reform, but things remain much the same." Part of the reason for the difficulty of innovation to take hold and have impact is defensive reasoning.

Gardner (1984) characterizes the defenses against high performance and poses a somewhat demoralizing position to optimists about high standards:

TABLE 5–5   Obstacles to Creative Thinking and Aids to Stifling Innovation

Obstacles to Creativity	Aids to Stifling Innovation
Self-censoring	Regard ideas with suspicion
Need approval/need to be right	Insist on approval to proceed
Eliminate possible connections	Require requests for information to be justified thoroughly
Listen to evaluate	Criticize/challenge each proposal
Follow precedent	Treat problem identification as a weakness
Avoid risks/obey rules	Withhold praise
Seek comfort and predictability	"Higher-ups" know everything and are responsible

Source: Lewis J. Perelman, Technology and Transformation of Schools (National School Boards Association, 1987), p. 113; and Rosabeth Moss Kanter, The Change Masters (New York: Simon and Schuster, 1984), p. 101.

There are large numbers of individuals who do not necessarily find unrelieved exhilaration in a system that emphasizes high performance. If these large numbers come to believe that the system exposes them unnecessarily to frustration and defeat, and if they enjoy the freedom of social action characteristic of a democracy, they will create elaborate institutional defenses to diminish the emphasis on performance as a determinant of status. We can observe such institutional defenses not only in education but in every aspect of our national life (p. 108).

Argyris (1985) studied defensive routines in organizations that stymie change efforts. He defines these routines as:

Thoughts and actions used to protect individuals', groups', and organizations' usual ways of dealing with reality. Defensive routines come between the individual or organization and any threats in the environment and can be productive and counterproductive. They are counterproductive when, in order to protect, they inhibit learning. . . . Defensive routines are productive when they protect the present level of competence without inhibiting learning (p. 5).

Defensive routines, according to Argyris, are used to protect people from pain—sometimes only in the short run because, if the routines inhibit learning, in the long term the pain may just be delayed. When dealing with threat, "we are programmed to create defensive routines and to cover them up with further defensive routines intended to bypass those that exist" (p. 3). Argyris believes that initially changes are made but then the people in the organization begin to face dilemmas, paradoxes, and threats. When that happens, defensive routines come into play, sometimes in the name of humaneness, civility, or realism. These routines are based on defensive reasoning, which is characteristic of soft data, inferences that are tacit and private, and conclusions that are not publicly testable. Some routines based on defensive reasoning are:

> Group think: Conforming thought that prevents people from seeing reality
>
> Soft reasoning: Deflecting issues by using "conventional wisdom" or impressions and not hard information or facts
>
> Bypass routines: Self-fulfilling prophecies with little potential for change; "that's human nature"

Symptoms of defensive routines are:

- Hidden informal organizations that subvert quality and productivity
- Inability to deal with problems everyone agrees exist
- Meaningless, nonchallenging bureaucratic work
- Middle managementitis—too many layers of management
- Employee desire for administrators to deal with others who are not productive
- Employees taking cover on difficult issues, then condemning administrators for unilateral action

Defensive reasoning can cause organizations to wither and die. People bring these routines with them, and they infect schools as well as private sector companies.

SUMMARY

Schools must be integrative systems to focus on innovation. Innovative organizations have team structures, networking, interdependence, creativity, and risk-taking opportunities. Professionals come together for participative decision making, bringing multiple perspectives to challenge established practices. But most people and organizations resist integrative and innovative activities because they disturb security and the status quo. Transformation of structures, thinking, leaders, and people will enable schools to become broader-based, multifaceted learning environments for all clients.

CONCEPTS

1. A school is an open social system, comprised of formal and informal structures in which coordination among its parts is necessary and communication among roles crucial to its successful operation.

2. Culture is an unwritten set of meanings, unique to each organization, which includes shared values, behavior patterns, mores, symbols, attitudes, and norms for "doing business." Culture defines organizational values and communicates to members how they should think and act, thus contributing to their security.

3. Leaders are intertwined with the culture's creation, management, and perhaps its destruction, so different leaders are needed at various phases in the organization's life.

4. Cultures can be positive forces in achieving organizational purposes or negative forces in inhibiting growth and change.

5. Organizational behavior and outcomes are also influenced by the informal organization—groups within the system that have their own practices, norms, values, and relationships. An organization's work culture is the product of both formal and informal influences.

6. School organizations are involved in both rational and political decision making.

7. Decision making is related to who has power. Vertical power comes from positions in the organization, and horizontal power is informal and related to expertise. Power tools include information, resources, and support.

8. Schools are information-based organizations, not because students and teachers deal with knowledge but because they require quality information to provide professional services and make decisions.

9. If transformation is to occur in bureaucracies, all subsystems must be involved (i.e., the formal organization; processes; political, production, and sociocultural subsystems; and people).

10. Leaders are needed for transformation to translate external demands to a commitment to change, to communicate infor-

mation to people, to develop confidence and trust, and to model transforming behavior.

11. Innovation involves the creation and implementation of new ideas, the redesign of all organizational subsystems, effecting change in the perception of people, flexible yet safe environments for experimentation, integrative actions on the part of the change agents, and leader champions who help form cultures.

PART III

TRANSFORMING LEADERSHIP

*Leaders define and express the dreams and visions
of the organization. They are the "polestars" who
communicate values and aspirations, and they are
able to inspire people to achieve organizational
goals while satisfying individual professional
needs. Without leadership, schools cannot be
successful.*

*Leaders must not be simplistically identified
by characteristics and traits. They come in all
sizes, shapes, dispositions, personalities,
philosophies, sexes, races, and educational levels.
They exist formally and informally, they can be
positive or negative, they can succeed or fail, but
they cannot be ignored. The forces of leadership
can sweep organizations forward and help people
revitalize, they can weaken desires and potential
through misguided efforts, or they can eliminate
possibilities by stifling creativity, commitment, and
initiative.*

*This section examines the concept of
transforming leadership and its impact on schools*

and people. In Chapter 6, a review of the leadership research provides an historical perspective as a backdrop for emerging theories. The world and work of contemporary leaders is examined, along with issues of management versus leadership, power, credibility, and impediments to leadership action. A case is built for transformational leadership in schools, drawing from the literature in the corporate and technological fields.

In Chapter 7, clear distinctions are made for the need for new leadership action, which centers around vision creation, core values, shared purposes, and commitment. In transforming schools, leadership density is the key in that many people can share the process. Teachers, principals, and superintendents must assume new roles, shed preconceived notions of job descriptions, and behave in significantly different ways to accomplish the schools' missions. Transformational leaders perceive the interconnectedness among themselves, the organization, and people they lead. They think about leading in broad, flexible configurations, are not bound by "what's always been," and engage in reflective practice. Their behavior models their values, expertise, confidence, and sense of purpose.

6 | Leadership Perspectives

Leadership is not an isolated concept. There can be no leaders without people to be led, causes to be championed, and organizations to be moved. The interconnectedness of people, structures, and leaders must be recognized as the key to understanding how transformation can occur. The goals, directions, and outcomes of change are set by the perceptions and thinking of the people in organizations, and their behavior measures whether changes produce success, quality, and productivity. Leaders must understand the power their perception and thinking have on affecting and directing organizational behavior.

Definitions of leadership are as varied as the number of researchers studying the concept. It has been viewed from the perspective of behavior, styles, personality traits, skills, interpersonal relationships, and level of power or influence. Yukl (1989) summarized the variations well by stating, "Leadership is defined broadly to include influence processes involving determination of the group's or organization's objectives, motivating task behavior in pursuit of these objectives, and influencing group maintenance and culture" (p. 5).

HISTORICAL PERSPECTIVE: A FRAME OF REFERENCE

Leadership is an intriguing and magnetic concept. As far back as the Middle Ages, much was written about leadership. In modern times, as the study of leadership reemerged, the concept was dissected into so many diverse parts that no clear and accepted definition existed.

Pfeffer (1978) builds a case for the ambiguity of the concept by reviewing most findings in leadership studies over the period of the 1950s to the 1980s, which have tried to define leadership in terms of traits, behavior, and relationships. He concluded, first, there is little evidence that the major dimensions of leader behavior, which emerged through literature and research, have any significant effect on organizational success; and second, in spite of all these varied studies, no clear definition resulted.

Burns (1978) agrees, stating that we had no school or central concept of leadership when he analyzed the subject in the late 1970s. He combined and synthesized the rich research, analysis, and experience into a comprehensive theory of leadership. The results of his work have contributed greatly to our understanding of how complex a concept leadership really is.

Leadership Traits

Charisma is that elusive but recognizable trait associated with many famous historical, political, and social figures. The notion of charismatic leadership evolved as researchers tried to isolate characteristics common to all leaders. They attributed certain personality or physical traits to a person, which were to account for his or her ability to lead or attract followers. Some estimates of how many personality traits were actually attributed to leaders in various studies are as high as 750, and obviously many were contradictory (Hoy & Miskel, 1978). The trait approach drew criticism by psychologists and sociologists in the 1940s and 1950s as being too limiting, which led the way to a focus on situational factors. When this idea appeared in the 1950s, it suggested that certain traits do set leaders and followers apart, but those traits might vary, depending on the situation.

Yukl (1989) suggests that "certain traits increase the likelihood that a leader will be effective, but they do not guarantee effectiveness" (p. 176). The characteristics found most frequently in successful leaders are:

- Adaptable to situations
- Alert to social environment
- Ambitious and achievement-oriented
- Assertive
- Cooperative
- Decisive
- Dependable

- Dominant (desire to influence others)
- Energetic (high activity level)
- Persistent
- Self-confident
- Tolerant of stress
- Willing to assume responsibility (p. 176)

Most recent studies on leadership acknowledge that traits and situations have an impact on effective leadership practices, along with many other factors. From traits, the focus changed to how leaders behave.

Leadership Behavior

The research on leadership conducted from the 1950s through the 1970s emphasized behavior and clustered around two general areas: *organizational tasks* and *interpersonal relationships* (Hoy & Miskel, 1978). No matter what behaviors are studied, described, or measured and then categorized, most terminology fits within these two dimensions.

Pioneering work in leader behavior was done at Ohio State University in the 1940s by Hemphill and Coons (1950) and revised in the 1950s by Halpin (1966). The Leader Behavior Description Questionnaire (LBDQ) measures two behaviors—initiating structure and consideration. *Initiating structure* is defined as "leader behavior that delineates the relationship between the leader and subordinates and, at the same time, establishes defined patterns of organization, channels of communication, and methods of procedure. *Consideration* is leader behavior that indicates friendship, trust, warmth, interest, and respect in the relationship between the leader and members of the work group" (Hoy & Miskel, 1978, p. 182).

The LBDQ has been widely used in private sector, military, and educational studies to determine leader-subordinate relationships. These two dimensions are placed on a continuum from low to high and result in four types of behavior. One who scores low on consideration and initiation is basically ineffective as a leader. The ideal leader behavior is displayed by a high score on initiating structure and consideration. Such a leader would have a strong relationship with subordinates, based on mutual trust, respect, and friendship, and would set clear, established patterns of operating, communicating, and achieving the organization's goals.

In school settings where the measure has been used, administrators have generally scored higher on consideration than on initiating structure. Halpin (1966) speculated that because schools are so concerned with human relations and group dynamics, they place more value on the consideration dimension and select leaders accordingly.

Using similar concepts, Blake and Mouton (1964) devised the *managerial grid* to explain leader behavior in terms of concern for production and concern for people. They determined five leadership styles along a horizontal and vertical axis, numbered 1 (low) to 9 (high) on each of the two dimensions. A manager with a 1,9 style would have a very high concern for the people in the organization and would establish friendly, comfortable work environments. In contrast, the 9,1 manager is characterized as very efficient, organizing tasks so that production is high and not hindered by the people in the system. The ideal style would be a 9,9 in which the results are high productivity created by committed, satisfied workers.

Hoy and Miskel's (1978) conclusions on leadership accurately summarize the state of the art in the late 1970s.

> First, while there has been considerable concern among scholars and practitioners in diverse fields, comprehensive empirically tested theories of leadership are still to be developed. Second, leader traits, situational components and effectiveness criteria must be considered simultaneously in leadership theory, research, and practice. Finally, the concept of good or bad leadership must be restricted to a particular situation (p. 208).

Situational Leadership/Contingency Models

The following models consider that personality is a stable characteristic of leadership style, but situations in which leaders must behave differ widely. The situational approach to leadership considers such variables as "the leader's authority and discretion, the nature of the work performed by the leader's unit, subordinate ability and motivation, the nature of the external environment, and the role requirements imposed on a manager by subordinates, peers, superiors, and outsiders" (Yukl, 1989, p. 9).

Fielder (1967) established a leadership model based on contingency theory, suggesting that both task- and relationship-oriented styles can be effective, given certain conditions of the situation or group to be led. He proposed that the style of the leader is a constant and the tasks to be performed or situations to be managed should be arranged to fit this style. Situations can be either favorable or unfavorable, depending on three variables: leader-member relations, task structure, and leader position power.

In contrast, Hersey and Blanchard (1977) developed a situational leadership model under the same assumption that styles and situations are both important. However, their model proposes that leadership style should be changed to match the situation—specifically, the maturity level of the followers. Four leadership styles are defined, in terms of relationship-oriented and task-oriented leadership, when matched with followers' level of experience, education, responsibility, and goal-setting ability. These styles are directive, persuasive, participatory, and delegatory.

McCall and Lombardo (1978) argue that leadership needs to be explained more comprehensively.

> Leaders may face an infinite variety of specific situations and engage in an infinite variety of overt behaviors. Trying to generate enough contingencies to explain all possible combinations of situations and behaviors may be fruitless. . . . Organizations, situations and individuals are constantly changing. To say . . . that leaders should be fitted to the situation is to deny reality (pp. 154–155).

Although situational leadership theory has not been well researched, it has added to our growing understanding by emphasizing leader behavior as a flexible, adaptable set of actions; an awareness of opportunities to build followers' skill and confidence levels to improve their performance; and a recognition that leader behavior does exist in some skill-oriented fashion.

Transactional Leadership

Situational and contingency models of leadership are concerned with the style of the leader, the relationship with followers, and the everchanging arena of leadership activities. These models describe *transactional* leadership, in which one person organizes an exchange of valued things with others. These valued things may be concrete or abstract, physical, emotional, monetary, or political. Transactional leadership focuses on observable behavior, self-interests, and situations. In this model, the leader and followers engage in a transaction in which the followers perform or move in a direction in exchange for support, autonomy, power, or other desired results. The interactions between leaders and followers are transactions based on mutual need and satisfaction.

Such descriptions of leader behavior are all based on an important assumption—that leadership is defined in terms of interactions with followers: "leaders inducing followers to act for certain goals that represent the values and the motivations—the wants and needs, the aspirations and expectations—*of both leaders and followers*" (Burns, 1978, p. 19).

"Transactional leaders were fine for the earlier era of expanding markets and non-existing competition. In return for compliance they issued rewards. For all intents and purposes these managers changed little. They managed what they found and left things pretty much as they found them when they moved on" (Tichy & Devanna, 1986, p. viii). Their role was to maintain the exchanges that were established and keep the organizational relationships stable.

Sergiovanni (1987c) related this type of leadership behavior to school organizations, saying that in transactional leadership, teachers and administrators barter to accomplish the separate purposes of each. They exchange services and meet each others' needs, largely based on extrinsic motives. Teachers work hard and receive rewards—monetary and psychological. Leaders achieve organizational goals and objectives and a working relationship with teachers and other staff.

Sergiovanni agrees with Tichy and Devanna, expressing that this leadership theory has little to offer for the future, as it is based on too narrow a view of people's potential and motivation and on an outmoded concept of management. Instead, the leader's behavior may not be as important as the meaning behind it, the commitment it generates, or the way it is perceived by the followers.

Transactional leadership does not consider motivation and higher purposes—values—of professionals. These factors are important because the perceptions and resulting behavior professionals express in schools are critical to understanding how to lead them effectively for change. Transactional leadership does not bind leaders and followers or motivate them to work collectively toward the overall purposes of the institution. Table 6–1 summarizes the historical approaches to transactional leadership.

Our premise is that significant changes must occur to transform schooling; consequently, former leader approaches will not work. Transactional leadership will keep schools the same—it may move people but it will not motivate them. It is a manager-versus-leader way of operating, ensuring that all the various parts of the system are functioning and regulated. Actions are ordinary and predictable, sustaining "what is" and never considering "what could be." Before examining new leadership for the future, a perplexing issue—management versus leadership—needs to be resolved.

TABLE 6–1   Summary of Historical Approaches to Leadership

Type	Approach	Description
Trait	Characteristics	Certain personality and physical attributes are necessary to become a leader.
Transactional	Behavior	Certain actions or styles can be defined and put into effect to describe what people must do to lead.
	Situation/Contingency	Conditions and people with whom leaders work determine effectiveness, not personality or actions.

MANAGEMENT VERSUS LEADERSHIP

Is the argument about differences between managers and leaders merely a semantic one? Don't managers and leaders do the same things? Can the roles, functions, and purposes these individuals enact be defined discreetly enough to warrant distinctions?

Most contemporary research draws the conclusion that there are significant differences between leaders and managers that provide dimensions for comparison and contrast. Zaleznik (1986) stated that managers and leaders are motivated by different types of situations, their historical perspectives are unlike one another's, and they think and behave in contrasting ways regardless of the type of organization. He believes that the managerial ethic is associated with a bureaucratic culture, whereas leaders create entrepreneurial cultures. Table 6–2 illustrates the differences in a number of dimensions.

Many organizations tend to be overmanaged and underled. Managers are efficient, whereas leaders are effective; also, leaders ask different questions than managers. The focus of managers' attention is on the physical resources, such as capital and workers' skills and technology, whereas leaders concern themselves with emotional and spiritual resources, like values, commitment, and aspirations (Bennis & Nanus, 1985).

TABLE 6-2   A Comparison of Leaders and Managers

Dimensions for Comparison	Leaders	Managers
Goal Direction	Personal; active	Impersonal; reactive; passive
Work Relationships	Create visions that excite people; develop options; inspire	Create processes to coordinate and balance; involvement but with limited options
Value Emphasis	Terminal, end-state	Instrumental; means
Problems	Create them	Solve them
Self and Environment	Separate from their environment; strong inner-identity; self-sufficient	Belong to their environment; depend on memberships, roles
Conducting Business	Transforming	Transacting

Source: Abraham Zaleznik, "Managers and Leaders: Are They Different?" *Harvard Business Review*, 64 (1986).

Deal and Kennedy (1982) differentiate between managers and leaders (whom they call "heroes"). "Managers run institutions; heroes create them. . . . Managers are routinizers; heroes are experimenters" (p. 37). They lament that such leaders have all but vanished from the corporate world of today and what remain are rational managers who write memos, plan by objectives, and work in careful, predictable fashion to maintain order. "While business certainly needs managers to make trains run on time, it more desperately needs heroes to get the engine going" (p. 38).

Managers maintain balance and seek compromises while they identify strongly with the organization. Leaders, on the other hand, take risks and imagine new areas, approaches, and images. They excite people in the organization and intuitively project creative alternatives. Both types of people may be useful to an organization. Managers tend to maintain the status quo, stability, order, and security, allowing the organization to perpetuate itself over time. In contrast, leaders operate with vision and have the ability to initiate and sustain change, to translate intentions into reality, to communicate and commit others to values, and to move people and organizations forward into new dimensions and directions.

Schon (1984) suggests that although the terms *management* and *leadership* are not the same, the separation of the functions of each need not necessarily cause problems. "One can be a leader without being a manager. One can, for example, fulfill many of the symbolic, inspirational, educational and normative functions of a leader and thus represent what an organization stands for without carrying out any of the formal burdens of management. Conversely, one can manage without leading" and perform functions of administration, resource allocation, and organizing the daily operations (p. 36). Scully (1987) disagrees; he does not think that both leadership and management have positive attributes. In fact, he says that leaders provide opportunities to succeed, whereas managers suppress ideas and talent of workers. Leaders allow people freedom and inspire them through visions, and managers simply seek to control.

In school organizations throughout history, there has been a preponderance of managers. Education has imitated the scientific management, bureaucratic model, so it is logical that those in charge would be expected to manage rather than lead. Schools have become the standard bearer for traditional values, passing on the culture of previous generations. They have never been charged with creating new visions, predicting what might be needed for an unknown future, or dreaming about possibilities. No one wanted education to "experiment" with children, sometimes making mistakes or failing. Yet, no dramatic learning or significant new dimensions can emerge without investigation, experimentation, and risk taking.

Scientific management has not served education well. In times when the external environment has changed for organizations like schools, leaders—not simply managers—are needed. Without visionary leadership, opportunities for growth are missed and adaptation to new circumstances does not occur.

TIP | **TRANSFORMATION INTO PRACTICE**

PRINCIPALS AS MANAGERS

A more managerial view of what executives do in their daily life was developed by Page (1985) and provides a complete nuts-and-bolts job description. Nine factors were found to be consistent in a number of studies that were tested in the Managerial Position Description Questionnaire (MPDQ): supervising, planning and organizing, decision making, monitoring indicators, controlling, representing, coordinating, consulting, and administering. Although these functions are defined in relation to corporate activity, they can be easily applied to education.

Principals supervise the curriculum and the teachers. They plan and organize the school calendar and activities, the schedules, and the budget expenditures; they constantly make decisions on class placement, teacher assignments, curricular materials, inservice speakers, and school programs. When principals monitor indicators, they review factors of effectiveness such as student performance, level of satisfaction of parents with the program, and productivity of teachers. Superintendents also monitor the community and political climate, the financial status of the district budget, and the effectiveness of middle managers.

Controlling activities include determining district policies, rules, and regulations for students; teacher contracts; and resource allocations. Dealing with the public, becoming a positive image and promoter of sound educational practices, and responding to concerns, questions, and complaints come under the category of representing. In accomplishing these tasks, the coordinating function emerges, as the administrator meets with many groups and tries to maintain a good relationship among all constituents in the school arena. Communication and information sharing are two important aspects in representing and coordinating.

The consulting role of an administrator involves sharing expertise as well as keeping current professionally by joining organizations and attending workshops and training sessions. Finally, the administering responsibilities described by Page are identical for business and education. Such duties as record keeping, report writing, and locating, disseminating, and analyzing information are common to all positions.

If principals follow this job description, will their schools be successful?
Could the activities described above be considered "transactional"?
Do executives who operate under these guidelines maintain the status quo or act as change agents?

THE CONTEXT OF LEADERSHIP

The context in which we study leadership today and in the future is vastly different than in the past.

Leadership theories have traditionally been short-range and atomistic, focusing on leader-group relations and passing over leader-group-system relationships. . . . Leaders and their groups are embedded in complex, often contradictory organizational systems, and to examine them outside this context ignores the richness of reality. How workers feel about themselves and their leaders is not everything—it is only important in the context of the tasks they are performing and the varied, external demands of the organization (McCall & Lombardo, 1978, p. 7).

Successful organizations of the future and their leaders will be described in a broader context, because it is important to consider the contemporary environment in which they work. The environmental context includes external influences upon the leader and the organization, and internal factors such as the people and the structure of the system. The external environment was discussed in detail in Chapter 4, in terms of the context in which schools respond to powerful forces, trends, and pressures.

Leaders are the bridge between the internal and external environments. To be successful, they need to develop the internal environment while struggling wth the ambiguity and complexity of the external context. Figure 6–1 summarizes the context in which leaders work, and serves as the framework for this next section.

Because of the involved interrelationships between all aspects of personal, business, and social life, leaders face a tough challenge in fostering change. Uncertainty is becoming a constant, and change is both interactive and discontinuous. These factors make workers uncomfortable and situations unstable, so leaders must use new ways to make sense of the accelerated complications they face (Bennis & Nanus, 1985). They need to read the environment well, interpret the impact it has on the organization, determine what changes are needed, and communicate clearly with people to keep them informed and committed.

Leaders must have a large repertoire of behavior to analyze and contend with the ever-changing internal and external environments. How leaders think, how they frame issues, and what questions they ask help to set the agenda and tempo for the entire organization. How people think and behave is a reflection of these leadership processes. In a school, the principal's leadership determines its responsiveness to par-

FIGURE 6–1   Context in Which Leaders Work

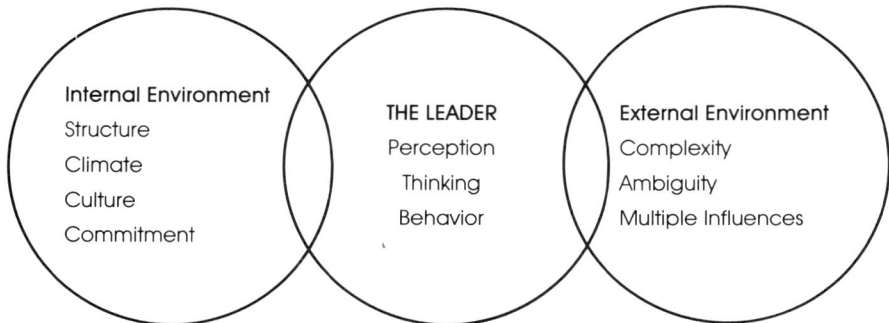

Internal Environment
Structure
Climate
Culture
Commitment

THE LEADER
Perception
Thinking
Behavior

External Environment
Complexity
Ambiguity
Multiple Influences

ents, its approach to problem solving, and its work climate and environment.

TIP | TRANSFORMATION INTO PRACTICE

LEADERSHIP AND PERCEPTION: COGNITIVE STYLE

Psychologists tell us that the fundamental basis for behavior is perception. Differences in perception create varied approaches and translate into many types of behavior. How leaders act, relate to followers, and accomplish purposes depend on the perspective from which they view the world and their place in it. Yet the study of leadership does not usually consider perception or cognitive style.

Cognitive style is based on qualities of the mind that determine "the message that is received from a situation, the personal meaning that we form. This perception and processing becomes the guide for individual behavior" (Guild, 1987, p. 83).

The greatest contributor to the development of the connection between perception and behavior was psychologist Carl Jung. Jung (1971) identified two types of perception—sensation and intuition—that affect behavior in very distinct ways. He proposed that judgment also affects how we make decisions, which then feeds into behavior. That judgment can be either objective (the thinking process) or subjective (the feeling process). Cognitive style, then, is determined by how leaders perceive—by sensing or intuiting—and how they make decisions or judgments—by thinking or feeling.

Those whose perception is based on sensation receive information in concrete, literal ways. They depend on their senses to provide precise, detailed, and accurate facts, and they behave in practical, stable, predictable ways. In contrast, people who primarily receive intuitively gain information in more subtle ways, from many sources, looking for intention, connections, and possibilities. They behave in a more random, imaginative fashion, and seek new challenges; they have difficulty with routine and detailed planning.

In terms of judgment, Jung believed people were either thinking (i.e., logical, rational, and cool) or feeling (i.e., sensitive, perceptive, and responsive). Their actions are also influenced by their attitude toward the world—extroverted or introverted.

In an extensive research undertaking during the early 1960s, Isabel Briggs Myers operationalized the psychological types theory into an instrument to measure these types. The Myers-Briggs Type Indicator (MBTI) provides a detailed profile of one's cognitive style by identifying 16 possible combinations of characteristics. The MBTI describes four basic preferences that direct the use of perception and judgment. The areas explored include extraversion-introversion, sensing-intuition, thinking-feeling, and judgment-perception (Myers & McCaulley, 1985).

Information gained from this perspective can aid leaders in several ways. First, it enhances self-awareness by pointing out the primary perceptual processes individuals use. Second, it assists one in working with others and understanding their behavior, by recognizing that people perceive and think in diverse ways. It can also help leaders to select effective teams to accomplish tasks by balancing different types, and to seek opinions for important decisions from colleagues who use different thought processes.

What implications does cognitive style have for school leaders?

> What does an intuiting-style principal focus on in classroom observations?
>
> Can a sensing-style principal effect change?
>
> Which administrator should be given the job of writing the master plan for curriculum?
>
> Who should be in charge of the new visions committee?
>
> Why do some teachers need detailed directions and a specific deadline to complete a project, whereas others take the task, run with it, and turn it in ahead of schedule?
>
> Which teachers should be assigned to a cooperative learning team and which should remain in individual, independent classrooms?
>
> Should we try to select administrators with cognitive styles different than our own?

"Cognitive complexity" is the leader's ability to use open and flexible thinking systems, to handle many issues simultaneously, and to integrate them for decision making. Leaders with cognitive complexity use multiple mindscapes and schemas and consider many points of view. They create fluid configurations and process large and varied amounts of information discriminately to analyze, evaluate, and ultimately come to conclusions (Lombardo, 1978). These descriptions illustrate the leader's need for continuously bridging the external and internal contexts in order to lead effectively.

Much of the leader's time is spent working through the internal environmental context—structure, climate, culture, and commitment. Organizational structure's (discussed in Chapter 4) effect on leadership needs to be considered. When leaders come to an organization, they find a structure in place, unless they are creating an entirely new institution. They must identify the structure—functional, product, hybrid, or matrix—and determine whether the structure fits with the intended goals of the organization and with the external environmental conditions. This determination is a very important one, because if the structure is dysfunctional, change will be the first order of business and will direct the leader's role.

In the case of school leaders, the structure they find is generally deeply embedded. With few exceptions, school structures have remained the same over decades; although brief periods of innovation have succeeded in making some structural changes, these have rarely lasted. Open classrooms, team teaching with shared decision making, individualized instruction for all students, and parental- and community-based school management are some examples of attempts at changing how schools function. Structural configurations are part of what leaders need to address in school transformation.

Another internal context of organizations is climate. Climate and culture have sometimes been used interchangeably to describe a subtle, but pervasive, influence in all institutions. The two concepts exist, but they are not synonymous. Organizational *climate* refers to the atmosphere or setting one finds in the workplace. Hoy and Miskel (1978) define climate in schools as a "set of internal characteristics that distinguishes one school from another and influences the behavior of people in it. . . . The climate is the end product of the school groups— students, teachers, administrators—as they work to balance the organizational and individual dimensions of a social system" (p. 137).

Climate of a school is like its personality—unique, complex, and evolving. As an enduring characteristic in educational research, climate studies have most often involved the relationship between leader (principal) and followers (teachers). It is an important concept for leaders because research has concluded that the most influential person in establishing a climate is the principal. Although leaders must accept some of the contextual conditions they find in an organization, there are characteristics over which they have control, and climate is one of these. The leader can alter the climate and make it a positive, productive, environmental force.

What about culture? It is a more difficult concept to measure than climate and a more powerful one. *Culture* was defined earlier as an informal set of rituals and values that communicates to people in the organization what kinds of behavior are important and expected in order to achieve the goals. Culture deals more with security and stability than climate does. Both affect people's feelings about what they are doing and their commitment to the organization. But climate is easier to change than culture, since culture is steeped in basic values and norms.

Culture can undermine or stimulate change, since it is a subtle and constant force, made up of values and norms that affect work processes, relationships, and people. Culture can assist in accomplishing the purposes of the organization, if the leader can tie the elements of change to the cultural framework.

The ability of leaders to shape organizational culture is often determined by the age of the system; that is, someone starting a new company or opening a new school is much more likely to be able to shape the culture of that institution than one that has existed for a long time. In new organizations, culture helps to build the system, because it is being formed at the same time as goals are established, staff is hired, and systems and facilities are designed. There is no history in a new organization. Legends, heroes, and stories that transmit values and purposes develop at this time. "The culture in young, successful organizations is likely to be very strong because it is instrumental to the success of the organization, the assumptions have been internalized by current members and transmitted to new members, and the founder is still present to symbolize and reinforce the culture" (Yukl, 1989, p. 216).

Leaders can be culture builders, however, in all ages of organizations by using the following mechanisms, according to Schein (1985):

1. Attention
2. Reaction to crises
3. Role modeling
4. Allocation of rewards
5. Criteria for selection and dismissal

The things that leaders attend to communicate what is valued. Conversely, what leaders choose to ignore also gives a value message. Attention, by a superintendent, would be shown by visiting schools often, talking with teachers and students, and attending school and parent functions. Whether the superintendent visits only academic classes and interacts with honor students or stops in at vocational and special needs programs communicates what is important. Events attended may be indicators of values—does the superintendent go just to plays and concerts, or only to athletic events? Attention is also demonstrated by the topics of administrative meetings: what is on the agenda and what is left off, what questions and concerns are raised, and how much time is spent on various issues.

Cultural norms are also reflected in reactions to crises. They determine which issues are classified as crises, and what approach will be used to resolve them. In some cases, dissonance and debate are perceived to be part of doing business—conflict is expected. In other organizations, any sign of discord creates a crisis, because conflict is outside the cultural norms. In a crisis situation like the defeat of a school budget, how leaders respond is important. Some may react defensively and assume a "bunker mentality," cutting off communication with segments of staff or community; others may employ broad problem-solving techniques to define alternatives and develop consensus on necessary reductions.

Role modeling may be the most effective culture builder because it can be a visible, everyday action. A principal who stays late to help a teacher demonstrates that he or she would value the same behavior of a teacher toward a student. Seeing a principal occasionally teach a class to illustrate a technique or assist a teacher in implementing a new strategy shows that the leader is an educator, not just an administrator. It also demonstrates a concern and understanding for other roles in the organization and offers an opportunity for individual growth. Likewise, a superintendent who runs a staff inservice workshop reminds the faculty of common values and a focus on continuing professional development.

The allocation of rewards, as a culture builder, is more difficult to do in an educational than a business setting, if only money is considered. In schools, salary schedules are negotiated and not open to change as rewards for performance. But there are other kinds of rewards administrators can give to teachers. For example, supervisory positions, such as department heads or team leaders, recognize staff leadership and expertise. Special awards and recognition programs can also reward service and good results. Teaching and administrative assignments to certain grades, classes, or schools, location of rooms, and duty schedules are ways people can be rewarded—or punished. In some schools, greater autonomy is given as a reward, providing growth opportunities, experimentation, and innovation.

Establishing strong criteria for staff selection and dismissal sets cultural standards for performance. One of the most important tasks leaders have is making decisions about who are the best people for the job—what skills and traits are necessary for success in the school environment. Hiring excellent people is one step; keeping them up to date professionally and improving those who have tenure are important responsibilities. The processes and values superintendents and principals apply in all of these cases influence the culture.

The final environmental context is commitment. A commitment gap exists between leaders and followers when followers do not perceive their values to be congruent with the leader's. If workers think their leaders have not created meaning or trust for them, then their behavior will reflect their perceptions. The vision that leaders need to communicate is missing when there is a commitment gap, because the workers feel no ownership, responsibility, or dedication to the goals of the organization (Bennis & Nanus, 1985).

This lack of commitment is expressed as loss of confidence. "Loss of confidence brings images of defeat and failure, helplessness, even self-contempt" (Gardner, 1986, p. 25). Workers cannot be responsible if they perceive themselves as powerless and uninvolved. In Part IV of this book, attention is given to the concept of teacher empowerment, which can generate faculty commitment to school goals and values.

Commitment requires a clear vision for the organization and development of credibility on the part of the leader. (Vision creation is a topic for the following chapter.) Credibility is established when leaders' values and purposes mesh, when resources follow those values, and when words and behavior are congruent. Credible leaders get their authority from their expertise; they know when they don't know something; their espoused theories and theories in use match; they establish trust through their fair and consistent actions; they are accurate, yet willing to take risks; and they can be counted on to follow through. Credibility depends on the leader's interaction with others; it is bestowed upon the leader based on followers' perceptions of actions over time.

This concept is a necessary component of effective leadership, in that the more credible the leader, the more likely it is that commitment of the followers will exist. Credibility is sorely challenged in political, societal, economic, and educational arenas. Followership by fiat does not work—autocratic or paternalistic "heroes" do not sway people to commit to work for very long periods of time. Charisma is not enough— people can become disillusioned if credibility is tarnished or lost.

Leadership has been an issue from school systems to the Oval Office, and it does not find itself in an open or trusting environment as the twentieth century ends. Reestablishing credibility is one of the major tasks for leaders, and how they use and apply power is a factor in this process.

LEADERSHIP AND POWER

"Power is the probability that one actor within a social relationship will be in a position to carry out his own will despite resistance, regardless of the basis on which this probability rests" (Weber, 1947, p. 152). Burns (1978) expands Weber's definition to point out that power wielders exert their influence to achieve their own goals regardless of whether these goals are shared by the respondents of that power. He also suggests that power can be better understood when viewed through a psychological perspective, which includes these assumptions:

"Power is first of all a *relationship* and not merely an entity."

Power "involves the *intention* or *purpose* of both power holder and power recipient."

Power "is *collective,* not merely the behavior of one person" (Burns, 1978, p. 13).

This view of power is more complex than Weber's because it connects the players in the power scene and assumes they all have reasons or motives for being part of that relationship. It also assists us in seeing how power fits into leadership. "All leaders are actual or potential power holders, but not all power holders are leaders" (Burns, 1978, p. 18). What, then, is the difference?

Bennis and Nanus (1985) describe power as misused throughout history when "leaders have controlled rather than organized, administered repression rather than expression, and held their followers in arrestment rather than in evolution" (p. 16). This is an example of the behavior of power holders, not leaders. Power, used properly by leaders "is the basic energy needed to initiate and sustain action, or the capacity to translate intention into reality and sustain it" (p. 17).

The answer to the difference between power holders and leaders lies in shared purpose. Leaders have goals, values, and motivation upon which they base their action. They also have the ability to recognize the followers' motives and desires and mesh them together to create a common purpose for all to embrace. The power in this shared purpose is that consensus can be developed around a core of values, yet autonomy is allowed in terms of reaching them.

Leaders who operate transactionally use their power to complete their exchanges successfully and move people to action, and they recognize the power resources of the bargainers. They have a separate but related purpose, as long as they have resources to trade. "To many contemporary theorists, the power of leadership is in the cleverness of the leader in sizing up situations and people, in managing the psychology of followers and in engineering the work place that makes the difference" (Sergiovanni, 1987c, p. 3). Leaders of the future will need to move beyond these transactions by creating and renewing shared purpose and commitment. They will be transforming—leaders and followers working toward higher levels of motivation and morality so that their collective power and purposes merge and become greater.

Successful leaders need to be able to distinguish between having power *to* influence and accomplish goals and motivate people, and having power *over* people, which implies compliance, dominance, and control. These leaders have a capital view of power—"They spend it to increase it" and they empower others with purposing (Sergiovanni, 1987b, p. 341). They pull people toward them. Because people are attracted to the ideas, values, and mission of the leader, they do not need to be pushed or moved. (The concept of leadership as purposing is discussed in the following chapter.)

Leaders have three types of power: position, personal, and political. Although distinctions can be made in the definitions, they often overlap to make it more difficult to isolate one from the other. *Position* power refers to the legitimacy and authority vested in the particular position one holds and the control the leader has over resources, rewards and punishments, information, and situations. *Personal* power includes both job expertise and interpersonal relationship skills. The leader must exhibit a certain degree of competence in the field, yet also be able to establish loyalty and commitment of followers, by the use of personal, charismatic qualities. The passion and intensity with which the leader communicates values and mission is included in this type of power. *Political* power does not suggest politics; rather, it is the power a leader has over decision-making processes in the organization and the ability to form coalitions with followers and change opponents into supporters (Yukl, 1989).

> Power alone is not sufficient to explain a leader's effectiveness in influencing people. A leader's influence behavior and skills must be considered also if we want to make progress in understanding how leaders influence people. Effective leaders have the skill to recognize when different types of influence attempts are appropriate, and the skill to carry out influence attempts in an effective manner (Yukl, 1989, p. 37).

These leaders perceive a situation and think about whether personal or position power is needed in that case. They also assess the followers' attitudes and perceptions in order to determine what actions or leader behavior to use to influence followers' behavior. Influence is the effect one person has on another's attitudes, perceptions, or behavior.

A final consideration on leadership and power is how much power is necessary or desirable.

> More influence is necessary in an organization where major changes in member attitudes and behaviors are required than in an organization that can continue to survive and prosper by doing things the same way as before. . . . It is especially difficult for a leader who recognizes that the

organization will face a major crisis in coming years, a crisis that can be overcome if preparations are begun immediately, but the evidence of the coming crisis is not yet sufficiently strong to persuade members to act now (Yukl, 1989, p. 50).

This is exactly the situation that exists in education at the conclusion of this century. Yukl concludes that, in such crises, "transformational leadership is especially relevant" (p. 50).

LEADERSHIP: NEW DEFINITIONS

Leadership "is one of the most observed and least understood phenomena on earth" (Burns, 1978, p. 2). We watch leaders all the time, but we may be concentrating on who they are, what their personalities are like, and what observable products they create, instead of noticing the subtle processes, complex interactions, and commitment that really characterize leadership. The media trivializes leaders and the masses idolize superficial giants—no wonder there has been no consensus about the essence of leadership. Bennis has remarked that in the face of enormous challenges confronting us, we seem to have a void where great ideas and people are needed. Yet he is hopeful that during "this moratorium new concepts of leadership have incubated," so that we can expect great men and women with "exciting new visions of power" (Bennis & Nanus, 1985, p. 2). The following examples of new definitions of leadership point to a significant change in what leaders must become to influence the organizations of the twenty-first century.

The new leader . . . is one who commits people to action, who converts followers into leaders, and who may convert leaders into agents of change (Bennis & Nanus, 1985, p. 3).

Leadership is the reciprocal process of mobilizing, by persons with certain motives and values, various economic, political and other resources, in a context of competition and conflict, in order to realize goals independently or mutually held by both leaders and followers (Burns, 1978, p. 425).

Leaders must also help people know what they can be at their best, calling for the kind of effort and restraint, drive and discipline that make for great performance. In leadership at its finest, the leader symbolizes the best in the community, the best in traditions, values, and purposes (Gardner, 1978, p. 133).

Leadership in the self-renewing and thriving enterprise is characterized by its willingness to move beyond tidy models of what leadership is and does. Leaders establish order and discipline, and simultaneously foster skepticism, incredulity, experimentation and change. They encourage the generation of new forms and actions that may have neither precedent nor accustomed approval. They inject creative enzymes into the system, with results that can be destabilizing and disorderly and are rarely parametric. They know that to achieve more and better results, more resourcefulness is as important as more resources (Levitt, 1988, p. 7).

Blumberg (1989) generated a description of a school administrator, gathered from members of his organization. These characteristics provide a practical example of the preceding definitions, applied to education:

An exquisite sense of timing
A passion about life
Self-definition rather than being defined by others
A belief in one's own ability to shape the world
Humor that works as glue to pull people together
A sense of the absurd and the ability to treat absurdity as just that
A vision like the biblical prophets
A ready-made image of a world that doesn't exist, but could
Patience and confidence that vision will come in its own time
An authentic compassion
An elegant sense of history
A sense of optimism such that the cup is always half full, never
    half empty (p. 227)

These definitions of leadership are values-based—not predicated on traits, behaviors, or situations. The values leaders bring to their work determine how they think, act, and respond to situations. Those values also pull people toward the leader and the organization, establishing shared purposes to accomplish new missions.

Concepts such as empowerment, trust, high self-regard, communication, and team building emerge as what leading is all about. Dreaming, creating a vision, defining a mission, and providing inspiration are also used to explain the subtle aspects of motivating people. Table 6–3 illustrates a similarity of contemporary thought about leadership. These descriptions create a view of leadership that is complex, value-driven, and multidimensional. Such leadership is concerned with perceiving, thinking, and behaving in new ways toward people and the organization. Active and challenging expectations are being set for those who will become successful and productive change agents.

For example, leaders have always been expected to set goals for the organization. In contrast, we now need leaders who are visionary and

TABLE 6–3   What Leaders Are About

Gardner	Garfield	Tichy & Devanna	Bennis & Nanus
Envisioning goals	Creating a	Change agents	Gaining attention
Affirming values	mission	Courageous:	through vision
Motivating	Concentrating on	—intellectually	Achieving
Managing	goals	—emotionally	meaning
Achieving a	Magnetism	Visionaries	through
workable level	Innovation	Lifelong learners	communication
of unity	Self-management	Belief in people	Creating trust
Explaining	Team building/	Value-driven	through
Serving as a	Playing	Ability to deal	positioning
symbol	Course correction	with complexity,	Deployment of
Representing the	Change	ambiguity	self
group	management		
externally			
Renewing			

inspirational, who can courageously create new missions through the visions they perceive. Leaders manage people, but now they must think about people as significant contributors to the achievement of goals, by recognizing their need to be empowered. Team building and shared meaning will help to encourage unity and coordinate action, thus increasing the level of motivation.

Leaders' behavior must be reliable and trustworthy, as they are called upon to be a symbol of high moral values in all facets of their lives. They need to possess integrity and positive self-regard, be tirelessly persistent in the pursuit of their mission, and manage themselves so they keep learning in an increasingly complex, ambiguous environment. These new leaders are necessary for the transformation we envision for the coming century. The next chapter on Transformational Leadership will explore all the dimensions of such leadership. Table 6–4 summarizes the approaches to leadership studies.

THE WORK OF LEADERS: WHAT LEADERS DO

Descriptions of what leaders do at work—how they perceive, think, and behave—are as varied as the definitions of leadership. One characterization of leaders' work combines three skills. "The nature of the job requires leaders to apply complexity/simplicity (certain types of

TABLE 6–4   Summary of Approaches to Leadership Studies

Type	Approach	Description
Trait	Characteristics	Certain personality and/or physical attributes are necessary to become a leader.
Transactional	Behavior	Certain actions or styles can be defined and put into effect to describe what people must do to lead.
	Situational/ Contingency	Conditions and people with whom leaders work determine effectiveness, not personality or actions.
Transformational	Integrated	Perception: —futuristic perspective —value-driven —visionary Thinking: —complex mental processes —optimistic confidence —power of information —creativity Behavior: —interacts with multiple environments —empowers and inspires people —creates organizational tension —instills meaning and purpose —initiates and manages change —uses many communication strategies —models values —synergistic

mental functioning); set up structures (a certain kind of technical skill); and use power to get things done (a social skill)" (Lombardo, 1978, p. 24). This view portrays leaders as having the ability to perceive in many different ways and apply all levels of thinking to their problem-solving tasks. They must also have enough technical expertise in their field to organize and implement structural configurations to make the organization run smoothly.

In education, technical skills include a knowledge of pedagogy as well as how people learn, the ability to set up school organizational patterns that promote the teaching-learning process, an understanding of effective teaching skills so supervision of instruction takes place, a deployment of staff for strategic use of strengths, and the establishment of communication vehicles both within and beyond the boundaries of the school and the district. Finally, the power or influence component suggests that leaders must not only set goals and develop visions but they must know how to motivate the workforce to feel ownership in the goals—sharing purposes—and understand their needs for security, satisfaction, and accomplishment in their jobs.

Another description of leaders' work is given in the form of a taxonomy of ten roles that cluster into three areas:

1. *Interpersonal behavior:* leader, liaison, figurehead
2. *Information-processing behavior:* monitor, disseminator, spokesperson
3. *Decision-making behavior:* entrepreneur, disturbance handler, resource allocator, negotiator (Mintzberg, 1973)

A third view of what leaders do is suggested by Cuban (1989) as he explains three roles of a superintendent of schools: instructional, managerial, and political. The instructional role is to change beliefs and behavior, whereas the managerial role is to ensure stability. These two roles are not easy to fulfill at the same time. The political role involves the process of determining and transforming goals into policies and programs. It includes the authority and influence used to work with a board and to govern a district.

TABLE 6–5   New Leadership—Summary

What It's About	How It's Done
Creating visions	Modeling values
Instilling values	Interpreting processes
Developing shared purposes	Creating conflict
Validating meaning	Exerting influence
Engendering trust	Making decisions
Mobilizing commitment	Managing change
Encouraging creativity	Creating new structures
Maintaining optimism	Building teams
Gaining credibility	Communicating mission
	Embracing technology
	Transforming data into information

Cuban points out that the instructional, managerial, and political roles are often at cross-purposes, creating role conflict for the leader. Conflict is also inherent because schools feel the repercussions created by competition for tax dollars, and changes in the economy, political culture, and values. Such conditions are examples of obstacles to the work of leaders. Table 6–5 provides an overview of the new dimensions of leadership.

WHY LEADERS CANNOT LEAD

If we are to understand what leaders must do to be successful in the future, then we need to be aware of conditions that interfere with the ability of leaders to lead. There are external and internal organizational forces that work against leadership. These include resistance to change on the part of people and the institution, pressure groups, divisive informal leaders, vested interests, bureaucratic structures, governmental requirements, union contract regulations, and leaders' own perceptions of their efficacy.

Because organizations often resist change, they can make it impossible for leaders to succeed, unless they are aware of the pressures working against them. "There is something in the nature of organizations and people that makes it difficult for them to change in a fundamental way. The transformational leader must understand the resistant forces and mobilize the energy needed to overcome them in order to transform the organization" (Tichy & Devanna, 1986, p. 72).

Organizations try to move toward compliance, stability, and routinization to perpetuate themselves. As they become more complex and sophisticated, they often establish many bureaucratic layers to insulate parts of the system from the whole. Within each system, specialists are added to handle more and more minute aspects of the operation until few have a clear or broad perception of the big picture. Overspecialization can damage the communication structure, inhibit broad-based decision making, and undermine the purpose of leaders.

Leaders must contend with technical, political, and cultural resistance to their change efforts. *Technical* resistance is described as (1) habit and inertia—"the way we've always done things"; (2) fear of the unknown and loss of predictability—which creates anxiety; and (3) sunk cost—investments made in established processes and procedures (Tichy & Devanna, 1986, pp. 74–75). People become concerned about how change will affect their role, status, norms, and values, and need to learn new ways of operating. If they have perceived that their performance "worked" in the past, why can't it continue? A great deal of time, energy, and money was invested in the initial processes or production. Does it mean that it was all wasted, if change is needed?

Political resistance comes in three forms:

1. A challenge to established leaders and practices—"Threats to Powerful Coalitions." Whenever new people or ideas are introduced into the organization, there is a tendency for the old guard to feel that they will be replaced or that their input will be ignored.
2. A do-more-with-less philosophy—"Zero Sum Decision-Making," which suggests that in tight economic times, new leaders will require greater productivity with fewer resources.
3. A necessity for leaders to admit that their earlier decisions may have contributed to the present difficulties—"The Indictment of Leadership Problem." Such a dilemma creates psychological barriers and defensiveness because it is hard to accept change when you helped create the problem (Tichy & Devanna, 1986, p. 77).

Three *cultural* reasons are also cited as contributors to the resistance movement against leaders. First, perceptions of people in the organization are deeply embedded and reinforced by the culture, as described earlier. "Cultural filters resulting in selective perceptions" form strong impediments to change (Tichy & Devanna, 1986, p. 79). Second, culture values tradition, stability, and security, so that when change begins, people regress to the past, which was a more comfortable time in their minds. Finally, most organizations have a "lack of climate for change," so this atmosphere must be brought about slowly by the leader, through personal attention, symbols, and consistent behavior, which reinforces all of the rhetoric and makes it real for the employees (p. 81). These examples of why leaders cannot lead examine organizational constraints, yet they imply that human factors are also involved.

People in the organization can erect impediments for leaders. In order to feel secure and comfortable in the work environment, people approach their work conservatively, developing routines and procedures. They fit in with the conservative nature of organizations in general, and together resist change strongly by making outcomes predictable and actions and decisions carefully structured. "Research supports the notion that people try to use their successful solutions even in situations where they are not the best fit. . . . People can go to great lengths to protect their view of the world" (Tichy & Devanna, 1986, p. 51). Success can become a barrier when applied to new problems or different cirumstances.

Bennis (1976) supports the claim of people creating impediments: "I had become a victim of an amorphous, unintentional conspiracy to prevent me from doing anything whatever to change the university's status quo. Even those of my associates who fully shared my hopes to set new goals and work toward creative change were unconsciously doing the most to ensure that I would never find the time to begin" (p. 10). The routine can drive out the nonroutine. Leaders' thinking can get clogged with detail instead of visions, as colleagues deposit their own problems on the leader's desk and expect solutions they could not find themselves. Such diversions have been colorfully labeled the "wet baby syndrome" and "monkey on my back."

A second and more obvious way people within the organization prevent leaders from accomplishing their purposes is by associating themselves with pressure groups, which can fragment the direction of the organization and divide the previously shared values and symbols. Concentrating on too many problems simultaneously dilutes effort and confuses purposes.

One way these groups resolve problems with the organization is through legal action, which contributes more toward the elimination of risk-taking behavior by leaders. They get worn down by having to re-solve issues in the courts instead of in the organization. Educational systems are particularly vulnerable in this arena, as political and legal pressure is applied to issues of equity, choice, malpractice, program opportunity, and policies. The litigous society freezes behavior, slows processes, and stops risk taking.

Compounding these problems is the emergence of informal leaders from each special interest group who all feel compelled to move their cause forward at any expense, even when outside the mission and values of the organization. Informal leadership can be positive if it furthers schools' mission and values, or it can be divisive if it is self-serving and inconsistent with client needs and organizational goals. Gardner (1984) states that damage results from such divisiveness, which is more self-indulgence than commitment. "One problem is that a high proportion of leaders in all segments and at all levels of our society—business, labor, the professions, and so on—are rewarded for single-minded pursuit of the interests of their group regardless of the damage it does to the common good" (Gardner, 1984, p. 137).

Blumberg (1989) addresses obstructions to leadership in the con-text of education. He observed four themes in schools that stand in the way: "Vested interests in particular ways of doing something, territorial concerns, teachers who resist changing their ideas about teaching, and occasions in which it appears that an individual is placing his or her personalized interest in a matter ahead of the district's or school's" (p. 156). These themes are consistent with previous examples and illustrate that education's impediments to leadership closely parallel those in other fields.

Leaders in institutionalized, political systems or bureaucracies like schools must constantly be alert to the pressures generated in those organizations. Institutions, by their very nature, try to draw in leaders and paralyze them with narrow, administrative demands, and eliminate their ability to pursue wider goals. In addition, the external environment intrudes, often hostilely, to influence the system and the leader.

External environmental influences have created multiple dependencies for leaders. Bennis (1978) feels that leaders' hands are tied in both public and private sector organizations, "by governmental requirements, by various agencies, by union rules, by the moral and sometimes legal pressures of organized consumers and environmentalists." He says of the external environment that "there is an incessant, dissonant clamor out there" and educational institutions that are dependent on external patronage structures are constantly being thwarted in their purposes (Bennis, 1978, p. 4).

A final interference with effective leadership comes from within leaders themselves. Bombarded by all of these pressures, leaders can begin to question their own efficacy. It is reasonable to expect some self-doubt, discouragement, and confusion when living in constant change and ambiguity, and with conflicting expectations and limited resources. Leaders must have defined themselves and know themselves well enough to withstand the questioning and challenging that occurs in political systems.

A strong sense of self and firm convictions of what needs to be done must be maintained by the leader. Self-understanding and a perception of competence are necessary for individuals to deal successfully with all situations, and even be able to use failure productively. It is important to take the time to look inwardly and to reassess periodically the visions and one's ability to maintain the dreams and create new ones. Garfield calls this "self-mastery" in his discussion of peak performers. "A peak performer's skills in self management emerge from the personal, internal skills of *self mastery*—the art of orchestrating and developing one's capabilities, after discovering what they are" (Garfield, 1986, p. 5).

TABLE 6–6   Summary of Obstacles to Leadership

Internal Forces	External Forces
Workers' resistance to change	Political resistance
Bureaucratic structures	Governmental requirements
Pressure groups	Pressure groups
Culture	Patronage structures
Informal leaders	Legal mandates
Negotiated contracts	
Leader's own self-doubt	

Bennis and Nanus (1985) concluded, "For successful leadership to occur there has to be a fusion between positive self-regard and optimism about a desired outcome" (p. 79). The leadership tasks of the future may not be able to be handled by rational, problem-solving techniques requiring complete information; instead, intuition and empathy will be powerful tools for future leaders. The internal and external forces that work against leadership are summarized in Table 6–6.

TIP | TRANSFORMATION INTO PRACTICE

PRACTICAL PROPOSALS FOR LEADERSHIP ACTION

An interesting set of proposed guidelines for effective action was designed by Yukl (1989), who cautions researchers that these activities are speculative and explorative. However, they present practical suggestions for how leaders should operate, based on patterns that have emerged through research, observation, and discussions with people in such roles. He proposes that leaders should:

1. Take advantage of reactive activities. Time management is essential, yet leaders often find themselves in unscheduled meetings or required obligations. Turning these potentially disruptive times into opportunities to accomplish aspects of work is an excellent technique to master.

2. Cultivate large networks of contacts. Leaders need to obtain and give information constantly and be ever conscious of changing conditions and developing problems. Establishing many resources, both in and out of the organization, helps the leader to keep on top of things and events.

3. Identify connections among problems. Within any organization, problems arise regularly but usually not in isolation. Recognition that problems

can be clustered to help solve them easier assists the leader in understanding the broad scope and complexity of work and can provide insight into many aspects of the system at one time.

4. Learn from surprises and failures. Negative information can become productive if it is used in the future to avoid decision-making errors. John Scully, of Apple Corporation, says of future leaders: "The new age leaders will not lead by toughness but with powerful ideas. . . . Yet the new age leader almost has to show his fallibility. Making mistakes is a very real and important part of succeeding. In a traditional corporation, too often a mistake is a sign of weakness. At Apple, making mistakes is a way to learn. If you fail to convey the idea at the top that you make mistakes, you can send the wrong message, isolate yourself from people" (Scully, 1987, p. 331).

5. Be willing to experiment. People are often too security and stability oriented, which makes them use the same techniques and approaches over and over. Innovative solutions and change can occur only when leaders are willing to be risk takers and sometimes fail.

6. Select problems judiciously. Some problems aren't worth the effort to solve; others may need to be temporarily ignored for political purposes. Assess which problems deserve attention, and do not give equal concern to every issue.

7. Learn how the political system works in the organization. To accomplish a goal, solve a problem, or initiate a change requires astute evaluation of who the key players are, where the informal power structures exist, and how to operate through the obstacles and resistance of opponents.

8. Make time for reflective planning. It is easy to fill time with the agenda of others and with responding to crises. But real and lasting progress on initiatives will only take place by carving out time to think, plan, and strategize—key elements in the leading process.

Source: Gary A. Yukl, *Leadership in Organizations*, 2nd ed., © 1989, pp. 68–72. Adapted by permission of Prentice Hall, Inc., Englewood Cliffs, New Jersey.

SUMMARY

Leaders are a critical component of the change process. The skills and expertise of leadership in schools will help determine whether they can transform our educational enterprises. There will be both assistance and resistance for leaders to handle; internal pressures come from the organization itself as well as from the people working in it, and external forces complicate the process. However, transformation of schools can be accomplished by courageous leaders with vision, purpose, values, and commitment.

CONCEPTS

1. The historical study of leadership involved traits, leader behavior, situational/contingency, and transactional approaches.
2. Management and leadership are different; managers maintain the status quo, whereas leaders initiate and sustain change.
3. Leaders operate in a dynamic context, composed of the internal and external environments of the system.
4. Leaders use "cognitive complexity" in thinking and decision making.
5. Two important contextual dimensions for leaders within organizations are climate and culture.
6. Commitment and credibility are the coins of leadership, and they must be present to convert subordinates to followers.
7. All leaders have power, but not all power holders are leaders. Leaders create and renew shared purpose. Leadership is value driven and idea driven.
8. New definitions of leadership include concrete concepts such as communication, empowerment, and defining a mission, and abstract ideas like creating visions, developing trust, and providing inspiration.
9. Leaders need cognitive, technical, and social skills to process information, make decisions, and interact with the environment.
10. Internal and external forces—some subtle and others overt—work to prevent leaders from leading.
11. New proposals for leadership action contribute to the concept of transformational leadership.

7 TRANSFORMATIONAL LEADERSHIP

Transformational leaders are needed to design and orchestrate the complex changes organizations must face, in both public and private arenas. They must be concerned with the people in these organizations to ensure that successful transitions are made from what was to what needs to be. They cannot simply restructure what is, but must question the fundamental core of schools' operation, to transform its purpose, values, and then its operation and people.

ESTABLISHING THE NEED

Transformational leaders are demanded not only because of the instability of today's environment and the unpredictability of future resources and economic conditions, but also because of moral pressures being placed on leaders' decision making and actions. Leaders are being called on to demonstrate high moral values in all facets of their lives. Political pressures have increased along with a global interdependency —all of which will continue into the next century.

> If our leaders at all levels are to be capable of lifting us and moving us toward excellence, they are going to have to believe in the people of this nation—a people able to perform splendidly and inclined to perform indifferently, a people deeply troubled in their efforts to find a future worthy of their past, a people capable of greatness and desperately in need of encouragement to achieve that greatness (Gardner, 1984, p. 152).

144

Motivating people to participate and believe in transformation of their organization will be the key.

In the business world, another enormous difficulty facing leaders is the necessity to reduce the workforce to maintain a competitive edge. Equity and justice issues abound when such cutbacks begin to take place. Tichy and Devanna (1986) point out that professionals and managers who are doing a good job may not receive raises or even have to be dismissed simply because the organization can no longer afford to employ as many people and still make a profit. Transformational leaders will be challenged to find new ways to keep people motivated, to ensure equity and justice prevail in the decision-making process of who keeps their jobs, and to remain competitive and successful in a world market.

A serious warning has been issued by Korn (1989) about the kind of leader needed for the year 2000. Korn feels that corporate leaders support his contention. He believes U.S. corporations are not developing tomorrow's CEOs; they are still operating under the belief that the same kinds of leaders we have had will continue to be needed in the future. If we do need distinctly different kinds of leaders, then we must identify new requirements for leadership and look—with entirely new perceptions—for people to fill those roles.

Korn conducted a study of 1,500 senior executives from all over the world to determine the characteristics currently possessed by leaders and those traits that will be necessary for success in the twenty-first century. Visionary leadership, instead of managerial skills, was mentioned by 98 percent of the respondents as the most valued standard for the future. Communication skills—and the frequency of that skill in operation—both in terms of employees and customers, will increase in importance in the future. Other highly ranked indicators include linking compensation to performance, emphasizing ethics, and planning for management succession.

Developing human resources, especially new kinds of leaders within organizations, was clearly described as a major thrust for corporations. Finally, the global awareness of international competition was stressed, and this theme has also emerged in education. Our students are being compared internationally and they pale in these comparisons on all academic subjects.

The educational world poses significant challenges that will need transformational leadership to address. Passow (1989) proposes several important questions in relation to reform movements, and equity is again mentioned. He wonders whether the current curriculum reforms will really prepare us for the twenty-first century and whether new knowledge bases and pedagogical strategies will be generated to deal with a changing student clientele.

> Do the schools and society really want to achieve the twin goals of equity and excellence beyond the level of rhetoric? Can the schools achieve equity and excellence without significant changes in the nature and structure of society? Do we have or are we generating the knowledge that will enable our schools to graduate the vast majority of students (with all their differences and similarities) with the knowledge, skills, insights, attitudes, commitments, motivations and concerns that will enable them to live successfully in the next century? (Passow, 1989, pp. 36–37).

Such provocative questions are being asked by both educators and the public, and it is felt that only with new, strong, and innovative leadership can answers be generated and visions designed to transform the educational structure and delivery system.

Sergiovanni (1987b) also suggests that "significant changes are taking place in how school leadership is viewed, understood, and practiced. . . . These changes . . . reflect the adoption of new values, visions, beliefs, and commitments for school leadership" (p. 337). He cites that many pressures have been brought to bear on the educational establishment, including blue-ribbon panels and reports, public pressure for higher expectations, and the belief that schools should meet the needs of all types of students. In addition, "New commitments to efficiency, requiring increased school productivity at the same costs, are strongly felt. Teachers are demanding improvements in the quality of work life they experience. These pressures are catalysts for change in the way schools are organized, managed, and led" (p. 337). We believe a new kind of leadership—transformational—is what is needed to meet these educational challenges.

> The old view of leadership, which emphasized style and behavior and the development of highly structured management systems, remains important. But now what leaders stand for and believe in, and their ability to communicate these values and ideals in a way that provides both meaning and significance to others is more important than how they behave (Sergiovanni, 1987d, p. 117).

Leaders are not simply to engage in transactions to promote achievement; they are to transform organizations through purpose and values.

Intellectual, Reform, and Revolutionary Leadership

Historical perspectives help us trace the development of leadership, as Burns (1978) has done, concluding that during significant political and economic times, three types of transforming leadership emerged: intellectual, reform, and revolutionary. *Intellectual* leaders not only consider analytical and normative ideas but they relate these ideas to their environment and they seek to change the social milieu by conscious purpose drawn from values. Such leaders have the capacity to *transform* power; that is, they have the ability to mesh means and ends with values into a cohesive purpose for action. Through their strong thinking and intelligence, they are able to develop a comprehensive plan and supply the intellectual foundations that unite purpose and action. School leaders of the future should be of this type, as they seek to accomplish educating students who come from various social backgrounds, contend with diverse values and standards, and attempt to rally their constituents toward the common purpose of improving the teaching-learning environment.

Reform leadership requires political skill—the ability to deal with large numbers of allies, some of whom have their own reform agendas. These leaders *transform* popular hopes into expectations and demands, yet they must do so with proper means, requiring the application of moral leadership to achieving purposes. Reform leaders "must be willing to transform society . . . if that is necessary to realize moral principles" (Burns, 1978, p. 170).

Educational leaders need to be reformers, as well. Superintendents contend with many agendas—from school boards, community groups, parents, senior citizens, staff, and students. All of these groups believe in education, yet their support depends on the ability of the superintendent to recognize their diverse needs and purposes and to unite them through high moral principles to improve the quality and productivity of the institution.

The third type of transforming leadership is *revolutionary*. Revolution, in its broadest terms, "is a complete and pervasive transformation of an entire social system" (Burns, 1978, p. 202). It raises the social and political consciousness of both leaders and followers. Revolutionary leadership is "passionate, dedicated, single-minded, ruthless, self-assured, courageous, tireless, usually humorless, often cruel. . . . Its success rests on a powerful value system, on responsiveness to popular need, and on systematic suppression of dissent" (Burns, 1978, p. 239). Some of these characteristics fit the need for transforming leaders in education, but they would not be successful or ethical by being cruel, humorless, and suppressing dissent.

A contemporary prototype of a transformational leader for the corporate world was created by Tichy and Devanna (1986), after having conducted extensive interviews with 12 executives. Some of the characteristics of the intellectual, reform, and revolutionary leaders appear in their description. Transformational leadership "is about change, innovation, and entrepreneurship. . . . This brand of leadership is a behavioral process capable of being learned and managed. It's a leadership process that is systematic, consisting of a purposeful and organized search for changes, systematic analysis, and the capacity to move resources from areas of lesser to greater productivity" (p. viii).

In the educational setting, Sergiovanni (1987c) explains transformational leadership as a building and bonding process, in that leadership *builds* higher-level professional relationships that are tied to moral, ethical conduct and values, and *bonds* people to the goals, purposes, and significance of a shared commitment. Politics and power struggles are dismissed for the greater good of establishing the best educational circumstances. "Transformational leadership works because of its ability to tap higher levels of human potential on the one hand and because it fits better the way in which the world of organizations work" (p. 10).

EMPOWERMENT OF FOLLOWERS

Leaders' relationship with subordinates is a key to understanding the transformation process. In transformational terms, subordinates are referred to as followers; a distinction is made because "subordinates are pushed from the outside, but followers are pulled by forces within themselves" (Sergiovanni, 1987c, p. 3).

The kind of leadership needed for successful schools creates followers, not subordinates. Cooperative change and progress do not occur when compliance is a factor. Members of school organizations are professionals, and, if treated as such, they will exceed expectations in order to meet their own established higher purposes, since their self-esteem is enhanced and they feel respected and valued. Followers are not pushed by external wants and needs; instead, they are attracted to their tasks because the work they do is significant and provides a sense of accomplishment. They perceive their role as important, and they commit their energy and talent to it. Followers have a sense that they can influence decisions and control elements of the school operation that involve them.

"The result of transforming leadership is a relationship of mutual stimulation and elevation that converts followers into leaders and may convert leaders into moral agents" (Burns, 1978, p. 4). Sergiovanni (1987c) similarly states that transformational leadership links the leader and followers through high purpose and shared values. "Here the focus is on arousing human potential, satisfying higher needs and raising expectations of both leader and follower that motivates both to higher levels of commitment and performance" (p. 7).

Bass (1985) adds that followers trust, admire, and are loyal and respectful to the leader, who transforms them through motivation—helping them recognize the importance of what they are doing for the organization, not for themselves, and activating their higher-order needs.

The followers in all of these descriptions are transformed by being empowered. Transformational leadership considers how power can assist others in becoming successful and accomplishing their goals. Leaders invest power in people and then expect a return on their investment. They are comfortable in delegating power to others in order to achieve the purposes of the organization. School leaders provide autonomy to teachers, confident in their ability to make decisions affecting their areas of expertise. Professionals desire a sense of efficacy—a belief that they influence decisions purposefully and have an impact on results.

Tichy and Devanna (1986) also found that the leaders they interviewed attempted to empower members of their corporation. The leaders "never pretended to be superhumans whose success was uniquely their own. On the contrary, they sought to empower others so that the necessary actions could be duplicated throughout the organization and, indeed, could survive their direct intervention and presence" (p. 47).

How Do Leaders Empower Others?

One cannot turn power over to the members of an organization and expect them to know what to do and how to accomplish the overall mission, in relation to their individual responsibility and position. The need to provide inservice opportunities and on-the-job training experiences in participative decision making, strategic planning, action research, and priority setting must be addressed. Leaders in all fields can prepare their staffs for empowerment by (1) creating clear visions, (2) connecting people to the purpose of the visions, (3) communicating effectively so that everyone understands and is working toward the same goals, (4) designing the plan for transformation, and (5) providing learning opportunities for followers to participate confidently and productively in the transformation process. Empowerment is discussed in detail in Chapter 10.

Educational leaders will be able to accomplish this activity only if they are aware of the need to change perceptions. Teachers need to see themselves and be seen in a new way. They must adequately value themselves and be valued by others. Their status, knowledge, and decision making need to be lifted. One of the ways leaders go about changing perceptions, thinking, and behavior of followers is by creating visions and gaining commitment to them.

CREATING VISIONS

Whether leaders are described as visionaries, mission creators, or goal envisioners, their task is basically the same. The dictionary defines *vision* as an unusual competence in discernment or perception; an intelligent forethought. Bennis and Nanus (1985) express the importance of vision, stating, "If there is a spark of genius in the leadership function at all, it must lie in this transcending ability, a kind of magic, to assemble—out of all the variety of images, signals, forecasts, and alternatives—a clearly articulated vision of the future that is at once simple, easily understood, clearly desirable, and energizing" (p. 103).

Transformational leaders must be able to meet the challenge of finding and creating a vision for their organization that is better than what currently exists and that can involve and convince all members of the organization to share the dream. Such leaders "must provide people with an image of what can be and motivate them to move ahead into the future they envision. . . . This vision of the future must be formulated in such a way that it will make the pain of changing worth the effort" (Tichy & Devanna, 1986, p. 122).

Educational leaders must have visions, just as corporate leaders do, in order to inspire staff and students to accomplish organizational goals. According to many of the effective schools' studies, one common element of success is leaders who have the ability to formulate and communicate an informed and specific vision of the future for their schools.

Ernest Boyer (1989) described his experience in higher educational as successful, not because the ideas in the college were unique or novel but because he and colleagues had a shared vision and worked loyally and enthusiastically toward it. He suggests that leaders must not only believe strongly in their vision but the vision has to be connected to the mission and purpose of the organization and be creatively expressed and shared with the constituents. It is the human factor that needs attention for transformation. Procedures and organizations will not change without the people's willingness to move in directions clearly communicated to them and accepted by them.

Vision is also mentioned by college president John Dempsey as one of the attributes necessary for successful leadership in education. He makes the point that it is not enough just to have clear visions for the future—they must be shared convincingly and optimistically with followers. "Clear vision, and the courage to articulate that vision, even under adverse circumstances, are essential elements of effective leaders," but "Good leaders must be good persuaders. People in organizations must be convinced, rather than told, what course of action they should follow" (Dempsey, 1989, p. 18).

In the face of demographic and social conditions, particularly in schools' future, this optimism and persuasive ability for educational leaders is crucial. School leaders have to redefine continually the values and purposes inherent in the vision for how teachers can accomplish their tasks, in spite of the social conditions children bring to school with them. The school may be the only encouraging experience in some students' lives, so a place has to be designed where they can find support and success. Such vision poses difficult challenges for our leaders.

How Do Leaders Create Visions?

Martin Luther King motivated thousands of people because he had a dream—a vision of a more just world—and he was able to communicate it dramatically to others. But his dream did not just come to him in the night. It took years of thinking, experiencing, and reacting with people. Visions, or dreams, in the context of transformational leadership, are more than ephemeral thoughts; they are value-based designs of what can be, where the organization's destiny rests. Creating a vision is hard work. It requires an understanding of the context and content of the educational system. Leaders cannot simply sit quietly and wait for visions to appear. They have to go out into the organization and beyond to gather information, diagnose needs, listen to people, ask probing questions, reflect quietly, argue and cajole, generate provocative discussions, experience the workplace, solicit outside opinions, and, finally, sift through the data and emotions to draw conclusions of what the future could be.

There is no blueprint for vision creation. In fact, it will be necessary to break down preconceived notions of the importance of strategic planning in order to allow both left (logical analysis) and right (intuition) brain thinking to occur. Creativity and intuition become valued commodities in vision producing, because visions are more than plans. The process of visioning can be explained in terms of a leader's perception, thought, and behavior, as illustrated in Figure 7–1.

A vision is made up of two elements. One is a "conceptual framework or paradigm for understanding the organization's purpose—the vision includes a roadmap. The second important element is the emotions appeal: the part of the vision that has a motivational pull with which people can identify" (Tichy & DeVanna, 1986, p. 130). Garfield (1986) uses the terminology "creating a mission," which closely parallels vision creation. He identifies six guideposts for leaders in this pursuit:

1. *Putting passion and preference to work:* Finding out what one really enjoys doing and does well, so commitment is easy to achieve
2. *Drawing on the past:* To use former successes in building future plans
3. *Trusting intuition:* Instead of relying solely on logic for creating a powerful, workable mission
4. *Having no preconceived limitations:* So that fear of failure doesn't enter into setting high goals
5. *Combining profit with contribution:* Recognizing that the orga-

FIGURE 7–1   Vision

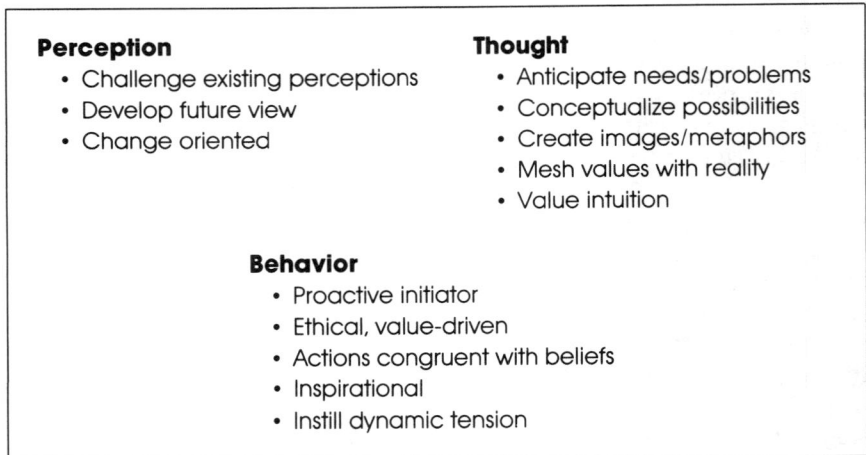

Perception
- Challenge existing perceptions
- Develop future view
- Change oriented

Thought
- Anticipate needs/problems
- Conceptualize possibilities
- Create images/metaphors
- Mesh values with reality
- Value intuition

Behavior
- Proactive initiator
- Ethical, value-driven
- Actions congruent with beliefs
- Inspirational
- Instill dynamic tension

nization is connected to people and community, not just to profits

6. *Seeing the need for quality:* Setting standards and producing value as well as goods or services (pp. 3–4)

Garfield confirms that setting visions or missions is a complex, sophisticated process for leaders.

Sometimes leaders create visions alone, but often the experience can be a shared one, with participants forming a team to investigate what the organization will look like when the vision is in place. In this process of deciding where they want to be at some future time, the roadmap emerges. This can be called a *mission statement*—a vision placed in operational terms.

It is easier to have followers accept the mission if they help to create it, but that is not always possible. The final step—setting the agenda for making the vision a reality—is another instance in which a team can be brought in to identify the discrepancy between the ideal and reality, to set priorities, to design strategies, and to determine evaluation measures. In this way, there is a blend of a qualitative statement of what should be and a quantitative measure of how to get there.

LEADERSHIP AS PURPOSING

The concept of purposing as a leadership act relates closely to establishing a vision for the organization, but purposing connects the participants to the vision created by the leader. Sergiovanni (1987) suggests, "Key to the concept of purposing is in the building of a *shared covenant,*" bonding all constituents in a common goal or cause. "The object of purposing is the stirring of human consciousness, the enhancement of meaning, the spelling out of key cultural strands that provides both excitement and significance to one's work" (p. 17).

Purposing includes related, continuous action on the part of the leader to ensure that followers understand and are committed to the organization's mission.

Purposing brings life and meaning into the day-to-day activities of people at work in schools. It helps people to interpret their contributions, their successes and failures, their efforts and energies in light of the school's purposes. Through this process, seemingly ordinary events become meaningful, with subsequent motivational benefit to the school. . . . Purposing represents as well the rallying point for bringing together all human resources into a common cause (Sergiovanni & Starratt, 1983, p. 201).

As purposing evolves, communication of what the leader believes in and where the organization should be going will result. Burns (1978) uses the term *collective purpose*, referring to the proposition that regardless of individual needs or interests, leaders and followers can come together to pursue higher goals collectively than they would independently. For leaders to effect change, this relationship and recognition of a common driving force must be established. It is possible for the leader's and the followers' needs or wants to be met at the same time as this overriding purpose is also achieved. Uniting in collective purpose means that all of the people in the organization accept a set of values toward which they work.

This concept is related to motivation, in Gardner's (1984) work, where he describes leaders as those who unlock motivation in their followers. Leaders capitalize on individual motives that work to achieve the purposes of the group's shared goals. When leaders enter into this arena of perception and thinking, they are stepping toward moral issues as well as motivational ones. Influential behavior in higher-order thinking levels requires leaders to take a plunge into the risky territory of values. Yet, it must be done; otherwise, the importance of shared values in determining collective purpose will be lost. "There is nothing so power-full, nothing so effective, nothing so causal as common purpose if that purpose informs all levels of a political system. Leadership mobilizes. . . . Utility of purpose and congruence of motivation foster causal influence far down the line" (Burns, 1978, p. 439).

Waterman (1987) describes this activity another way, by noting "an important leadership challenge is to find ways of articulating causes so that they make meaning for people. Causes that speak only to the needs of the organization—or to individual needs—are not the stuff of permanent renewal. A cause, put forward with some inspiration, can be what turns a dreary issue into a catalyst for renewal" (p. 289). The ultimate causal impact of leadership can be measured only when real and lasting change is implemented. Leaders, as change agents, must be judged by their ability to commit followers to the intended change and to motivate those followers to take ownership in the change to make it succeed.

MEANING THROUGH COMMUNICATION

Communication is woven throughout the discussion of setting purposes and establishing meaning for all participants in an organization. Understanding the subtleties of meaning are important to a leader's overall effectiveness. Pondy (1978) suggests that it is not enough simply for people to work in the same environment, or to create a set of shared experiences in an organization. The activities must be talked about, *meaning* must be communicated—not just *words*, and the leader should be the instrumental force in the creation of shared meanings.

Talking about one's work is especially important in school settings, where teachers are isolated from one another for most of their work day. They do communicate with their students, but sharing with colleagues or administrators does not occur regularly or naturally. Situations need to be structured to encourage dialogue, sharing, problem solving, decision making, and verification that their work is meaningful and important.

Principals who view continuing communication as a high priority will ensure that their ideas, missions, and dreams are shared. "Great leaders articulate and share their dreams with others, and through this understanding make their dreams accessible. This access is to the things people care about most: meaning, good feelings, a sense of control. How leaders share themselves, and through this sharing breathe power and purpose into others, is an intriguing area for research" (McCall & Lombardo, 1978, pp. 100–101).

Pondy (1982) has pursued such research and concludes that language sharing is a powerful tool for influencing the behavior of others. It is a subtle, invisible way, with innumerable variation, to convey expectations, to explain events, to provide insight into the purpose of activities, and to bring people's ideas together. Common language, shared concepts, and a sense of understanding allow leaders and followers to communicate and move toward the same goals. Pondy explains, "Some of these expressions refer to an internal, non-articulated sense of understanding. But the content of the feeling cannot be communicated. If, in addition the leader can put it into words, then the meaning of what the group is doing becomes a social fact. . . . The meaning can be talked about, exchanged, modified, amplified, and used for internal processing of information" (p. 94).

Leaders have much information at their disposal and they have the power to use that information to enhance or impede communication. They must process, analyze, and decide how and with whom to share data, so that as they develop and explain their vision for change, leaders gain commitment from constituents. First, the leader's symbolic role comes into play as stories and myths are created to build a new culture for transformation. But communication does not stop at this point.

When reorganizing a corporation, Blumenthal said, "A commitment to the vision and the mobilization of positive energy really don't come into play until there is some success . . . it became positive when the numbers became positive" (Tichy & Devanna, 1986, p. 181). The leader needs to continue communicating during the early stages of change, when people are skeptical or uneasy, to share progress, and to convince them that the new direction will be successful.

Setting up a communication network is a necessary task for the leader, since it is difficult and impractical to speak directly to all workers. As discussed earlier, information networks are important structures to establish who holds the power of information and who exchanges information with whom, through planned interactions. Leaders must ensure that they build a team at the top that has all the information, that can communicate the plans and vision accurately through the organization, and that will receive legitimate feedback from the workforce (internally) and from the clients or consumers (externally). Only by developing an extensive yet tight network can the leader be assured that two-way communication is happening.

EFFECTING CHANGE

If the purpose of transformational leadership is to change the organization and people, how does the leader move from what is to what can be? What are the components of the transforming process through which the leader must assist the followers and the system?

The process can be described in terms of (1) building a human support base, (2) creative destruction, (3) managing the transition, (4) organizational redesign, (5) ensuring recommitment, and (6) reconciling external forces. Sometimes these processes are orderly and proceed from 1 to 6, but since most organizations are in constant, dynamic flow, the order may be reversed, the tasks may occur simultaneously, and the process may be messy rather than neatly prescribed.

Step 1, building a human support base, involves all the components previously considered in establishing a vision, translating the vision into a mission, communicating it with constituents, and gaining their support or at least understanding and creating the shared purpose toward which all can work. This step includes teachers, middle-management educators (supervisors, support staff, principals), and parents and students.

Even though commitment may not be given at this time, everyone who will be affected by the change must understand the purpose, direction, beliefs, and values that formed the new mission. "One of the most difficult transformational tasks is to create a sense of urgency before there is an emergency" (Tichy & Devanna, 1986, p. 47). In the best cases, everyone has opportunities to participate in the process and realize its importance.

The second step, creative destruction, is a concept developed by Tichy and Devanna (1986), who say we are all part of extended webs of social networks. Organizations contain these social networks in their technical, political, and cultural systems. They help to define our roles and relationships and can be both formal and informal. The process of destruction must be handled very carefully because people rely on these webs to find purpose in their work life. While the old networks are being broken down, workers still need a sense of belonging. Keeping them involved in the process, instead of treating them as outsiders, will ease the tension of transition.

A third step for the leader in effecting change is managing the transition between the former organization and the transforming one. Albert (1984) outlines four tasks:

1. Summarize the past, so that objectives and dreams of participants come to closure.
2. Justify a change, or explain the rationale, deliberations, and need for the transformation.
3. Create continuity between the past and future by recognizing what elements of the past, if any, can be carried forward into the new plan. There are almost always certain historical perspectives that will have value for the change process.
4. Eulogize the past to acknowledge that former structures, systems, ideas, goals, and values worked for a particular time and will be respected in the future.

The fourth step in change is organizational redesign. Much discussion has taken place in previous chapters on the structures and contexts of organizations. They are designed to be strong, lasting systems, so redesign becomes a challenge for transformational leaders. These leaders must become social architects to reshape the roles, networks, and structure of the organization.

When people are commissioned to change an institution, they often go about the process in small, incremental, and even superficial ways. New coats of paints, different names for rooms and programs, or slight structural alterations are offered as blueprints for the new workplace. But transformational leaders must be bold, creative, and critical change agents, daring to demolish major structural connections in order to make drastic statements about how differently people need to perceive the possibilities.

As well as making changes in the structure, moving people becomes an organizational redesign tool. Such movement helps the creation of additional networks, which brings groups together for new purposes (Tichy & Devanna, 1986, pp. 210–213).

It is sometimes necessary to destroy perceptions as well as systems (as stated in Step 3) to gain acceptance for future visions that will bear little resemblance to the past. When Tichy and Devanna explained the corporate renovation achieved at IBM, they stated, "Unique organizational configurations were designed to make this possible. There was a need to accommodate new political relationships that would empower a different set of actors, and to support a culture that differed from the dominant culture of the firm at the time" (p. 188). Organizational redesign of schools is a major component of the transformational process.

Step 5 in the change focuses on recommitment, which can be defined as the strategies the leader must use to check on the accuracy of messages and meanings communicated during the transformation stages. It is essential that all the constituents be a part of the social network, which gives and receives data concerning the change activities. Important information is being transmitted and decisions are made constantly, so people must feel included in the ownership building and communication process. The leader must be very visible and accessible during this phase to establish new cultural ties and validate the transformation.

Reconciling the external forces is the final step in the initial transformation strategies for the leader. It is similar to the preceding phase of being sure people are supportive and committed, but considering external influences suggests the need to read outside pressures and demands continuously and make appropriate responses to them. The political arena, societal pressures, economic factors, and cultural complexity compel the leader's attention to integrate transformation between the internal system and the external environment.

TIP | TRANSFORMATION INTO PRACTICE

LEADERSHIP, EDUCATION, AND TRAINING

Where will the leaders come from? Demographics indicate that retirements may cause a shortage of qualified principals, superintendents, and other leaders. In schools, formal leaders must be licensed, requiring the completion of an advanced degree or training program. But can leaders be made in these programs as they currently exist?

Leadership is a critical factor in successful schools, Without a qualified corps of prospective candidates, crucial positions may be filled by people incapable of providing transformational leadership. And without it, our schools will fail.

There seems to be an education and practice gap. Even in other places, like military leadership, academics and training do not predict extraordinary leadership. Some of the great leaders in history (e.g., Patton, Eisenhower, and Grant) were modest students who did not excel in the designated course of study. Yet in the field, they led brilliantly in motivating troops and employing tactics. Their success may not have been predictable in the classroom. In politics, a similar pattern appears with John Kennedy, Abraham Lincoln, and Harry Truman.

This is not a treatise advocating *against* education or training programs, or *for* placing the mantle of leadership on people with less than stellar academic records. Nor is it advocating that leaders are born and that their traits are easily recognizable. Leaders come in all shapes and sizes, and vary in personal style and articulateness. The issue is the education and performance gap in leadership programs. This gap has been recognized by the evaluation of graduate programs, the development of leadership academies in some states, and the institution of formal inservice and staff development programs for administrators.

Many of these programs try to link theory and practice through simulations and other participatory experiences. "In-basket" activities, which require prospective leaders to sort through a series of issues, place them in priority, and then determine a course of action toward each, are frequently used. A panel of professors, and sometimes practitioners, then rate each person's response and provide feedback about the approach, content, and rationale of each response.

Although the candidates gain experience in handling problems, they may not be realistic or they may promote a mechanistic, scientific-management approach to leadership. The tendency may be to make schools highly rational, logical places, with problems that can be solved by systematic predesignated approaches. School organizations, and the people in them, may be reduced to a simple cause-and-effect game, devoid of the subtleties of commitment, ambiguity, alliances, feelings, philosophy, or tradition. Intuition is not a factor because it is difficult to explain or rationalize. The very things that make schools challenging and make leadership a critical, uncertain science are not measurable or obvious.

Simulations or in-baskets are good tools, but how they are used depends on the perception of leadership, people, and organizations that the evaluators have. That perception, in our estimation, must include:

- *Organizational dynamics:* An understanding of the complex, uncertain and political places requiring cognitive complexity, not scientific management that presupposes a rational environment.
- *"Knowing the knitting":* Ensuring that potential leaders have com-

prehensive knowledge of curriculum and instruction —the major purpose of schools. Without strong working knowledge in these areas, leaders' credibility, in the eyes of professionals, will be compromised. Peters and Waterman (1982) state that excellent companies "stick to the knitting."

- *Human motivation:* Leaders must know people and be able to understand and respond to human behavior. People react to change, to organizations, and to other people and circumstances. Successful school leaders can analyze behavior and life-cycle changes and understand how to motivate people, build commitment, and stimulate growth and development needs.
- *Ethical practice:* Professional service cannot be provided unless it meets ethical standards. Without anchors in ethics, school leaders cannot practice "leadership by outrage" or meet the value of "do no harm" to clients.

Certainly management practices, business affairs, legal issues, and other aspects of school leadership are important, but they relate to knowledge, comprehension, and skills, which are easily measured. Requisite knowledge is needed, but so is dynamic, transformational leadership.

What should leadership development activities look like?

What is the role of public schools and practitioners in this process?

Can mentors help develop leaders and provide insight into what school organizations are really like?

Can the private sector assist in providing interdisciplinary training and broad perspective to school leaders?

How can potential leaders become conceptual thinkers who can apply theory in practice and recognize practice in theory?

Values

Throughout this chapter descriptions of transformational leaders have included the concepts of values, beliefs, and shared purposes. "In general, transformational leaders formulate a vision, develop commitment to it among internal and external stakeholders, implement strategies to accomplish the vision, and embed the new values and assumptions in the culture of the organization" (Yukl, 1989, p. 231).

The notion of new leadership values in education is treated comprehensively by Sergiovanni (1987b). He proposes a set of nine values, used by successful leaders who understand the need to coordinate bureaucratic and cultural linkages to bring about change. These values contribute to our picture of the transformational leader and provide an excellent summary, related specifically to education.

1. *Leadership by purpose,* discussed earlier, consists of those continual acts that communicate what is important and valued in the school organization. Purposing helps people to feel the significance and meaning of their work, so that they are motivated to continue.

2. *Leadership by empowerment,* also previously addressed, is giving teachers opportunities and tools for decision making. When people feel they have power to make things happen and are given the respect that they can handle the situation well, they usually do. When school leaders invest power in their staff to contribute to the organization's goals, the return is generally great.

3. *Leadership as power to accomplish* is similar to the above, but it emphasizes the leader as facilitator. Effective school leaders do not rule by edict, rewards, and punishments. Instead, they focus on what their staff is able to accomplish and they assist their efforts. It is a positive, rather than negative, view of the use of power.

4. *Leadership density* is related to empowerment. It suggests spreading school leadership roles and activities among the staff. Just as the principal can be viewed as a teacher, so can the teachers be given leadership responsibility within their areas of expertise.

5. *Leadership and quality control* in schools is different than in corporations. It has less to do with programming, prescribing, checking, and controlling, and more to do with teachers' attitudes toward their work. Quality control involves what people believe in, how much they identify with their role, and how much satisfaction they feel in the accomplishment of their purposes.

6. *Leadership by conversion* epitomizes the act of transforming by changing workers with limited commitment to the purposes of the school into professionals, who share the meaning, enthusiasm, and belief that they can significantly contribute to and influence the outcomes of the organization.

7. *Leadership by simplicity* is just what is sounds like—do not complicate matters by too many procedures and regulations. It also implies that small is not only better but more personal—for ease of communication and establishment of good working relationships. For example, large high schools can be depersonalized, and "schools within a school," house plans, or team structures are being designed to eliminate the cumbersome and impersonal dimensions of such organizations. Gardner (1984) cautioned against large organizations, stating, "But we were slow to reckon the cost—in the dimming of initiative, the deadening of creativity, and the sheer frustration to the individual of being caught in vast, impersonal systems" (p. 143).

8. *Leadership by outrage* is a powerful concept that is focused totally on values. It simply says that the core values around which the organization is built cannot be compromised. Since the leader establishes that there are many acceptable ways for the values to be implemented, much autonomy and discretion is left to the professionals to do so; however, strict adherence to the overall beliefs is demanded. If these values are altered or misrepresented, the leader expresses outrage, because the real purpose of the institution can be jeopardized. Then change is demanded, to conform to the school's vision of what it should be.

9. *Leadership as reflection in action* portrays leaders as complex thinkers, who recognize they operate in a multidimensional framework. They cannot approach problem solving in a simplistic way, given the circumstances. Lombardo (1978) describes this distinction in cognitive terms: "Cognitive simplicity suggests responses, predictable, hierarchical behavior, and stress away from diversity and conflict. Leaders who are not cognitively complex tend to make decisions too quickly, to think in a linear fashion, to ignore varied points of view" (p. 16).

TIP | TRANSFORMATION INTO PRACTICE

TRANSFORMATIONAL LEADERS

The Principal

> It is not the teachers, or the central office people, or the university people who are really causing schools to be the way they are or changing the way they might be. It is whoever lives in the principal's office (Barth, in Lieberman & Miller, 1984, p. 61).

The role of school principal will be expanded in transforming schools. That is not to say the principal will have even more to do than before, however. The role should be enhanced, with more leadership opportunities and less management obligations.

Principals will:

- Meet with teaching teams to collaboratively plan, make decisions, and design strategies to meet the school's mission.
- Lead staff-development efforts at the school level.
- Demonstrate the values of the school in daily activities.
- Work closely with parent groups to increase their involvement in and commitment to children's learning.
- Evaluate staff based on goals set together for the accomplishment of certain annual objectives, which may be individualized or a part of a team or schoolwide goal.

- Be in classrooms to watch students learn, to demonstrate techniques, to assist teachers, and to try out a new strategy.
- Visit other learning environments that extend beyond the walls of the schools—museums, laboratories, businesses, community centers, and so on.
- Participate in research and development activities to keep the learning community up to date on the latest technology, theory, and practices as they apply to schools.
- Develop cooperative relationships with local universities and businesses for the betterment of education in each community.
- Have time to think, dream, and create new visions to inspire the organization and its people to move forward.

What will be gone:

- The need to "check on" people—tardiness, lesson plans, follow-up with parents. If teachers are operating as professionals, they assume greater responsibility for all their actions and can be trusted.
- The need to memorize volumes of do's and don't's that comprise the negotiated agreement. Empowered professionals do not need the "protection" of labor-oriented unions to see to it that their rights are not being violated.
- The need to single-handedly assume the burden of supervision and evaluation. Peer coaching techniques will free the principal from some routine duties.
- Attending parent conferences where parents insist on removing their child from a teacher's class but want to have their complaint anonymous for fear of retribution on their child. Teaching teams will discuss student and parent concerns and work together to find the most productive learning environment for all children.
- Designing the master schedule at elementary and middle schools. Technology has finally arrived, so the computer can easily adjust multiple variables to ensure the most efficient use of everyone's time. Also, remember that there will not be just one schedule. Staggered hours, flextime, extended school days/years, and differentiated learning environments will provide "choice" options for staff, students, and parents.

The Superintendent

The chief school administrator, as a transformational leader, will deemphasize the role of administrator and heighten the leadership aspects of this key position. As such, many of the tasks in the typical job description will be new. Lewis (1987) suggests that "school district success will depend, as never before, on the ability of the superintendent to visualize, participate and realize change" (p. 145).

Superintendents will:

- Perform as a social architect, restructuring the organization and building a new culture by creating future-oriented visions that reflect the core values of schools.

- Design these visions based on new knowledge and consider how education can meet the needs of all student populations.
- Invent excellent futures for the twenty-first century and communicate as a "strategic actor" to ensure the realization of long-range goals and the articulation of the vision (Lewis, 1987, p. 150).
- Act as an inspiring model for the visions and values adopted by all.
- Promote empowerment through the creation of team structures for joint planning and decision making about school operations, students, and long-range objectives.
- Behave as an entrepreneur, creating innovations within the organization by working with teams and giving them autonomy, discretionary resources, and freedom to experiment (Lewis, 1987, pp. 110–111).

SUMMARY

There is no recipe for transformational leaders. People who are devoid of a sense of purpose and a concept of what can be cannot follow a list of steps to behave transformationally. Transformational leaders are conceptual thinkers who see the big picture, understand trends, and identify the essential purpose and values behind schools or other organizations. They know what they stand for and can provide a sense of direction and vision that attracts and inspires others.

Transforming leadership will pull schooling and all of its participants into the twenty-first century, confident and armed with the abilities to be successful. Smith and Andrews (1989) suggest that a transforming educational leader

> must first be able to manage the meaning of schooling, which means that the leader has a clear understanding of the purpose for schools and can manage the symbols of the organization toward fulfilling that purpose— the primary theme about which all activity must be organized. Management of attention is the educational leader's ability to get teachers to focus and expand their energies toward fulfilling the purpose of school; e.g., they will use their talents to teach children. Management of trust means that leaders behave in such a way that others believe in them and their style of leadership does not become an issue. Management of self is simply, "I know who I am; I know my strengths and weaknesses. I play to my strengths and shore up my weaknesses" (p. 5).

Lewis (1987) refers to these leaders as "Renaissance school administrators." Their characteristics are:

- They believe in school people.
- They are value-driven.
- They are committed to learning.
- They are courageous leaders.
- They are visionaries.
- They identify themselves as change agents.
- They are skillful in dealing with complexity, ambiguity, and uncertainty (pp. 281–285).

CONCEPTS

1. There are three types of transformational leadership: intellectual, reform, and revolutionary.
2. Subordinates are different from followers. Followers are pulled by mission, accomplishments, high purpose, and shared values.
3. Transformational leadership is an empowering process that allows participation and discretion in decision making.
4. Creating visions is an integral component of transformational leadership that has the magnetic quality of attracting, motivating, and committing followers.
5. Purposing is a shared covenant that bonds all people in a common goal or cause, which creates meaning and motivation.
6. Communication is more than words—it must create meaning and allow sharing to take place among all people in the organization. Creating meaning is the job of the leader.
7. Transformational leaders effect change, which includes purpose, structure, social networks, and the process of commitment.

PART IV | TRANSFORMING PEOPLE

Organizations are only as effective as the people in them. The needs of workers must be fused with the mission of the institution. Strong linkages between the roles and expectations of the organization and the motivation and developmental needs of people are required for success. Formal structures can enhance performance or stymie growth of professionals. Renewal and continued learning contribute to the capacity of the organization and its people to be dynamic and productive.

Organizations need leaders, but they are dependent on people for their existence, survival, and success. In Chapter 8, the relationships between organizations and people are analyzed, with a focus on professionals. The perception people have of teachers as professionals, technicians, craftspersons, or laborers is explored, as well as the current condition of teaching.

In Chapter 9, adult growth and learning are reviewed to assist in understanding the needs of professionals at various career and personal levels.

Professional growth opportunities in schools are presented, including staff development, inservice education, and supervision. These processes are described in terms of transforming perceiving, thinking, and behavior to create new models.

Finally, Chapter 10 explores the educational professionals' need for empowerment and participation, as related to the outcomes of transformation. Intriguing concepts such as the positives of uncertainty, the negatives of participation, empowerment as responsibility, and overspecialization are introduced.

8 Professionals and Organizations

We have all heard the expression, "Busy as a bee"—a phrase intended to demonstrate industriousness and motion. The metaphor of schools as beehives of activity would be viewed positively by most people—students and teachers going about their work and fulfilling their roles according to plan and expectation. Do we want schools to be beehives? Do we want beelike behavior from professionals?

Our perceptions influence how we treat people. Mike Cooley, President of the British Union of Engineers, proposes:

> Either we will have a future in which human beings are reduced to a sort of bee-like behavior, reacting to the systems and equipment specified for them; or we will have a future in which masses of people, conscious of their skills in both a political and technical sense, decide they are going to be the architects of a new form of technological development which will enhance human creativity and mean more freedom of choice and expression rather than less (Wirth, 1989, p. 535).

Bees or architects? Reactive or proactive behavior? How are we to perceive professionals in schools? How can we develop commitment and motivation?

ORGANIZATIONS AND PEOPLE

Professional training programs often assume that organizations are logical and rational places. Although teachers and administrators receive the knowledge and skills necessary to practice professionally, many are naive about working in a complex organization. As discussed in the last chapters, school operations and decisions are not always rational or orderly—ambiguity and uncertainty are a part of organizational life.

Conflict between the organization and the individual has been written about for decades. Some organizations perceive their workers as adversaries or as replaceable cogs in the corporate machine who toil anonymously and who are motivated by greed (Bennis, 1989, pp. 86–88). The conflict that results from that perception is detrimental—squandering human resources that must help the organization meet its goals and survive in the greater environment. Quality people are the key to productivity, not material resources. Satisfying clients can only be accomplished by talented and commited employees.

When Gardner (1964) considered the individual-organizational conflict, he advocated examining the impact organizations have on individuals and defining when organizations become a threat to people so safeguards can be built into the system. "We must discover how to design organizations and technological systems in such a way that individual talents are used to the maximum and human satisfaction and dignity preserved" (p. 79). Bennis (1989) cites that the common good and individualism are sometimes at odds. The explosive 1960s assaulted authority in every institution, as people fought for their identity, the melting pot disappeared, and fragmentation and loss of consensus resulted. He cautioned, "We are in danger of losing individualism's opposite, a sense of community, of collective aspirations, of public service" (p. 72).

Wirth (1989, p. 537) addressed the notion of fragmentation describing some workplaces as "crazy," coming from the Norwegian word krasa, meaning fragmented or segmented. Industry fractured work so that "idiots could do it." Schools are also segmented in that learning is separated into information bits, grade levels, and discrete courses with no relationship to other disciplines. In the process, meaning is often wrung out of work. "If scientific-efficiency rationale is having crazy-making effects in schools, is anyone in management questioning its effects?" (Wirth, p. 536). According to Peters and Waterman (1982), "man seeks meaning from organizations," which is necessary for survival, and organizations must be structured to promote it. Without meaning, people spend their time at work in quiet desperation (pp. 276–277).

Commitment and Motivation

Commitment and success go hand in hand. Stories deluge periodicals about athletes, businesspeople, and professionals of all ages and sexes achieving success because they committed themselves absolutely to the task or goal they wanted to attain. Yet, we often hear that the trouble with public schools is that today's teachers are not as "committed" as the teachers of the past.

Do people plod through work in a lackadaisical manner, without care or interest? The National Education Association (1988) study on the condition of teaching concluded that once jobs are mastered, they can become routine, tedious, and monotonous. People need meaningful challenges to push their talents and abilities. Sculley (1987) believes that loyalty cannot be bought through pensions and cradle-to-grave security. Commitment is created through opportunities, rewards, and challenges. Block (1988) bluntly states, "The reason people leave the office at exactly five o'clock, lobby for longer coffee breaks, and negotiate for more pay for less hours is because they're viewing their work as an act of sacrifice and obligation, something that's being done to pay the mortgage" (pp. 76–77). To eliminate this behavior and build commitment, Block advocates that workers must have the freedom to choose their own path to achieve results, work must be structured so that people concentrate on the entire project rather than just a piece of it, and passive behavior must be discouraged. Passive behavior is "an extreme form of withholding. Passive people remain silent as a strategy for getting what they want. Passive behavior often makes us feel sorry for quiet people. We have to keep in mind that passivity is political, a goal-seeking stance, and other people are nowhere as near as vulnerable as they seem" (p. 78).

Not all organizations make people into unmotivated clock watchers. Patriarchal organizational cultures reduce commitment; entrepreneurial ones build it. Table 8–1 identifies the differences between the two concerning the locus of authority, self-expression, and commitment. Schools have been accused of being patriarchal—with top-down management distrusting teachers. Being trusted is the "elixir of commitment" (Boyer, 1983, pp. 218–219). The National Education Association (1988) identified several factors that contribute to motivation and commitment. They need clear goals and knowledge of their efforts through feedback. Teachers get psychic rewards from successful and strong relationships with students and recognition from valued colleagues. Like others, they need professional independence and discretion—

TABLE 8–1   Commitment in Patriarchal and Entrepreneurial Organizations

	Patriarchal	Entrepreneurial
Authority	External	Internal/within
	Decisions from elsewhere	Employees decide
Self-Expression	Self-restraint essential	Accept emotional side
	Feelings do not matter	Care about others and their jobs
	Subjectivity has no place	Trust intuition
Commitment	Work is sacrifice	Work is commitment
	Actions based on external motivation	Internal responsibility for outcomes

control over their own fate—with opportunity for growth. Finally, for work to be meaningful, it must be related to their beliefs and values.

Committed people are also motivated individuals, whose feelings are tied to how well they perform at work. When they do well, they attain psychic rewards—satisfaction and the internal incentive to continue to perform. Poorly motivated people make mistakes, have high absenteeism rates, and become alienated from the organization's mission. Motivation has been likened to energy, the level of which is influenced by the thermostat of management control.

> Many individuals who are being controlled (or who feel controlled) by someone else or an organization have their freedom of movement diminished and experience a simultaneous diminution of energy. To the extent that people are able to increase their autonomy in a situation, their freedom of movement increases and their energy levels rise. There is an observable behavior change showing joy, freedom, exhilaration and greater spontaneity (Patten, 1980, p. 7).

Leaders have a lot to do with energy, and their perception of human nature determines the autonomy and control they allow. Dowling (1979, pp. 29–31) summarized that the major thinkers on motivation and human nature generally fall into two camps: monolithic and pluralistic. In the *monolithic* camp, he places Herzberg, Argyris, Likert, Skinner, Homans, and Whyte. *Pluralists* are listed as McClelland, Roethlisberger, Drucker, Boulding, Bell, and Bennis.

The monolithic camp has two groups. *Universalists* (e.g., Herzberg, Likert, and Argyris) believe that human nature is uniform and unalterable and that there is one best way to change organizational behavior and one right organizational design. *Behaviorists* (e.g., Skinner, Homans, and Whyte) believe that people can be controlled by the environment because they seek pleasure and want to avoid pain.

The pluralists believe that human behavior can be influenced and that it is alterable. People can shift their behavior patterns and learn new ones. The environmental determinists in this group (Bell, Boulding, and Bennis) believe that humans cannot be controlled by the environment.

Dowling states that while there are two general camps, there is a basic core of agreement that "economic man is dead; self-fulfilling man is very much alive. The central purpose of any organization is to fulfill human needs, variously defined, of which economic need is but one, and not the strongest need in any of our thinkers' hierarchy" (p. 32). A summary of the monolithic and pluralist views of organizational design and human nature is presented in Table 8–2. The chart is not parallel in that it presents contrasts, but it does define the major perceptions of both groups.

Argyris (1964) believes the basic assumption of formal structure "is to make employees feel dependent, submissive and passive, and to require them to utilize only a few of their less important abilities" (p. 278). But he points to hopeful developmental trends concerning people and organizations, which include moving people from:

- A state of passivity to activity
- Dependence to independence
- Behaving in few ways to behaving in alternate/different ways

TABLE 8–2   Human Nature and Organizational Design: Two Views

Monolithic (Human Nature Uniform)	Pluralistic (Human Nature Alterable)
* Job enrichment	* Decentralization: Communication and decision making
* Certainty of self-actualization	*Autonomous units with responsibility
* Consensus in decisions in a hierarchy of interlocking groups linked by management	* Achievement motive: Challenge and R & D
* Senior executives encourage conformity, limit risk taking	* Incentives and affiliation of group and working relations
* Positive reinforcers	* Lessen controls that restrict autonomy in decisions
* Participation increases productivity	

- Having erratic, casual, shallow interests to deeper interests
- A short time perspective to a longer one
- Being in a subordinate position to aspiring to being in an equal or superordinate position
- Lack of awareness of self to an awareness of and control over self

These trends emphasize and parallel the issues identified by the monolithic and pluralistic views in Table 8–2. Motivated people need room to operate—autonomy and decisions, challenge and responsibility, enrichment and participation, and cooperative working arrangements and affiliation. Motivation, coupled with success, leads to satisfaction.

PROFESSIONALS

Professionals have different needs than laborers or technicians because the expectations and demands on them are stronger and more diverse. Of all professionals working in 1984, 75 percent were in places like schools, hospitals, laboratories, and courtrooms, rather than in private practice (Raelin, 1986). Yet, little formal attention is given to training professionals for the idiosyncracies of organizational life. Sergiovanni (1987a) states:

> Professionals and bureaucrats function differently at work. The work of bureaucrats is programmed by the system, and they are subordinate to it. Professionals, too, are part of a system but their work emerges from an interaction between available knowledge and individual needs. Professional work requires that practitioners be *superordinate* to their system and use it to make sensible decisions according to the decision they face (p. 49).

The orientation of professionals establishes conflict with bureaucracies because their loyalty is to their profession and not to the organization (Gardner, 1981).

The assumptions about work and knowledge that underlie a bureaucratic or professional approach to teachers is identified by Bacharach and Conley (Sergiovanni & Moore, 1989). Bureaucratic views assume that the nature of work knowledge can be specified, that people high in the hierarchy can control substantive and administrative knowledge, and that the work of teachers can be standardized. Professional assumptions about the nature of job-related knowledge are that it can be defined only in broad limits, that the control of knowledge must be done by hired professionals, and that knowledge cannot be standardized.

Knowledge, in fact, distinguishes professionals from other workers. Raelin (1986) defines a profession as an "occupation requiring expert knowledge that justifies a monopoly of services granted by government licensing" (p. 47). Under this definition, teachers are professionals, even though they do not control entrance into the field, teaching practices, salaries, or working conditions. Raelin believes there are structural components to professions (formal education, standards, and entrance requirements) and attitudinal attributes (disposition to colleagues and sense of autonomy).

Weick and McDaniel (Sergiovanni & Moore, 1989, p. 332) believe that a professional relies on deep commitment of the organization's members beyond pecuniary gain, that he or she has a base of scientific or scholarly knowledge, that his or her work improves the human condition, and that members meet rigorous standards of education and selection. The characteristics of professionals, according to Raelin (1986, p. 9) are:

Expertise: Specialized training in abstract knowledge

Autonomy: The ability to choose the examination of and means to solve problems

Commitment: Primary interest in pursuing the practice of the profession

Identification: Identify with the profession or fellow professionals through formal associations or external referents

Ethics: Rendering service without regard for oneself or without becoming emotionally involved with the client

Standards: Committing oneself to policing the conduct of fellow professionals

Professional work involves autonomy, challenge, variety, and meaning. "Professionals are also typically interested in jobs that tap their creative or entrepreneurial instincts, that treat them in a personal way, that emphasize professional standards, and that allow them to operate without excessive supervision" (Raelin, 1986, pp. 19–20).

The behavior of administrators toward the professional staff is also related to the developmental stage of the organization. There is higher tolerance for autonomous and innovative professionals in the beginning or growth phases of an organization. In mature or declining phases—especially in tough economic times—there is less tolerance of professional entrepreneurship and discretion. In times of organizational stress, Raelin points out, administrators follow the wrong instinct and centralize authority and decision making, which results in greater control, more management, more rules and procedures, and greater fragmentation of effort. The stress and pressure on schools in some states has led to greater centralization, increased standardization, and more specifications and rule-driven requirements.

It would be overly simplistic to state that all professionals have the same needs, commitment, and attitudes. Like organizations, professionals move through stages or phases of development. Doctors just out of residency have divergent needs and perform their roles differently than highly experienced physicians. Teachers are similar. Beginning teachers have different levels of confidence, skill development, and perception than master teachers. Raelin (1986) identifies three career stages that are applicable to all professionals:

> Stage 1—Finding a niche (Early career): Individuals are idealistic about the profession, engage in routine work, and seek out a mentor. They want to make the most of experiences and work with older, proven professionals.
>
> Stage 2—Digging-in (Midcareer): Committed to work, these people endure long hours and their skills are at their peak. Many become specialists in their area and develop trusting relationships with their peers. Feedback about performance is less forthcoming than earlier.
>
> Stage 3—Entrenchment (End career): Individuals begin to lose touch with recent changes and developments in their field. There are two possible roles at this stage: mentor to younger professionals or sponsor of professional ideas and activities.

Regardless of their level of development, professionals aspire to have control over their work. Many desire autonomy, or at least a strong voice, over ends as well as means. Because of commitment to professional values, deference to bureaucratic needs is resisted. Professionals are more likely to gain autonomy over their work in organizations when administrators recognize and value their expertise, knowledge, practice, and concerns. (Chapter 9 addresses the issues of adult growth in the development of professionals.)

PROFESSIONALS AND BUREAUCRACIES

The topic of organizations as bureaucracies has been discussed earlier. The impact of bureaucracies is important to understand because teachers, as professionals, must work in them. A typical bureaucracy is dysfunctional to professionals because it operates in low-trust ways and it emphasizes standard behavior.

Jokes have been made about bureaucrats and the bureaucratic mentality. This mentality is characterized by being strategic in relationships to gain advantage, rather than building bonds and cooperation. Managing information and maneuvering situations and people is a prime component of this approach. Caution in telling the truth or sharing plans is emphasized, along with seeking approval from those higher in the hierarchy. Certainly this is not the environment in which professionals can thrive.

Professionals are more comfortable in an entrepreneurial, not a patriarchal, bureaucratic environment. Block (1988) states, "It is only the bureaucrat who has no feelings, makes no exceptions, does everything by the book, follows the rules and lives a life of total predictability. The objectivity and rationality we yearn for in organizations is only partially attainable. Organizations are too complicated to be totally predictable and operate on a plan" (p. 71). Many schools function in just such a manner; unfortunately, teachers are expected to behave in this way—following rules, adhering to a formula, and going by the book.

Conflict: Bureaucracies and Professionals

The contrast between professional and bureaucratic principles leads to role conflict: the incongruence between the needs of individuals, driven by professional standards, and the organizational expectations of bureaucracies. Bureaucratic principles include job specialization, standardization, and centralization of authority. Professionals have a different perspective, however. They stress the uniqueness of clients' needs, achievement, research, change, and skill based on knowledge. Authority is based on competence, not position, and loyalty is to professional standards and clients. Table 8–3 summarizes bureaucratic and professional principles.

Several practical role conflicts occur for teachers because of the clash of these principles. For example, teachers are supposed to defend the welfare of students and implement teaching strategies and methods to help them learn. However, as bureaucratic employees, teachers are supposed to follow school procedures and regulations. If they are using a method that goes against the grain of the accepted practice, then there is conflict between bureaucratic expectations and professional obligations.

TABLE 8-3   Bureaucratic and Professional Principles

	Bureaucratic	Professional
Standardization	Stress uniformity of client problems	Stress uniqueness of client problems
	Rules as universals	Rules as alternatives
	Stress recordkeeping	Stress research and change
Specialization	Efficiency of techniques: task orientation	Achievement of goals: client orientation
	Skill based on practice	Skill based on knowledge
Authority	Decisions based on application of rules	Decisions based on unique problems
	Loyalty to organization	Loyalty to client
	Authority from position	Authority from competence

Source: Ronald G. Corwin, "Professional Persons in Public Organizations," in Fred Carver and Thomas Sergiovanni (Eds.), *Organizations and Human Behavior* (New York: McGraw-Hill, 1969). Adapted by permission.

Administrators and Professionals

The conflict of professionals with bureaucratic organizational expectations also expands to friction between administrators and professionals. In theory, administrators represent organizational or corporate culture, whereas teachers are driven by professional culture. Teachers undergo professional socialization (Raelin, 1986), which creates identity with a professional group. Managers view their role from an organizational perspective and practical approaches to problem solving. Administrators and professionals occupy different roles in organizations, and these roles could lead to conflict.

One of the major differences in orientation is administrators' desire and responsibility for maintaining organizational order. They place emphasis on predictability, control, and organization, whereas "teachers . . . owe their primary allegiance to professional norms and claim that their daily activities require discretion and on-the-spot decisions. Therefore, they tend to find the proper performance of their jobs to be inconsistent with bureaucratic demands of administrators" (Bacharach & Conley, in Sergiovanni & Moore, 1989, p. 314).

Some of the resentment of teachers toward administrative control and dicta is reasonable, particularly when viewed from a professional's perspective. It is difficult for people not to resent, to some degree, others with control or authority over them who do not have the knowledge about their jobs that they do. This is the challenge for principals and others in administrative positions—to be able to lead people who may know more about their curricular and instructional areas than they do. Instruction becomes the organizing force for professionalism in schools, and resource allocation becomes the organizing force for administrators (Hanson, 1985, p. 103). In light of this, there could be the penchant for principals to become managers only instead of leaders—paper pushers who cite regulations and procedures and escalate the conflict between themselves and other professionals. (The differences between managers and leaders were outlined in Chapter 6.)

Conflict can also be related to the size of the unit and the integration of the individual professional. The smaller the unit, the greater the identification with supervisors, which generally results in less conflict and higher morale. Raelin (1986) points out, however, that a large organization does not automatically spell integration difficulties for professionals. Large organizations that are aware of the need for autonomy will flatten the structure (or decentralize) to allow for decision making by professionals. The restructuring reforms in schools address this issue.

Finally, conflict is influenced by the nature of supervision. Professionals prefer to work for supervisors who have professional training or a strong appreciation for the norms and standards of professional practice (Raelin, 1986, p. 22). Supervisors who lose identity with professional practice are more likely to be perceived negatively with greater potential for conflict.

The perception of administrators toward teachers is important in determining whether schools are professionalized or deprofessionalized. Professionalism in organizations is a function of how people are treated, which is the result of how they are perceived by school boards, administrators, and the community.

What Do Professional Organizations Look Like?

Professional organizations "embody the transformation process in people rather than in machines and represent a strategy to deal with uncertainty in the work place. The decision to adopt a professional strategy is of fundamental importance, because it means work will be left intact and delegated to a professional workforce rather than subdivided and hierarchically controlled for a nonprofessional workforce" (Weick & McDaniel, in Sergiovanni & Moore, 1989, p. 338). Work should be dispersed but not subdivided as if part of an industrialized assembly line.

Two types of professional work organizations can be identified: *autonomous (or organic)* and *heteronomous (or mechanistic)*. The difference between the two rests on the extent of discretion or autonomy professionals have. Heteronomous/mechanistic organizations keep professionals subordinate to administrative controls, and discretion or autonomy is limited. In autonomous/organic organizations, officials delegate to professionals the responsibility for defining and implementing goals, establishing performance standards, and ensuring that these standards are maintained.

A major issue is how to move a professional organization toward a common goal if decisions are delegated and decentralized. One way professional organizations can be identified, according to Weick and McDaniel, is by congruence of organizational and professional goals or "the professional's interpretation of the world and the organization's interpretation of the world" (Sergiovanni & Moore, 1989, p. 339). In these organizations, professionals have influence on goals and resource allocation so the fit between goals and aspirations of professionals and organizational mission is tight. Once established, these goals should not be compromised.

Goal setting relies on values, which, in conjunction with expertise, are the mainstays of professionals. Weick and McDaniel define values as "a rationalized normative system of preferences for certain courses of action or certain outcomes" (Sergiovanni & Moore, 1989, p. 334). All professionals have values that are transmitted through training, education, and socialization. Values and the norms that go with them are the informal controls on professional behavior in a decentralized system where decisions are made closest to their impact on the client. Ensuring a tight fit between professional and organizational values can be achieved through a value-based selection process, mentoring systems, and adherence to a code of ethics.

Values are not esoteric abstractions. Metaphorically, values are like the core of a baseball around which processes, structures, and strategies are wound in the form of decisions. Values are anchors that tie people together in turbulent times and when they are confronted by nonroutine information. Values are necessary for teachers to process and interpret nonroutine and critical information. They drive decisions about curriculum, instruction, organization, and teaching approaches.

School structure should support values and norms, not stifle them. Chubb (1988) stated that effective schools are organized differently than ineffective ones because they have clearer goals, are directed in their mission by educational leaders who work with teachers inside the school rather than trying to please central office, and encourage teachers' influence within the school.

Not all schools function this way, however. Clark and Meloy (Sergiovanni & Moore, 1989, pp. 279–281) specified some prevalent assumptions others have made about how schools should be organized. This perception is more bureaucratically oriented. They cite:

- The basic bureaucratic form is the only way to organize schools —hierarchical, with high specialization.
- All schools need principals, who are appointed by the board on recommendation of the superintendent, to serve as managers and represent the authority system.
- Goals are established at the system level with high centralization.
- The teacher's role is limited to the classroom and not involved with goal, curriculum, or operational decisions.

Tightly bureaucratized structures straitjacket teachers and do not allow them to participate in meaningful decisions. Many of the initial reforms of the 1980s were based on these assumptions and spearheaded movements to remove uncertainty from classrooms by tightening control. Excellence was to be ordered by increasing control over teachers (Bacharach & Conley, in Sergiovanni & Moore, 1989, p. 312), even though they must respond spontaneously to diverse student and program needs.

In contrast, Clark and Meloy (Sergiovanni & Moore, 1989) identified new democratic principles for enhancing professionalism:

- New schools must be built on the consent of the governed, with principals and teachers chosen by teachers.
- Authority and responsibility must be shared; staff, not a designated leader, would assume responsibility.
- Staff members would trade assignments and work collaboratively in groups—teachers would lead, manage, and instruct.
- Teachers would control formal awards—salary, promotion, and tenure—and there would be peer evaluation.
- Goals for the school would be developed through a consensus process involving professionals and the community.

Whether these principles can be implemented without teachers having more time is questionable because becoming involved in governance as well as curriculum and instruction will require reflection, study, evaluation, and new skills and training. Altering the work year or the way teachers are organized may have to take place to really effect democratic principles. Longer or more flexible contracts and the reorganization of the work calendar will need to be considered as part of the transformation process.

TIP | TRANSFORMATION INTO PRACTICE

UNIONISM AND PROFESSIONALISM: AN OXYMORON?

How can professionals subscribe to the tenets of unionism? There seems to be a direct conflict between professional values and those of the labor-unionist perception of work. However, the drive for union participation has, at its heart, an antibureaucratic tinge. Unionization of teachers has been based on trying to gain control and to influence educational policy in a system that disregarded their input.

Teachers unionized to influence the bureaucratic structures that constrained them. According to Spring (1989), unionizing provided several things for teachers:

1. A means to increase self-worth and influence educational policy
2. Psychic rewards that enhance their sense of efficacy
3. Opportunities to increase their knowledge and expertise, which is the best way for professionals to maintain control and autonomy

Corwin (1969, p. 214) stated that "militant professionalism" intended to compromise the control that administrators gained over public education, as well as lay influence over educational policy. Unions have represented teacher interests in salary, fringe benefits, and working conditions, but have also moved their focus to policy issues such as textbook selection, class size, and governance.

Raelin (1986) cites that unionization was opposed by some who felt that the movement itself compromised professional interests. He states that unionism, with its base in the values of standardized treatment and uniformity has dampening effects on autonomy and initiative. "Professionals sustain an intense individualism and ambition, and hence fear any collective system that does not reflect the individual's responsibility, performance, or qualifications" (p. 115). Consequently, seniority systems, which are cemented in time and that disregard talent and performance, become repulsive.

However, as the world has changed, so has the face of unionism. Perceptions of the old adversarial relationships between labor and management are softening even in hard-core union bastions like that of the auto workers. Cooperation—induced by the need for the very survival of the industry—has unions and management talking.

Gone are the days when management and labor met only at the negotiating table to trade insults and accusations. Today, the U.A.W. and auto executives travel to Japan together, go on retreats together, even publish newspapers together. . . . Jointness heralds a new era of industrial democracy, affording workers a genuine voice on the shop floor. To others, jointness marks an identity crisis for the union, a time of doubt and indecision (Massing, 1988, p. 20).

Teacher unions must change in this new era as well. Rigid enforcement of contract provisions can work against teachers having the autonomy and decision-making ability they need. Flexibility does not come from the rhetoric of old-style master agreements.

What is the role of teacher unions in transforming schools?

Can unions themselves transform?

Are unions more comfortable with a bureaucratic rather than a professional organization?

Why are issues of unionism not at the forefront of discussions on educational reform?

Is there a difference between a professional organization and a union?

Professional Ethics

"Bureaucracies are beautiful mechanisms for the evasion of responsibility and guilt" (Bennis, 1989, p. 96). In any case of wrong doing, those in the bureaucracy plead ignorance, stating they "were out of loop," were simply following orders, or did not see the whole picture. It is all a matter of ethics. As stated earlier, professional behavior rests on ethics and values. Ethics are the cornerstone of any professional service or treatment; without them, what security do clients really have?

Ethics, defined in the *Oxford Dictionary*, is "a system of rules to which we are constrained to conform, or to which we perhaps internalize and take for our own standard." Nutt (1989) and Harmon and Jacobs (1985) both add the dimension of ethics as standards for moral judgment. Nutt indicates that group, organizational, and cultural ethics all exist and attempt to define acceptable behavior. Together, they express the values adopted by each individual to govern ethical conduct, which includes overt behavior or inaction. Nutt states that there can be conflict between what is acceptable ethically in organizations and what is acceptable personally.

Professions have ethical standards based on service to the client. Teachers' clients are students. Teachers' responsibility, therefore, is to maintain their knowledge and skills in order to provide the best education possible, and defend, if necessary, conditions that will enhance the success of learning (Spring, 1989). If teaching circumstances are repressive and teachers struggle for survival—facing large classes, a poor working environment, masses of paperwork, or unsafe conditions—it will be difficult for them to focus on the needs of students.

Some general ethical responsibilities for people working in organizations include (Dunham 1984):

- Responsibility for their own actions and for the actions they initiate and undertake at the direction of others. Following orders does not relieve responsibility.
- Responsibility for their actions if they are a part of a group. They must defend against "group-think" or going along with the crowd.
- Responsibility for subordinates, peers, or others if they encourage them to behave in a way they would consider unethical.
- Inaction, like overt conduct, can result in unethical behavior.

The behavior most closely related to ethics is decision making. Unless steps are taken to encourage an open discussion of ethics, they can be overlooked in the the decision-making process. Nutt (1989) identifies two steps that can be taken to introduce ethics into this process. One step is to point out that people raising ethical questions will not be subject to sanctions or penalty. Second, ethical considerations must be reviewed when objectives are selected and alternatives are identified. Nutt points out some pitfalls that can cause ethical problems:

Self-protection: Some people get caught up in buck passing and "going along." Sometimes organizational life suggests that compromises and accommodations are expected. Data are slicked over to meet the boss's desires, and people tell individuals what they want to hear.

Self-righteousness: Organizations have zealots who are convinced of the rightness of their cause. These people will pursue any means to accomplish their ends under the guise that the outcome is justified.

Self-deception: Buying into a superior's agenda may require small compromises in one's values until the agenda overtakes and supercedes them. The individual rationalizes this behavior as not unjustified and not unethical. People put the "best face" on a situation that creates a conflict of values.

Unethical behavior can be caused by severe competition, by people in authority "looking the other way" and not modeling or expecting high standards, or by people with "Machiavellian" personalities (i.e., the ends justify the means) (Dunham, 1984). Sometimes individuals' ideological standards (those they hold personally) are different from their operational ones (those used in their role performance). A statement of ethical standards is a powerful force in having people reflect on ethical practice and decisions.

One ethical predicament that can occur when professionals or others work collaboratively in groups is "group shift." This problem is related to the group process, when groups make decisions and engage in behavior that is more extreme than those undertaken by individual members. Members diffuse responsibility and rationalize the decision, even though they may have qualms about it, because it was not made by conscious intent or even consent. It is difficult for individuals to raise ethical issues in groups because of the desire to be an accepted member. Keeping the focus on client needs is not easy, especially when the problem is not clear, the information is ambiguous, and all parties may not have personal contact with the issue. Clients can become depersonalized. Therefore, *premum non nocere*—above all, do no harm—should be the ethic in professions like law, medicine, and education.

Ethics and integrity are often confused. A good summary of the difference is made by Srivastva and Barrett (1988):

> When I think about the difference between integrity and ethics, I intuit that the major difference is that integrity is something that is characteristic of any living system, person, or organization. Integrity for that system is the state of being itself, of fully operating according to its highest purpose, of realizing its potential as a life form. The definition of integrity comes from within the individual or system. Ethics, in contrast, is a set of rules agreed upon or imposed from the outside. It cannot exist without a social system, for which ethics become the "rules of conduct recognized in certain limited departments of human life." It is clear that when people do not agree among themselves on those rules, the rules can be effective only if they are imposed by power (p. 49).

Integrity is an interactive phenomenon. *Wholeness* and *completeness* are the keys. Relationships must be whole, and organizational integrity requires that the commitments be in alignment with the standards and dominant values of the system. A school that espouses a set of values and then makes a commitment to the contrary does not have integrity. Organizations must hold fast to their mission and interests, even in the face of resistance from individuals. Individual integrity

TABLE 8–4   Principles of Integrity

1. *Tell the truth:* Communicate honestly, fully, and openly. Give reasons for the decisions and action taken.
2. *Obey the law.*
3. *Reduce ambiguity:* Clarify organizational values and priorities, as well as individual rights and responsibilities.
4. *Demonstrate concern for others:* Treat others as you would have them treat you. Artificial rank and status differential should be minimized. Reinforce that all people have individual rights that cannot be denied.
5. *Accept responsibility for the growth and nurturing of clients/subordinates:* Respect people's unique characteristics, allow people to function as whole entities, and practice *premum non nocere* (above all, do no harm).
6. *Practice participation, not paternalism:* Give reasons and justifications for decisions and communicate them to people before they are binding and irreversible.
7. *Provide freedom from corrupting influences:* Protect members from forces that challenge unethical practices and from any cultural or reward systems that discourage integrity. Respect people's right to act on conscience.
8. *Always act:* When resources are available to act with integrity or when someone needs help, integrity requires that action be taken.
9. *Provide consistency across cases:* Handle people's problems in the same manner and do not show preferential treatment.
10. *Provide consistency between values and action:* Have a "tightness-of-fit" between espoused theories and theories-in-use. Otherwise, action is hypocritical.

Source: Adapted from Suresh Srivastva and associates, *Executive Integrity* (San Francisco: Jossey-Bass, 1988), pp. 126–127.

means acting on valued established principles, even when asked to do otherwise.

Srivastva and Barrett (1988) identify 10 commandments for executive integrity. These principles, listed in Table 8–4, can apply to all professionals, including teachers, and the conditions in which they practice.

THE CONDITION OF TEACHING

The job of teaching is perceived and described in many different ways. Teachers view themselves as professionals, sometimes downtrodden by bureaucracy and regulations. Within their field, some see teaching as scientifically inclined. They value research on brain development, motivation, learning, and other disciplines that require precise cause and effect outcomes. Others believe teaching is more art than science, filled with an incalculable magnetism of wonder, attraction, and concentration. These characteristics cannot be defined or measured behaviorally or scientifically because good teachers know intuitively how to motivate and instruct, especially in serendipitous teachable moments. And still others believe that teaching is both art and science— a blend of applied knowledge and intuition.

Outside the field of teaching, people's perceptions of teachers are not limited to the notion of professionalism. *Laborers* is a prominent designation when people are viewed as members of a union, applying political clout to achieve influence or economic gain. In some circles, teachers are perceived as craftspersons, who apply knowledge and skill but who lack a strong research and scientific theoretical base and clear standards and procedures. These differences in perception—from professional to craftsperson to laborer—can create problems in the way teachers are treated. As Bacharach and Conley (Sergiovanni & Moore, 1989) point out, teachers are not viewed as professionals because the complexity of teaching is hidden beneath the apparent simplicity of its execution and because it is not cloaked in unfamiliar language or jargon. Bacharach and Conley contend that teaching *is* a profession because it meets three specifications: (1) structural criteria (formal code of ethics and lengthy training process); (2) attitude disposition (degree to which members believe in service to the public, self-regulation, and autonomy); and (3) societal recognition (degree to which society views the occupation as a profession).

Goodlad (1984) supports the differences in perception in his major study of schools. "In general the practicing teacher . . . functions in a context where beliefs and expectations are those of a profession but where realities tend to constrain, likening actual practice more to a trade" (p. 193). He maintains that individuals become teachers because of the professional values of autonomy in decision making and the application of knowledge and skills learned in training. But when they begin to hone those skills in practice, they encounter realities in schools that restrict professional growth.

In discussing high schools, Boyer (1983) concurs that teachers lack control over many factors crucial to instruction and, consequently, some of them do not see themselves as professionals adorned with commensurate responsibilities. They fall back to standard procedures of lecturing, question and answer, recitation, seatwork, and homework because of heavy class and student loads and the pressure of time.

Bacharach and Conley (Sergiovanni & Moore, 1989) make distinctions about how teachers behave based on how they deal with uncertainty, the variation and number of problems they encounter, and the number of possible solutions they identify. They suggest four labels for teachers: bureaucrats, technicians, craftspersons, and professionals (pp. 318–320). From their vantage point, teachers as *bureaucrats* are appendages of bureaucracy in which problems are identified and specified for them. Individuals are managed through expectations and modes of operation, and administrators are held accountable for teachers' results. The notion of *technician* emphasizes the limited range of solutions available to teachers, who behave in predictable ways under the direction of others. Administrators (principals and others) specify solutions for them. An example of teachers being treated as technicians is the development of teacher-proof curriculum materials.

With the third label, teachers as *craftspersons*, accountability changes from principals to teachers but the problems for which they are accountable are narrow and restricted. Finally, in the *professional* context, the dimensions of uncertainty and problem identification and solution are recognized. Administrators realize the possibility of failure, and they accord teachers great discretion in performing their work. Teachers are assisted in developing a repertoire of skills they can apply to multiple problems. Figure 8–1 defines the relationship of uncertainty in problems and solutions and their connection to the four roles used in these descriptions.

How administrators perceive the work of teachers may help resolve the conflict between professional values (demands for autonomy and participation) and bureaucratic values (need for coordination and predictability). The key component is how much uncertainty principals and others believe teachers must handle (Bacharach & Conley, in Sergiovanni & Moore, 1989, p. 327). Management assumptions about teachers and professionalism include:

- Teachers, as line professionals, cope with a critical level of uncertainty.
- Teachers already make informal decisions in carrying out their work.
- Teachers should have a structure to allow them to participate in decisions outside their classrooms.

The professionalization of teaching demands changes that are internal and external to the classroom. Classroom issues focus on instruc-

FIGURE 8–1   Perception of Teacher Roles and Problems and Solutions

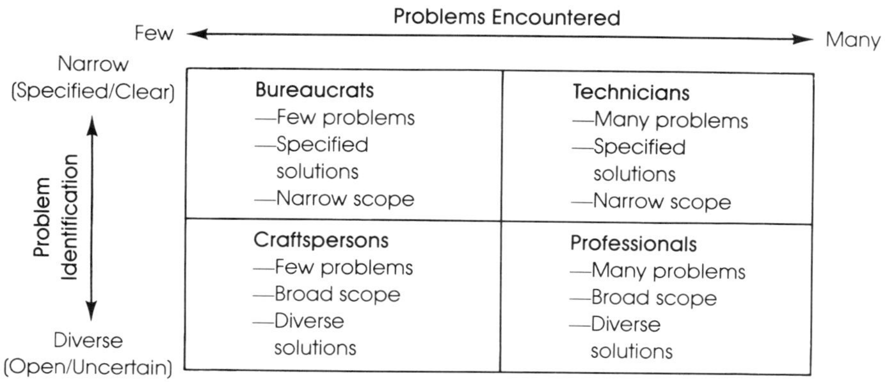

	Problems Encountered	
Few ←		→ Many
Narrow (Specified/Clear)	**Bureaucrats** —Few problems —Specified solutions —Narrow scope	**Technicians** —Many problems —Specified solutions —Narrow scope
Problem Identification	**Craftspersons** —Few problems —Broad scope —Diverse solutions	**Professionals** —Many problems —Broad scope —Diverse solutions
Diverse (Open/Uncertain)		

Source: Adapted from Bacharach and Conley, in *Schooling for Tomorrow*, Edited by T. Sergiovanni and J. Moore (Boston: Allyn and Bacon, 1989), p. 319

tional practices, the methods and practices used in teaching and curriculum implementation. External issues include control over licensing procedures, teacher preparation and selection, professional development, and evaluation. In addition, Spring (1989, p. 56) specifies that teachers will need new skills in a knowledge-based economy. Those skills for "new teachers" include the ability to act independently and collaborate with others, to think for themselves, and to make critical judgments. These teachers will need in-depth knowledge and understanding.

Teacher Satisfaction

Teacher behavior is one of the factors affecting the quality of a school (Goodlad, 1984) and the teachers' work environment. Boyer (1983) agrees, stating, "Improving working conditions is, we believe, at the center of our effort to improve teaching. We cannot expect teachers to exhibit a high degree of professional competence when they are accorded such a low degree of professional treatment in their workaday world" (p. 161).

According to Boyer (1983), these working conditions are often composed of overcrowded classrooms, large class loads, lack of professional surroundings, and a hierarchical, bureaucratic structure, all of which work to sap teacher energy and enthusiasm. Goodlad (1984), in fact, found that personal frustration and dissatisfaction were the major reasons for teachers leaving their jobs. Actually, conflicts with administrators, students, and fellow teachers ranked low as reasons for leaving. Many teachers work for intrinsic, not extrinsic, rewards like salary or fringe benefits. Satisfaction, then, rests on the fulfillment of these expectations. Boyer (1983), however, found that teachers quit for the same reasons other workers do. He indicated that when teachers want to be of service and want to teach but are stymied and frustrated in meeting these expectations, then dissatisfaction occurs. "Surveys reveal that teachers are deeply troubled, not only about salaries, but also about their loss of status, the bureaucratic pressures, a negative public image, the lack of recognition and rewards" (p. 145).

Raelin (1986) asserts that teachers have unionized because of these concerns but that this unionizing may have further tarnished their professional image. "This loss of respect, coupled with gradual loss of autonomy, has led salaried professionals even to consider unionizing as a means of retaining their professional rights within their employing organizations" (p. 88). Under difficult situations, teachers begin to compromise. That was the major premise in Sizer's (1984) work, *Horace's Compromise*, in which teachers made concessions and shortcuts to deal with the working conditions in busy days. These shortcuts affect planning, class preparation, assignments, and grading.

However, conditions do not have to be dire for teachers. Situations that are supportive through sensitive leadership, involvement in schoolwide decisions, and the availability of help are associated with enthusiasm, professionalism, and fulfillment (Goodlad, 1984). Goodlad also states that teachers feel they have substantial influence over curriculum, instruction, student behavior, and communication with parents. They have some influence on extracurricular issues, community-related topics, dress codes, and assignment to classes and grades taught. But they feel their influence is minimal regarding fiscal management, teaching assistants, and the hiring of professional personnel (p. 190).

The National Education Association's study (1988) on teacher working conditions found:

- Teachers do not feel that they have the resources they need to carry out their jobs.
- Teachers do not have the opportunity to bring their professional knowledge to bear in decision making.
- Teachers feel that communication between them and their principals is less frequent than desired.
- Teachers believe that administrators do not provide enough support.

TIP | **TRANSFORMATION**
INTO
PRACTICE

PSYCHIC REWARDS AND TEACHING

Why do teachers want to teach? According to John Goodlad in *A Place Called School* (1984, p. 171), liking kids is not a prime reason. Teachers teach because of the following:

1. The nature of teaching itself	57%
2. Desire to teach in general or to teach a specific subject	22%
3. The idea that teaching is a good and worthy profession	18%
4. Desire to be of service to others	17%

All of these motivations are psychic ones, not associated with compensation or standard of living. People become teachers for internally satisfying reasons. Goodlad found that those who became teachers because of other people or for economic purposes were the least likely to find fulfillment of career expectations. A vast majority (74 percent) of teachers reported that their career expectations have been fulfilled.

Lortie, in *Schoolteacher: A Sociological Study* (1975), states that psychic rewards are associated with the psychological satisfaction derived from the job. They vary from person to person, but there are strands that cut across people and the occupation. Teachers report that "reaching" students and making them learn was an extremely motivating psychic reward. A chance to "associate with children or young people" is another example. On the other hand, extrinsic rewards concern salary and community status. Lortie's findings parallel Goodlad's research. Of 5,800 teachers surveyed by Lortie, over 76 percent gave top priority to psychic rewards, whereas only 11.9 percent selected extrinsic rewards.

What happens when these psychic rewards are not felt? Spring (1989), in *American Education,* believes that teachers burn out, feel bitter, or leave the profession. If a student resists learning and does not care about school, then a major satisfaction in teaching does not exist.

Spring (1989) mentions that the denial of some psychic rewards may be intrinsic to teaching. Students "are not rewarded by the system for demonstrating the joy of learning" (p. 44). Spring believes that teachers are frequently trying to figure out how to make students learn, while some pupils are figuring out how to "get by" with minimum effort. This situation will not meet teachers' psychic needs. Boyer (1983) states, "Most teachers feel their work is negatively influenced by students who are unmotivated, by parents who are nonsupporting, by administrators who saddle them with trivial tasks or burdensome paperwork, by schools that permit students to slide through with any course just as long as they meet ADA (average daily attendance) expectations" (p. 142).

What can leaders do to stimulate psychic rewards?
Does the way schools are structured affect teacher satisfaction?
Would teachers' psychic reward potential increase if they were not as isolated as they are?
Would better measurement of teacher productivity and student achievement influence teachers' psychic needs?
Do ambiguity and uncertainty increase the chances of dissatisfaction?

Conley, Bacharach, and Bauer (1989) indicate that the major dissatisfiers for elementary teachers were role ambiguity, student behavior problems, routinization of work, and large classes. For secondary teachers, role ambiguity and negative supervisory behavior are problems. The authors indicate that talented people will become disillusioned with their careers if their work environment stymies their intrinsic motivation.

Although Conley, Bacharach, and Bauer found differences between elementary and secondary teachers, role ambiguity was a constant. This finding supports the research on professionals in bureaucracies, which suggests that professionals accept bureaucratization to the degree that it clarifies their role. The expectations for teachers and their behavior are not always clearly defined due to differences in philosophy, lack of agreement on professional standards of practice, and debate on the role of teachers and the purpose of education itself. Bureaucratization of teaching, on the other hand, encourages routinization of work—a dissatisfier for elementary staff.

Mundane and routine work and approaches to instruction will result in dissatisfaction. "When routinization does occur, i.e., when there is a preponderance of rules defining and enforcing what is to be done, professionals tend to react negatively" (Raelin, 1986, p. 117). Negative reactions may include disappointment with professional development, the inability to meet professional standards, and dissatisfaction with colleagues and supervisors. Many states are increasing regularized classroom procedures and approaches to instruction that will only add to the routine and dissatisfaction, particularly among the most talented teachers.

Bacharach and Bauer (1989) assert that professionals can only be effective in schools if talented people are recruited. However, talent will demand the ability to be creative and autonomous in achieving goals. They also believe that teachers must be rewarded for their accomplishments. Talent rather than time ought to be a major consideration in remuneration and employment.

Teacher Isolation

Autonomy is different from isolation. Goodlad (1984) stated

> The teachers we studied appeared, in general, to function quite autono-
> mously. But their autonomy seemed to be exercised in a context more of
> isolation than of rich professional dialogue about a plethora of challenging
> educational alternatives. The classroom cells in which teachers spend
> much of their time appear to me to be symbolic and predictive of their
> relative isolation from one another and from sources of ideas beyond their
> own background of experience (p. 187).

Despite the trend toward collaboration in the private sector through quality circles and other means for people to work cooperatively to produce high-quality outcomes, schools still rely on the individual teacher, assisted at times by specialists, all of whom perform their role independently.

Teachers rarely work with peers in collaborative efforts on district committees or projects, nor do they observe each other or visit other schools very frequently (Goodlad, 1984). Boyer (1983) found that high school teachers suffer this isolation because of the weight of their sched-ules and the self-contained classroom, which restrict opportunities for intellectual discussion or sharing common problems. It is possible for teachers to spend very little time in the company of adults while working.

Collegiality is all but nonexistent among teachers, according to Maeroff (1988), who stated, "Knowledge is the currency in which a teacher deals; yet the teacher's own knowledge is allowed to become stale and devalued, as though ideas were not the lifeblood of the occupa-tion. The circumstances of teaching cause teachers not to respect them-selves, much less each other " (p. 474).

Isolation has a significant impact on teachers' behavior and self-renewal. Without the ability to communicate with each other or see the larger context of their roles, teachers limit their perception to their classroom. They derive their ideas from past experience, the individual success in their own classrooms, and the teachers they had while in school. Without horizontal communication among and between teachers, they are walled off, left to their own devices.

The structure of the school year and the length of teachers' work year (generally 10 months, or around 190 work days) contribute to their isolation. A longer work year might allow teachers to participate in more teacher-initiated staff development, to share ideas and opportunities, to think collectively, and to check perceptions against realities.

Teacher Disenfranchisement

A final condition of teaching concerns disenfranchisement. Goodman (1988) believes that disenfranchisement occurs when "the conceptualization of instruction and the curriculum is separated from those who actually teach. That is, decisions about what should be taught, why it should be taught, and how it should be taught are made without (or with limited) input from the classroom teacher" (p. 202). Teachers in this process are not perceived as reflective professionals or practitioners capable of establishing meaningful curricular goals, developing thoughtful lessons, or designing stimulating instructional strategies. They are seen to use teacher-proof materials, apply direct instruction, or teach to specific test objectives.

In this view, teachers are perceived as technicians (see Figure 8–1) who coordinate the day and work to ensure that students get through the specified curriculum in a timely manner. Teaching is viewed as an automated process and teachers as "automated functionaries" (Goodman, 1988, p. 202). The culprit in this approach to teacher and teaching is scientific management and its methods of control. Control and disenfranchisement of teachers comes from supervisors monitoring behavior —governing workers by impersonal rules and regulations, which are enforced by a sanction system. Control can also be achieved technically by embedding workers' tasks in structure, schedules, tools, and standardization. Many schools are controlled technically by bell schedules, textbook expectations, and direct instruction (one approach is best for all). Goodman states:

> The curricular and instructional programs that have dominated classroom activity have been based primarily on principles of fundamental efficiency and social control. These programs emphasize the study of utilitarian skills over substantive content or artistic talent; the sequential segmentation and memorization of knowledge over synthesis and wholistic understanding; and the standardized, quantitative evaluation of pupil's work over the informed judgment of the teacher (p. 212).

SUMMARY

Better working conditions for teachers will require less bureaucracy, greater autonomy, and more leadership opportunities. Teachers learn from each other and from other professionals. As we have stated, however, many schools are bureaucracies, and Raelin (1986) believes that young professionals are inadequately prepared to deal with them. Wirth (1989) states that the studies of teacher burnout, isolation, job satisfaction, and sense of efficacy are rooted in working relations and institutional structures.

CONCEPTS

1. How people who work in complex institutions are treated directly influences whether conflict will exist between individuals and the organization.
2. Organizations must be designed and function to enhance the role and participation of workers in order to survive and be successful in the future.
3. The structure and perceptions of organizations relate directly to the level of motivation and commitment of the people who work there.
4. Patriarchal organizations reduce commitment; entrepreneurial organizations build commitment.
5. The connection between human nature and organizational design can be viewed from two perspectives: monolithic and pluralistic.
6. Motivation of people in organizations is dependent on factors like autonomy, decision making, participation, responsibility, and affiliation.
7. Professionals working in bureaucracies create conflict.
8. The characteristics of professionals are expertise, autonomy, commitment, identification, ethics, and standards.
9. Organic organizations encourage professionalism, whereas mechanistic organizations impede professional behavior and satisfaction.
10. Values connect professionals and organizations toward common purposes.
11. Schools are highly bureaucratized structures that must now become professional organizations with new values and principles.
12. Professional behavior rests on ethics and values; ethics are standards for moral judgment.
13. Ethics and integrity are related but not identical concepts. Integrity comes from within the individual system, whereas ethics are imposed from without.

14. The condition of teaching can be described from various perceptions—teachers as professionals, bureaucrats, laborers, technicians, or craftpersons.
15. The level of satisfaction for teachers is linked to the degree of psychic rewards they experience.
16. Isolation, fragmentation, and disenfranchisement interfere with efforts to professionalize teaching.
17. The transformation of schools from bureaucracies to professional organizations will enhance the condition of teaching and the role of teachers.

9 The Development of Professionals

In at least one way education is like any other business or profession: the quality of personnel is of central importance. No matter how sophisticated or extensive a school's resources or how carefully developed its policies, without the skill and commitment of teachers and administrators, a school cannot succeed. Effective education depends on effective professionals (Fielding & Schalock, 1985, p. 1).

A school that strives for quality and success without continuous investment in human resources sows its own seeds of mediocrity and failure. Teachers need continued growth and development to maintain their vigor and upgrade their expertise.

The numerous theories that explain human growth and development have three concepts in common: (1) there is a predictable pattern and sequence; (2) individuals seek growth and help to determine its direction; and (3) growth happens when people interact with others, with the environment, and ultimately with themselves. Although patterns do exist and are helpful in understanding how people change throughout their lives, it would be misleading to conclude that everyone moves through all these stages in a planned, organized manner.

Developmental psychologists agree that growth is a complicated and interactive process influenced by many forces both inside and outside the individual. The environment is not only a context within which growth takes place. More fundamentally, it is a major component of a dynamic interaction. To understand the potentials for adult growth in schools, adults *and* schools must be examined (Levine, 1989, p. 23).

ADULT GROWTH

Levine (1989) concludes that the theories of adult growth can be divided into two types—those that discuss *phases* of adult development and those that explain developmental changes as *stages*. Phase and stage theories have the three previously mentioned aspects in common, but they differ in their focus. Phase theories emphasize major life tasks or conflicts that arise at relatively specific times in people's lives and stimulate growth. Stage theories view development as "a series of sequentially ordered stages whose progression, in contrast to phase progressions, is *not* dependent upon age." Instead, development occurs "as an organic process of alternating periods of balance, transition and reintegration" (Levine, 1989, p. 85). An example of each type of developmental theory should help in delineating the differences.

Erik Erikson was one of the early phase theorists who described eight life phases: infancy, early childhood, play age, school age, adolescence, young adulthood, maturity, and old age. At each phase, there is a specific, prominent issue that must be resolved in order for growth to occur. When this happens, the person develops a new capacity. For example, in the young adult years, from age 20 to 40, the major conflict is intimacy versus isolation. When an individual has successfully resolved this conflict, the ability to love is created.

During the maturity phase, ages 40 to 60, adults are struggling with generativity versus self-absorption. Generativity refers to nurturing, providing guidance for the next generation, and re-creation or revival. Parenting issues are a specific example of the focus of this phase, yet the adults also need generative experiences with other adults for their own continued growth. Resolving generativity/self-absorption conflicts results in the ability to care.

Finally, at the old age phase, age 60 and older, the primary concern is integrity versus despair.

> Erikson's theory suggests that a sense of integrity must prevail over feeling of despair and disgust. Older adults thrive when they are able to integrate their past experiences into the present. Advanced status, recognition from others, and chances to share the accumulated wisdom of growth are inherent in the resolution of the developmental conflict of old age (Levine, 1989, p. 63).

Adults do not move through these phases automatically. They may stay in one phase and never experience growth if the conflict issues do not get resolved. Feelings of guilt, inferiority, and despair can be created when people are unsuccessful in dealing with these life conflicts.

This phase theory closely parallels the description in the preceding chapter of the three professional career cycles—finding a niche, digging in, and ending a career. Knowledge of these phases can influence how the work environment is structured and will encourage —rather than stifle—growth experiences. In schools, for example, attention should be given to the conflict occurring within those teachers who are in the young adulthood phase. If the primary concern is to avoid isolation and achieve intimacy, the current structure of schools contributes to the conflict, not to its resolution. As we have mentioned, teachers often describe their feelings of isolation—teaching in individual classrooms, moving through a highly structured schedule, and experiencing limited exposure to other adults. Administrators have more interactions with adults than do teachers, but their positions as evaluators separate them from the collegiality of fellow professionals in the schools; therefore, they also experience isolation. These realities have implications for professional development, which will be addressed later in this chapter.

Kegan (1982) provides an example of the stage theory of adult growth. He believes growth happens as a process with alternating periods of stability, instability, and temporary rebalance. The five stages he describes are not discrete entities; rather, they are transitions that are constantly occurring. His theory is based on changing relationships between self and others and how people create meaning—of themselves, others, and their world. Perception plays a large role in his efforts to explain how people behave at the various stages. He focuses not just on the behavior but on the meaning behind it.

The first stages refer to childhood and pre-adult, when the orientation is completely on the self. Beginning with stage 2, the person moves out of childhood and into the Imperial Balance stage. This is usually at a pre-adult time, but adults can experience this stage as well. The person's orientation to self and the world is through one's own perception and needs. The self is built on meeting its goals and it relates to others only as a means for getting its purposes. Adults in this stage are viewed as self-centered, opportunistic, and unresponsive to others' needs.

In stage 3, Interpersonal Balance, people become very important. There is great reliance on others for the establishment of identity and there is no self-independence. The individual is compliant and avoids conflict because of a great need to be accepted and to establish and maintain good relationships. A person in this stage, always seeking interpersonal balance, is agreeable, goes along with the group, and has no differing opinions or independent thought.

In contrast, stage 4, called Institutional Balance, evolves a new sense of self-ownership. The person is more independent than in the previous stage, but relationships with others also exist. Now the individual feels comfortable with relating to many people and can develop mutual interactions because of a strong sense of self-control. The person can be with a group or separate from it without causing any discomfort or anxiety, since new individual standards and values are forming. Prominent characteristics of this stage and are personal achievement, competence, and responsibility (Levine, 1989, p. 105).

Finally, in stage 5, Interindividual Balance, interdependence and individuality are both present. The self has become very well developed so that the person can easily manage all the complex relationships and organizations formed in his or her life. The orientation of self is no longer to achievement; instead, it focuses more inwardly on broadening the psychological dimension. The individual in stage 5 can be autonomous yet maintain strong connections with others. Balance is achieved between intimacy and independence.

As these stages unfold, the individual obtains increased opportunities to interact with the self, others, and the world. Each stage has both positive and negative aspects to it, and everyone does not necessarily pass through all of them. People can move in and out of any stage throughout their development—sometimes backward as well as forward. Such movement is not as likely in phase theories, which tend to correspond to clusters of ages and only move forward or stop.

Loevinger's work (1976) on stages of development provides a view from the ego and is interesting to consider because of its implications for change. She describes the ego as a process, or function, that is social in origin and constantly interacting and evolving to form relationships with the outside world, while striving for order, security, stability, and balance. The ego can move through these seven stages:

1. *Self-protective:* externalization, blaming others, concerned with control, manipulative; this stage is usually associated with young people, not adults.
2. *Conformist:* approval and belonging important, social acceptability, following all the rules, stress on outward appearance, materialism.
3. *Conscientious conformist:* an in-between stage, still conforming but beginning to develop more independence in thinking.
4. *Conscientious:* interpersonal communication very important, self-evaluative, often critical, becoming reflective and motivated.

5. *Individualistic:* growing tolerance of self and others, recognition of life's complexity, sense of individualism yet strong emotional ties and values for interpersonal relationships.
6. *Autonomous:* beginning to search for self-fulfillment, understanding of others' need for autonomy, high tolerance for ambiguity, broadened outlook toward life.
7. *Integrated:* firm sense of identity, respect for self and others, acceptance of reality.

These descriptions have much in common with Kegan's stage theory, and, as was the case with his ideas, many people never experience all of these levels. Stages 6 and 7 are very sophisticated and mature stages of ego development.

Just as understanding phase theory can assist us in working with others in schools, stage theories have similar applications. "Stage theories point to the importance of understanding how the individuals with whom we are working understand themselves, their world and others. This understanding helps us to recognize an individual's major preoccupations and assumptions, as well as to anticipate his or her interpersonal style, affect, and motivation" (Levine, 1989, p. 115).

For example, Kegan's Imperial Balance stage orientation has been related to the structure of self-contained classrooms. This organization may discourage growth or advancement to another stage because of its inherent separation and competition. The Interpersonal Balance stage is relevant to new teachers. Their need to be accepted and to conform can be helpful in acclimating them to the norms and expectations of the school culture. But this process can be either positive or negative, depending on the culture established. If cooperation, sharing, and creativity are valued, the new teacher will assimilate these characteristics. If strict adherence to the rules, hours, contract language, and compliance are stressed, those behaviors will be shaped. Considering stage 5, Interindividual Balance, those characteristics of autonomy and interconnections may be desirable and easily met for a superintendent, but not fit the role of a principal or teacher.

Levine (1989) applies Loevinger's stage theory to adults working in schools.

> Development is conceived of as ongoing. The individual, engaging in a constant process of active exchange with the environment, constructs meanings, strives for competence and protects the self from changes that threaten to undermine the assumptions or inner logic with which the self-system is maintained. Changing relationships between self and others are the interpersonal arena for the activity of making meaning (p. 101).

A major concern then for educators interested in growth is the recognition of the large array of developmental places people may be at any given time.

In addition to acknowledging that people pass through various phases or stages that affect their behavior, we also should consider their psychological states, which closely parallel the preceding theories. Growth opportunities that are offered will be ignored or rejected if people are incapable of learning or if they are unmotivated because of their psychological orientation. Maslow's (1962) work is the most well known in this field; his hierarchy of needs resemble the phase theories in their orderly progression and the stage theories in the behavior exhibited at each level.

The five levels of psychological development are based on needs.

1. *Physiological needs:* to satisfy the basics—food, clothing, shelter, economic security.
2. *Safety needs:* to establish psychological safety and security in one's world; a nonthreatening social context and a predictable future.
3. *Social needs:* to belong and feel loved; respect and acceptance by others is important.
4. *Ego needs:* for achievement; competence, self-esteem, and confidence emerge.
5. *Self-fulfillment needs:* for self-actualization, expanding horizons, seeking challenges, autonomous because of role security, optimistic, future-oriented.

Professional growth would not be a high priority for people in the first three states. Their orientations are more practical and concrete, and they have not reached levels of psychological maturity that would accept such opportunities. Individuals at level 4 would be most interested in development that would enhance their status, skills, level of job, or advanced degrees. Teachers in this state would be motivated by courses toward higher degrees. They might be considering moving into supervisory or administrative roles. They would be receptive to ideas that enhance teaching skills and would not be threatened to try or experiment with new approaches or programs. People at level 5 are completely open to new experiences and view professional growth as a personal responsibility. They would welcome sophisticated, challenging growth opportunities and would easily adapt to or initiate change.

A final perspective from which growth can be viewed is cognitive developmental theory, summarized by Sprinthall and Sprinthall (1980):

1. All humans process experience through cognitive structures called stages—Piaget's concept of schemata.
2. Such cognitive structures are organized in a hierarchical sequence of stages from the less complex to the more complex.
3. Growth occurs first within a particular stage and then only to the next stage in the sequence. This latter change is a qualitative shift—a major quantum leap to a significantly more complex system of processing experience.
4. Growth is not automatic nor unilateral but occurs only with appropriate interaction between the human and the environment.
5. Behavior can be determined and predicted by an individual's particular stage of development. Predictions, however, are not exact (p. 279).

If one subscribes to this concise view of cognitive growth, professional development might take a different direction than if one believed stages to be erratic, forward as well as backward, and highly unpredictable. Interestingly, the Sprinthalls (1980) raise the question as to whether the knowledge that people move through these stages has any implications for thinking, action, and practice in the real world. They conclude that such knowledge is valuable, because numerous researchers have accurately predicted individuals' future success based on levels of psychological maturity. Table 9–1 summarizes theories of adult growth and development.

All schools have a mixture of persons at various stages of cognitive development and at different levels of Maslow's hierarchy, who come to the workplace with complex needs and expectations. Facilitating growth and ensuring that professionals continue to develop is a major challenge for the future.

> Growth, as we have seen, implies change and uncertainty. Yet schools demand stability and knowledge from the adults who serve as teachers and administrators. Might the demands of the profession be incompatible, or at least in tension, with the needs and realities of adult growth? Should adults expect to be growing in a setting designed for children? Will a context compatible with the growing needs of adults be a provocative or a disruptive environment for children? These are the kinds of questions that surface when school is considered as a context for the development of both children and adults (Levine, 1989, p. 113).

PROFESSIONAL DEVELOPMENT

Before answering these questions, we should clarify what development of individuals in organizations really means. Various terms are

TABLE 9–1 Summary of Adult Growth and Development

Phases (Erikson)	Career Cycles (Raelin)	Stages (Kegan)	Ego Stages (Loevinger)	Psychological Development (Maslow)	Implications
Young Adult— Intimacy	Early Career— Finding a niche	Imperial Balance	Self-Protective	Physiological Needs	Skill-oriented Practical training
			Conformist	Safety Needs	Competence development Individualized opportunities
		Interpersonal Balance	Conscientious— Conformist		Prescribed, directive
			Conscientious— Interpersonal	Social Needs	
Maturity— Generativity	Midcareer— Digging in	Institutional Balance	Individualistic	Ego Needs	Team building Colleague support Group-oriented Experiments Conceptualize
Old Age— Integrity	End Career— Entrenchment	Interindividual Balance	Autonomous	Self-fulfillment Needs	Mentoring focus Leadership Personalized, creative options Alternatives
			Integrated		

used for specific activities: *training, inservice, staff development, retreats, workshops, professional improvement plans,* and so on. "Employee development can be defined as a planned process to provide employees with learning experiences designed to enhance their contributions to organizational goals" (Heneman, Schwab, Fossum, & Dyer, 1980, p. 331). In general, the three types of development programs are:

1. Orientation of new employees
2. Improving performance on the present job
3. Retraining for new jobs

In this context, employee development is more than just training; its basic objective is learning and behavior change. Likewise, professional development should be goal-directed, purposeful, and intentional, highlighting the status of educators as professionals. The outcome of this development is expected to be increased effectiveness for people, programs, and organizations.

Context for Professional Development

All professional development is influenced by the context in which it occurs, as summarized in Figure 9–1. Three internal context dimensions are technical, interpersonal, and cultural (Fielding & Schalock, 1985). The technical context is all of the resources and procedures in the organization that can either stimulate or stifle growth. The interpersonal dimension includes the amount of support colleagues give one another; the sharing and cooperation that exist with materials, resources, and ideas; and the frequency level of interpersonal communication that takes place in the organization. The cultural is the shared

FIGURE 9–1   Context for Professional Growth and Development

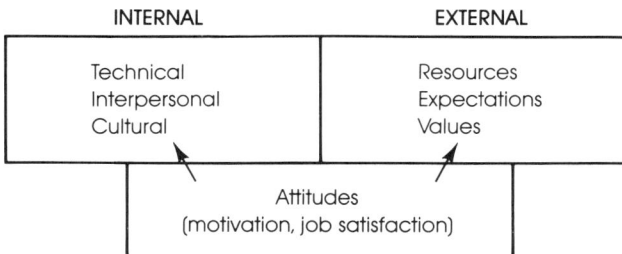

values, beliefs, and ideals that are powerful tools to communicate purposes, roles, and missions in the development of professionals. Without the proper context, growth cannot occur. Some cultures support and nurture growth, providing comfort at critical moments of self-doubt and allowing risk and change through security and encouragement.

Attitudes of professionals also play a significant role in the establishment of cultural norms for growth. Lieberman and Miller (1984) describe four themes that affect the daily life and shape the attitudes of teachers—rhythms, rules, interactions, and feelings. *Rhythms* refer to the notion of the cyclical pattern of school years (one can always start again, try new things, yet also observe that what was done can be undone). *Rules* provide limits and sanctions, yet set forth plans and suggest the potential power of individual classrooms. *Interactions* mean teachers and children communicating, teachers and teachers sharing as colleagues, and teachers and administrators setting the tone for success or failure. *Feelings* certainly influence attitudes and play a crucial role in how professional development will be perceived. "By understanding feelings, we appreciate ambiguity, vulnerability, and defensiveness as camouflages for commitment, concern and hope" (Lieberman & Miller, 1984, p. 15). Attitudes—both of and toward professionals—are key to understanding the internal and external contexts that influence growth. Before examining the external attitudinal influences, job satisfaction and motivation will be discussed, because attitudes are closely interwoven in these concepts.

Job Satisfaction and Motivation

Job satisfaction involves employees' attitudes and feelings of well-being in the workplace. A common definition relates job satisfaction to two perceptions on the part of the worker: (1) what the person thinks the job and work environment are providing, and (2) what the person believes the job should provide. Job satisfaction is the congruence between the needs of the individual and the expectations and outcomes of the organization.

Three areas in which satisfaction is considered are: the work itself; coworkers; and organizational policy and practice, which includes items such as salary, promotion possibilities, and job security/stability. Fielding and Schalock (1985) describe these three areas from a different perception. They suggest that organizations can provide satisfaction to their members through "achievement (being successful in accomplishing tasks)"—which corresponds to the work itself; "affiliation (feeling of belonging and affection)"—relating to coworkers; and "power (having reasonable control over one's work)"—which is part of organizational policy and practice.

Providing job satisfaction in education is a challenge when viewed through the achievement, affiliation, and power perspective. A teacher's level of achievement is most often defined by linking it to evaluation of performance of self and students. Yet, if being successful in accomplishing tasks means that children are taught well and learn well, teachers may not experience enough satisfaction. We discussed psychic rewards and satisfaction in the previous chapter, pointing out that the very things teachers value are difficult to measure and express. It is based on some factors over which teachers have no control, such as student ability, quality of instructional materials and curriculum, and the value placed on education in the community. Achievement can also be measured in terms of doing a job well and being promoted to a higher level. There are few promotional positions in schools, and those that do exist require leaving the classroom to do something different than that which was done well.

The organization must provide opportunities to enhance the performance level of the professionals, adequate finances to support the instructional programs and school buildings, and feedback mechanisms for teachers to check (with students and parents) their perceptions of how well they are doing. This feedback can validate their achievement and add to job satisfaction. Teachers need a sense of efficacy—the ability to influence outcomes and events. More creative options must be developed for teachers to stay in the profession and yet feel advancement. Such changes may necessitate more flexible scheduling, a new description of duties, differentiated staffing, combinations of teaching and administrative duties, and changes in the ten-month work year. Although most of these suggestions will create difficulty in the bargaining unit, they must be explored seriously. These provisions will improve job satisfaction in terms of achievement.

The affiliation dimension of satisfaction has drawn much attention, and we have dealt with the feelings of teachers working in separated classrooms with limited access to coworkers. Some schools have addressed this problem by creating teaching teams, providing common planning time, and establishing instructional advisory committees to increase opportunities for staff interaction, but more needs to be done to strengthen feelings of belonging and participation.

Closely related to the affiliation need is the power concern, defined as having reasonable control over one's work. We discuss empowerment in detail in this book, and the fact that this concept has emerged as a national issue illustrates how significant this issue is in the area of job satisfaction.

All of these issues also influence motivation, a closely related concept. Maslow's theory of psychological stages is often used to explain human motivation. Each level in his hierarchy needs to be fulfilled before a higher-level need emerges, and once a need has been gratified, it no longer serves as a motivator. The lower-order needs of physiological and safety factors do not provide much motivational potency for teachers. These needs are generally gratified at the beginning of the work agreement.

There is a difference between motivation and movement. Power and extrinsic rewards—if applied potently enough—can *move* people to action to complete tasks and be productive. Organizations often try to move people through the power of positional authority, monitoring, evaluating, sanctions, or compensation, all of which may not produce growth or motivation. In fact, the application of power has diminishing effects because as it is applied over time, greater power is needed to move people to action. Motivation, however, can be induced by providing the climate and opportunities in which people can meet their professional needs for continued growth and self-actualization, which will have a reciprocal effect on organizational effectiveness and success. The carrot of professional development is more powerful than the stick of organizational power. Motivation comes from within, whereas control is imposed from without.

Sergiovanni and Starratt (1983) discuss motivation theory and connect such needs to the degree of investment people place in their work. "Participation investments" relate to these lower-order needs mentioned earlier. For example, teachers must participate in schools by preparing lessons, interacting with students, attending meetings, following regulations, and being evaluated. If they do so successfully, they will be rewarded by benefits that satisfy their needs for security, social, and some esteem factors. Participation investment is not linked to the level of professionalism experienced on the job; it deals more with routine expectations.

Continued motivation of professionals must focus on their higher-order needs—for advanced esteem, autonomy, and self-actualization. Sergiovanni and Starratt term this level of activity "performance," which links to the professional's need for autonomy and self-fulfillment. This investment goes far beyond the expected work relationship to consider commitment, quality of work, dedication, and consistently high professional performance.

External Context for Growth

The context in which professional growth, job satisfaction, and motivation occurs seems to be primarily internal, but external factors also influence the existence and direction of such development. The values and expectations placed by clients on continuing education as well as the available resources determine the external environmental conditions.

For example, patients demand that doctors keep abreast of the latest medical research, procedures, and advancements in curing diseases. Clients expect their attorneys to keep current with new laws, court decisions, and judicial precedents. Corporate executives are regularly sent to retreats, training seminars, and courses to enhance their skills. Emphasis on areas like strategic planning, decision making, stress reduction, and handling conflict illustrate that developmental needs are broadly based and encompass more than job-related skills. People and organizations hire consultants regularly to ensure that they are getting the best advice and know the most current trends and practices to assist in their decision making or problem solving. Those professionals and organizations that are successful take the time to continuously learn and expand their expertise.

Is this the case in education? Do all of the participants and recipients of the educational process value continuing education and professional development? Traditionally, districts and communities have not recognized this need of the professionals to keep learning, and so have not been willing to provide the time and financial backing for such activity. But educational research has given us important information, and technology has placed new dimensions on teaching and learning. Providing high-quality educational service places the same development demands and requirements as on other professionals who depend on knowledge and information as a basis for their authority.

Context for Adult Growth in Schools: Summary

"Most schools are not organized to facilitate the developmental work of adulthood," concludes Levine (1989, p. 61). She raises a few additional issues that point out the complicated and problematic context of professional development. First, teaching keeps adults connected to the world of children and may prevent teachers' growth. Conflict can occur if teachers attempt to remain sensitive to childlike perspectives and understand and relate to children, yet develop maturity for themselves.

Second, the positive aspects of working in schools seem to favor those who may have a limited commitment to teaching—who have other priorities along with their job—because the advantages are short days and long vacation periods. There is a sense that some people select teaching because it fits into their lifestyle and affords time for other pursuits, such as further education, outside business, or raising a family. For these reasons, people in education would have little interest in professional development, and if they did, the structure of the work year discourages it on an in-depth, coordinated basis.

A third context to consider is the source of rewards and recognition. Development must focus on opportunities for interaction with significant other adults, such as colleagues and administrators. Designing growth activities should also recognize the repetitive nature of teaching, which can become tiresome. Each year, one must start over, acclimating students and adhering to the prescribed curriculum and programs. Teaching can be a very standardized occupation with limited chances for new experiences, unless teachers see different perspectives, are able to try new ideas, and can measure their impact. This starting over can be an exciting opportunity or a boring repetition, depending on attitudes and expectations.

These contexts pose some constraints in efforts for staff development. New structures, positive environments, and creative alternatives will characterize the transformation necessary in this important dimension. In order to design effective staff-development programs that translate transformation into practice, we need to understand the following:

- How organizations encourage or impede professional growth
- How adults grow, develop, and learn
- What the condition of teaching is in today's world
- Professionals' need for empowerment and participation
- How staff development, inservice training, and supervision are related

STAFF DEVELOPMENT

We're doing teacher education the same way we've been doing it for fifty years, the process is fundamentally flawed, and we need some utterly new models (Shulman, in Brandt, 1988).

If teachers are to shed their time honored role as transmitters of the present culture and assume the role of continuous learners, staff development practices must shift radically (McKenzie, 1987).

Are these minority opinions of recalcitrant educators who have given up on the system, or does the area of professional preparation and development fit into the transformation picture we have created? As early as 1980, Sanders and Schwab noted, "Despite forces operative among teachers that might move them naturally toward improvement of their skill, possibilities for teacher development are blocked by the same barrier of schooling's social structure. The picture is depressing but hardly unfamiliar" (p. 271).

In light of the previous discussions on professionals in organizations, the various stages adults pass through as they develop, the conflicts teaching presents in its current condition, and the needs professionals have for empowerment, it is obvious that successful transformation of schools considers how development programs must change to fit the future.

Many terms are used interchangeably to describe distinct processes of learning. Harris (1989) provides a clear contrast between staff development and inservice education. *Staff development* is the broadest term, which includes planning, career development, recruitment, creative assignment, personnel evaluation, as well as inservice education. The *inservice education* component of staff development relates specifically to "any planned program of learning opportunities afforded staff members of schools, colleges or other educational agencies for purposes of improving the performance of the individual in already assigned positions" (Harris, 1989, p. 18).

The entire process of staff development is important in transforming schools. Many states are currently evaluating their teacher preparation programs in colleges, licensing requirements for teachers and administrators, and testing and performance qualifications for permanent certification. They are also investigating the profiles of students who enter the teaching profession, and providing greater incentives to do so, because concerns have been raised that the best and the brightest choose other professions. School districts across the country regularly assess their programs for supervision and performance evaluation, but most of these programs are tied to a traditional model of teachers as subordinates.

For our purposes in looking at transforming schools, we will concentrate on the inservice education and supervision components of staff development to focus on the people who are already in the field. As we suggest the kinds of training programs necessary for those who are providing educational services, it is also true that these skills, attitudes, values, and perceptions should be built into teacher preparation programs. Teachers and administrators often say they did not feel adequately prepared through their formal undergraduate and graduate work to take on the complete responsibilities of their positions and that the on-the-job experience became the real training. These comments are understandable, based on what we believe educators need. Throughout the text, we have said they will need to know how to do the following:

- Deal with complexity and ambiguity
- View uncertainty as a positive force
- Challenge their perceptions of reality
- Understand how to work in nonrational organizations
- Blend individual needs with institutional roles
- Embrace technological innovation and respond humanely to clients
- Recognize that change may be the only constant of the future
- Maintain professional standards and meet organizational goals
- Protect autonomy and participate in team building
- Bring to the decision-making process both an individual and an organizational perspective
- Translate and apply research and theory to professional practice

How are these complicated tasks learned? How are such sophisticated skills practiced by teachers and students desiring to become teachers?

Neither preparation programs nor inservice training have begun to tackle these complex skills. There are few, if any, courses to help people understand the workplace environment in which and the people with whom they will work. The focus has been on tangible, observable activities, generic aspects of teaching and management, the "bee-like" reactive behavior, and prescriptive, step-by-step recipes for program implementation. In the context of thinking, perceiving, and behaving, the programs have targeted only the behavior aspect—the how-to's—instead of addressing pedagogy and higher-level thinking, perception, and intuition as they apply to educating children.

New "basic skills for adults" are emerging, both in education and other fields. The Center on Education and Employment at Teachers' College, Columbia University, has looked at new workplace needs in such fields as banking, insurance, and textiles. They concluded, "Employees at all levels must apply multiple criteria and deal with problems that have multiple solutions; be comfortable with nuances, interpretations and uncertainties; contribute to innovative solutions; understand the whole production process, not just a piece of it; and work collaboratively to solve problems" (Lewis, 1988, p. 469). These skills coincide with the descriptions we have suggested for educators and they set a clear, if very different, direction for the design of inservice programs.

A New Design: Assumptions

Programs to help staff members develop to their full potential are comprised of staff-development activities, inservice, and transforming supervision. These initiatives must do more than provide teachers with recipes, methods, and other practical ventures. They must help teachers use their talent to self-manage, by checking their perceptions and reviewing their cognitive structures, and by designing and implementing productive, quality programs. Table 9–2 illustrates the perception and thinking needed to redesign professional development, which will in turn alter behavior.

The design for professional development must take into consideration the need to change perception, thinking, and behavior of the people in schools—to have them continually question their practices and check them against the reality of their context and outcomes. Professional development is a "deliberate effort to alter the professional practices, beliefs and understandings of school persons toward an articulated end" (Fielding & Schalock, 1985, p. 5). Its purpose is to foster growth and to increase individual and school effectiveness as well as to improve instruction for student learning.

As programs begin to foster growth, educators' roles should become expanded. That articulated end should include (1) more opportu-

TABLE 9–2   Perception and Thinking for Professional Development

	Staff Development	Inservice	Supervision
Perception:	Individual- and group-oriented	Group-oriented	Individual-oriented
	Geared to the improvement of the profession	Geared to the improvement of the organization	Geared to the improvement of the individual
	Professional growth is valued	All professionals can enhance skills	Supervisors can be peers, partners
Thinking:	Global	Customized	Prescriptive
	Collaborative	Assessment, analysis	Analytical
	Broad focus	System focus	Specific focus
	Change established modes	Create new skills	Experimental
	Research, development	Higher-order processes	Multiple strategies

nities to make decisions in areas affecting work and in which the participants have expertise; (2) more options (for teachers) to work on
educational projects beyond the classroom and (for principals) beyond
the management aspects (research and experimentation, curriculum
development, long-range planning); and (3) new job roles to combine
teaching and leadership (Levine, 1989). The most important point to
understand in the development of new programs is that one blueprint
will not work. Guidelines, principles, and foundations will drive the
design, but each activity must reflect the people and places it is supposed to serve.

Lieberman and Miller (1984) researched the work and world of
teachers and concluded that because of the great variation in educators'
needs, single-purpose staff development or inservice will make no lasting difference or impact on the professionals. Some of the guiding
principles they suggested should be a part of transforming staff development. For example, programs should have a developmental nature, a
long-term focus, and far-reaching interaction and continuity.

There are common elements for these designs. Each must:

- Offer immersion and transformation in conceptual under-
  standing
- Inspire teachers to invent and create
- Be experience-based, so learning comes from doing and ex-
  ploring
- Hook the curiosity, wonder, and passion of teachers
- Consider the feelings, fears, and anxiety of the learners
- Engage the perspective of teachers (McKenzie, 1987, pp.
  101–108)
- Challenge mindsets and paradigms-in-use

Before creating new programs, however, we need to find out what
professional development looks like in other fields, to help us know
what those outside education think we may need for the future. This
reality check will ensure that we are up to date and connected to the
context in which education works. Greater effort should be made to
examine and apply approaches from innovative industries. There are
"links between schools and modern industrial firms that are centrally
concerned with the development and use of knowledge. New forms of
management, supervision and training that are emerging from knowledge industries may well have relevance for the design of professional
development programs in schools" (Fielding & Schalock, 1985, p. 72).

Instead of telling teachers what to do and how to do it, we must provide mechanisms for them to conduct research and investigations, experiment with ideas and not be evaluated at the same time, discuss successful practices, generate changes based on their accumulated knowledge, and practice problem-solving and decision-making skills as they apply to real situations in our schools. Time has to be creatively restructured to allow these activities to occur without eliminating learning time for students or shortening the school day. If contractual obligations get in the way of professional development and role experimentation, then negotiated agreements and unions will have to change radically.

Lambert (1989) proposes that these staff-development efforts are part of empowering the professionals as they participate in new ventures. She includes options, choice, authority, and responsibility as elements of empowerment. Options are the acknowledgment that various roles exist, there are many ways of accomplishing the work of teaching, alternatives in curriculum are possible, strategies for planning and implementation can vary, and time can be used in an infinite variety of ways. Linked to these notions is the fact that since there are alternatives, there are also choices to be made, and no one way is best. The recognition that teachers have options and can make choices suggests an increased authority in areas of decision making; and, finally, a renewed responsibility for those decisions—to plan and see them through, to share and communicate, and to train newcomers in the profession to value these elements. Such activities begin to make teachers educational leaders, who can contribute to the vision creation and missions needed to move schools forward. "Staff development must fulfill three needs"—that of the society to regenerate itself to create nurturing environments for all children; that of the school, which must develop the personal, social, and academic potential of its young people; and that of the individual professional's need to live a satisfying and stimulating life (McKibben & Joyce, 1980, p. 253).

Inservice Education

Inservice education in transforming schools will be driven by some basic assumptions gathered from research:

1. Inservice must offer the opportunity for teachers to work together in supporting, collegial ways to concentrate on important dimensions of teaching, learning, and their profession.
2. We must help teachers be pioneers, inventors, and discoverers —at the forefront of innovation, not in the background of secu-

rity and tradition. We need entrepreneurs—risk takers that move beyond the "adapt and adopt" philosophy of inservice.

3. New designs must be customized; that is, they must take into consideration the needs and interests of staff, cycles of professional growth, staff turnover, curves of learning, and variety in approaches and methods.

4. The focus of training will be long-term, not bandwagon, efforts, so that change can be nurtured and measured.

5. All activities must be congruent with the value system of the organization.

6. "So long as people make the crucial difference in school operation, their inservice education will be a vital concern. Even if a fully qualified, ideally competent staff were available, time would gradually erode that competence as conditions change and old competencies become obsolete. Even if new learnings could be gained from on-the-job experiences, staff turnover and the need to speed learning processes for some would still demand inservice education" (Harris, 1989, p. 12).

Challenges to Inservice Education

Unfortunately, the task of designing a comprehensive plan for inservice education is not as easy as accepting the research assumptions and charging forward with the specific activities to meet those assumed needs. Our knowledge of the enormous variety in the recipients of the plan sends messages of caution. Before creating any design, it is important to recognize that the professionals we hope to inservice are at various levels of interest and motivation, adult growth and development, and career and personal needs.

Levine (1989) describes school staffs as getting newer and getting older, in that approximately one-third of teachers have 3 years or less of experience, whereas most of the other two-thirds have over 15 years of experience. Staffs are now made up of young professionals with new ideas (in the first cycle of their professional lives) and veterans (at the third cycle—entrenchment). The majority is still a very experienced group. Finding programs that are challenging and interesting, that enhance their professional skills and change their perceptions and thinking, is a difficult assignment. Customized inservice is necessary and can be provided by matching people in cooperative ventures, through technology or by offering a variety of choices so people can select the one that best fits their needs.

As we have stated, not everyone is ever at the same readiness or acceptance level for change. Teachers at different stages of career development need different kinds of inservice. Some teachers have no interest, others need help in the most routine aspects of classroom instruction, and still others are extremely competent and want opportunities to share their expertise and work collaboratively. Some want leadership opportunities, whereas others are threatened by anything new. Teachers and administrators may be reluctant to experiment with innovations that may upset their routine and create uncertainty.

Another challenge is the fact elementary and secondary teachers generally focus on different concerns. Elementary teachers face dilemmas about coverage of a subject versus mastery of it, large- versus small-group instruction, and fitting in all the subjects they have to teach. Secondary teachers struggle with fitting instruction into structured time periods, operating within the organizational structure, and loyalty to colleagues versus students. These are nuts-and-bolts concerns. People whose focus is at this level are not ready to explore innovation, future visions, and transformational change. Because they are immersed in the everyday activities, they often do not know what they need, so their attitudes and perspectives toward inservice pose a further challenge. If inservice addresses their perceived needs, they will be receptive. Yet those individual, day-to-day needs may not be in consort with the mission of the school and the broader issues of education with which transforming schools must deal. We must end the superficial involvement in meaningless practicality that categorizes many inservice activities. To change perception and attitudes will require more complex and integrated plans, which are demanding and tied to specified outcomes.

Finally, as was mentioned earlier, the attitude of staff is not the only concern. The value placed on professional development in schools—by administration, boards of education, and the public—greatly influences the content, quality, frequency, and availability of programs. Time and funding for research and development are crucial to the creation and well-being of inservice programs. A long-standing criticism of public schools is that no time is devoted to research in districts. Research and theory building that is carried out in R & D centers of universities never gets applied to its intended source—the schools. Even when research findings clearly show directions for educators to take, the data are often ignored at the local level. For research to be applied, teachers must be directly involved in its design, implementation, and analysis.

The real problems confronting schools are enormous in comparison with any ideal situations. The gap between what is known and what is in practice is enormous in nearly every school setting. The gap between what people can do and what they are potentially capable of doing is also enormous for most staff members. Even the gap between what people are doing and what they want to do is very great for many staff members (Harris, 1989, p. 12).

Future professional development programs must rely on sound theory and research and then apply findings to professional practice in schools, if transformation is to become a reality.

In summary, inservice programs to professionalize teaching must allow teachers to reexamine and question their perceptions, to analyze and challenge their thinking, and to discover and experiment with new roles and behavior that will transform them from recipients and transmitters of knowledge to creators of it. Table 9–3 outlines transforming inservice in terms of perception, thinking, and behavioral dimensions.

Transforming Supervision

The process of supervision has undergone many changes over the last decade, primarily in attempting to refocus on supporting instructional efforts, building relationships between supervisors and teachers, and providing technical assistance. When schools transform, so must supervisory practices. The following assumptions will guide that process:

1. Supervision must be closely linked to professional development, since the purpose of supervision is to improve teaching and learning.
2. Supervision must be perceived as a growth-enhancing process, not as a way to determine who is not doing the job well.
3. New teachers need to receive regular instruction and feedback, have frequent visitations from the supervisor, and engage in dialogue about their instructional strategies and the curriculum they are teaching. They need opportunities to watch good teachers work and to discuss what they observe in order to incorporate ideas into their repertoire. They must feel comfortable to question and ask for help, both from colleagues and their supervisors. They must have the opportunity to learn the culture of the organization and the core values around which it operates.

TABLE 9–3   Inservice Education for Transformation

Perception	Thinking	Behavior/Outcomes
Congruent with values of school	Collaborative assessing	Staff works together toward common goals
Tied to mission of what school would like to become	Evaluating	Time is provided for reflection, investigation, research
Challenge present viewpoints, create discomfort	Use/value intuition	Learning strategies, assumptions, curriculum regularly evaluated
Foster innovation, experimentation	Research orientation	Teachers seek new places to visit, learn
Change mindscapes	Open-ended, divergent	Views, opinions from other professionals are sought
Cannot be isolated	Interdisciplinary ideas	Staff interacts with other fields to gain ideas, to keep in touch with outside world
Deal with subtantive issues, no recipes	Broad-based, flexible	Commitment to develop/improve culture
	Analysis/Synthesis	Programs and structures respond to emerging client needs
		Teachers are highly trained professionals, engaged in complex, important work
		Cooperative learning ventures that link teacher needs and professional cycles
		Input is sought from students, parents, and community
		Action research is conducted with and by staff in the schools, in conjunction with universities

4. New people coming into a system must be made to feel there is a strong commitment to helping them succeed. Support networks can make this happen.
5. Experienced teachers need different kinds of supervisory activities, not just fewer observations, as is often the case between nontenured and tenured staff. They need to feel free to experiment with new ideas and to develop creative approaches to the implementation of mandated curriculum. They need collegial discussions with supervisors where ideas are exchanged and suggestions come from both parties.

Supervision must be data-based, so that perceptions and schemas can be validated or changed. Otherwise, individual teacher behavior will remain the same.

New Design Ideas

One of the most promising supervisory practices for experienced teachers is peer coaching, or peer assistance. Peer programs are well received because they assume professional support as a guiding principle. Teachers help each other learn new skills and provide insight, assistance, and guidance in a nonthreatening atmosphere. Staff in one peer assistance program point to three major benefits: communication, rehearsal, and awareness (Chrisco, 1989). Obviously, if peers are planning together, observing each other, and learning additional techniques from colleagues, communication will increase and be based on professional sharing and dialogue. They refer to rehearsal as discussing a lesson about to be observed. As parts of the lesson are considered, there is reflection as to what will occur and therefore more examination into the teaching practices. Finally, awareness is heightened, in acknowledgment of unconscious processes coming to a conscious level and the ability to share problem solving with others (Chrisco, 1989). *Peer assistance* is often considered a broader term than *peer coaching*, because it can encompass more than observing classroom instruction. It can involve activities such as teachers teaching each other, sharing a unit across grades or subjects, or doing a combined research project.

The term *peer coaching* has gained wide recognition through the Madeline Hunter model for teaching and the work of Bruce Joyce. Its purpose is similar to peer assistance programs, but it is used mainly to provide support to new teachers and to create leadership opportunities for experienced ones. Chase and Wolfe (1989) define *peer coaching* as "a confidential arrangement between peers that includes a focused classroom observation and feedback on that observation. It is not evaluation; it does not certify a teacher's effectiveness. Instead, coaching provides teachers a means of examining and reflecting on what they do in a psychologically safe environment where it is all right to experiment, fail, revise and try again" (p. 37).

Hyman (1989) provides a comprehensive look at the positives and negatives of peer coaching, as he lists the premises around which this process was built:

- Teachers have the ability to help each other.
- Teachers want to change.
- If teachers do not presently have the skills to perform peer coaching, then they can learn them in a relatively short period of time and apply them.
- Teachers are professionals, who can act as do professionals in other fields to upgrade their actions.
- Teachers will accept and believe what their peers will say to them.
- Teachers can and will trust other teachers to lead them to positive change.
- Teachers are or can become reliable observers of other teachers.
- Teachers have or will learn adequate conceptual framework for observing and interpreting classroom talk and other events.
- Teachers are in control of their lives as teachers such that they can consciously determine to counter the forces that have created today's status quo.
- The people in control of the schools will permit the changes flowing from the implementation of peer coaching to take effect permanently no matter how these changes affect them (pp. 64–65).

Those changes, however, must be congruent with the values of the school district. We cannot make the assumption that all of these premises exist in schools today. If this is a significant concept, time and effort need to be spent to make them realities in transforming schools.

Innovations such as this offer promise to the professionalization of teaching by involving staff members in another segment of the educational process that directly impacts on their performance. In transforming schools, the emphasis of supervision matches what peer coaching is trying to do. "This innovation promises to reduce teachers' isolation, to create a collegial and professional environment in the school and to promote the transfer of skills from training to the workplace" (Chase & Wolfe, 1989, p. 37).

Hyman (1989) also advocates this approach and suggests that everyone involved in the educational enterprise should rally around it, because of its potential positive impact. "Peer coaching emphasizes staff development through self-renewal and self-improvement rather than by edict. Peer coaching seeks education which is humane; it counter-acts resentment, burn-out and self-destruction" (pp. 72–73).

In many places, principals are the supervisors, or central-office positions are created superordinate to teachers, thus all supervisory activities are conducted by "the boss." In these cases, strong efforts must be made to separate supervision and evaluation of teaching performance. A summary of supervision for transformation is found in Table 9–4.

Evaluation is a different process and even it can be built on some new premises. The process used for new teachers to determine whether

TABLE 9–4   Supervision for Transformation

Perception	Thinking	Behavior
Developmental, not evaluative	Integrated/ interdisciplinary	Validate effectiveness of ideas, methods, techniques
Not isolated activity	High order: analysis, synthesis, evaluation	Individual action research
		Focus on affective, cognitive, psychomotor skills
Foster innovation	Research-oriented: data, information	Collaborate with other teachers, mentors for feedback
Change mindscapes	Intuitive/analytical	Peer coaching
Create/feel passion for growth		Objective, goal-directed
		Networking, externships, links
Information-based		Divergent programs, not uniform profiles for supervision
Build on strengths		Value-added activities, to demonstrate growth
		Feedback-based, with parents, student input
		Measurement portfolios
		Data-based, validate perception, thinking

employment will be continued should not be the same as that used for experienced teachers. Evaluation for tenured teachers can be based on individual goals set by the staff member and supervisor, so that it too can be a shared process, not an adversarial one. Supervisors and principals must be trained as coaches and be willing to develop collaborative strategies with teachers to focus on transforming professional development.

SUMMARY

Adults learn and grow in different stages, and their values, motivation, learning styles, and receptivity to change vary greatly. Times, conditions, and factors within and beyond the school environment can influence growth and development.

Staff development and professional growth are powerful concepts, integral to the transformation of schools. Therefore, everyone involved in this process must understand adult learning, factors that contribute to job satisfaction, and the role of inservice, supervision, and evaluation in motivating growth. Competent professionals, confident with their expertise, are what we need and must insist on for all children to have successful school experiences.

When reexamining supervision in the context of transformation, these questions may guide perception and thought in new directions:

- Who should be responsible for supervision in an empowered environment?
- What is the destiny of an externally imposed, hierarchical structure for the supervision of professionals?
- If professional development results in increased competence and heightened self-esteem, is supervision necessary?
- Are professionals in other fields supervised, and if so, how?

CONCEPTS

1. Adults pass through various phases or stages as they develop, grow, and mature. Growth is subject to interactions individuals have with others, with the environment, and with themselves.
2. There is debate as to whether developmental patterns are precise and predictable or nonrational and sometimes unstable.

3. Adult growth patterns are important to understand when considering developmental activities in organizations.
4. Professional development is comprised of staff development, inservice education, and supervision.
5. Professional development should result in increased effectiveness for people, programs, and organizations.
6. Job satisfaction and motivation are desired outcomes of professional development.
7. The success of developmental programs is linked to internal and external environmental conditions, influences, and attitudes.
8. Staff development in education must be transformed to prepare professionals to deal with the complexities they will find in schools and to prepare them for education in the twenty-first century.
9. Transforming inservice must encompass the perception, thinking, and behavior of professionals so that they become both creators and transmitters of new knowledge, not simply recipients of it.
10. Peer coaching offers promise as a professional strategy to transform supervision in schools.
11. Supervision and evaluation of teachers and administrators will be based on collaborative techniques and the accomplishment of shared missions and purposes.

10 Professionals: Empowerment and Participation

> An Eastern European economist was discussing the economy of his country with a Western journalist. He said, "There are only two ways to restore and revive the economy—the natural way or the miraculous way."
>
> "The natural or miraculous way?" the journalist questioned.
>
> "Yes. The natural way would be if a group of angels came down from heaven and created jobs and prosperity for everyone."
>
> "That's the natural way?" the journalist blurted, "Then what's the miraculous way?"
>
> "If we took the initiative and did it ourselves," he retorted.

According to this thinking, schools will have to transform the miraculous way—through the initiative and action of professionals. In order to take initiative, people need some semblance of authority and power to deal with the challenges they face in school situations.

Contrary to popular thought, the level of uncertainty and ambiguity can be an advantage because it enables professionals to control their own destiny—to seek, explore, cooperate, and use their expertise to find answers. In effect, uncertainty is power inducing because it places knowledge, expertise, and research at the center of problem solving. Professional judgment carries weight, along with collaborating with others to find answers. Individuals will explore, define, and take risks and responsibility to solve issues, instead of relying on some external, controlling authority.

Using uncertainty as a positive force is an example of a paradigm shift discussed in Part I of this book.

225

When we believe with certainty that someone else can decide for us or that we can control what will happen, we lose the capacity to receive and use information. Instructional improvement is a constant cycle of decisions, discoveries, and further decisions. As we explore the unknown in accepting uncertainty, we unlock school reform and enter a new phase of professionalism (Glickman, 1987, p. 122).

Bacharach & Conley (Sergiovanni & Moore, 1989) state that the greater the uncertainty and ambiguity teachers confront in their classrooms, the less effective bureaucratic strategies are. The more unpredictability that exists, the more effective professional strategies can be.

Uncertainty is vital to most professions and is at the heart of teaching. It revolves around what students know, what they are learning, and what instructional content they need to learn. With the variety and number of students teachers see each day, there is doubt about how well each is learning and comprehending. There is also the problem of knowing how students learn best. These ambiguities are endemic to teaching at all levels. The second uncertainty—instructional content and methods—concerns selecting content appropriate for the students. Teachers are also uncertain about what instructional methods work best or are most productive. For elementary teachers, who are not subject-matter specialists, there may also be some doubt about their own knowledge in certain content areas (Floder & Clark, 1988).

Such uncertainty may not bring out exploring and risk taking, as Glickman expects. People fall into routines to reduce uncertainty and to adapt to complexities, even when the results are not satisfactory (Floder & Clark, 1988, p. 516). Routines are nothing more than habitualized thought and action, which increase predictability and provide security.

Uncertainty, however, can provide opportunity for professionals to control their destiny through knowledge and expertise if they perceive and think about it differently. Control and power, when viewed as complementary principles, describe the empowerment of teachers suggested by the reform movement.

POWER AND EMPOWERMENT

Confusion often results whenever discussions of power take place. Related terms are used interchangeably, such as *authority*, *control*, *autonomy*, and recently *empowerment*. Power is defined in detail in Chapter 4; our purpose here is to explain the link between power and the concept of empowerment.

From a traditional view, control comes from power. Power is a positive force without which little would get accomplished. One definition of *power* is "the need to control other persons, to influence their behavior and to be responsible for others (Dunham, 1984, p. 116). There are two general ways that people satisfy their need for power—through personalized or socialized means. Personalized power seekers attempt to dominate others because that domination provides satisfaction. Socialized power seekers, on the other hand, are concerned with group goals. It is this socialized type of power that is connected with empowerment.

Power and autonomy, however, are not the same thing. *Autonomy* is independence from the control of other subunits in the organization. *Power* is the ability of one unit to impose its will on an other (Hanson, 1985, p. 100). The dictionary defines *empowerment* as giving authority or power to others. How effectively this power is used to produce results determines the efficacy of those empowered.

Bennis (1989) indicates that empowerment is the collective effect of leadership, which has four strands. First, empowered people feel like they can make a critical difference, are significant, and have meaning. Second, learning and competence do matter. Leaders value mastery and mistakes are allowable because they provide knowledge and feedback. Third, empowered people feel a sense of community. Unity, team, and family are evident. Finally, in an empowered environment, work is exciting and challenging. Empowerment by leadership is magnetic in that it pulls people to a sense of mission and energizes them to act individually in the pursuit of collective goals (pp. 22–23).

In an interview, Ann Lieberman (Brandt, 1989) states that empowerment means involving other people authentically in dealing with their professional lives. This allows real participation in making decisions; unfortunately, however, decision making is often seen as the bottom line of empowerment. To many, empowerment is defined only in terms of governance —who makes what decisions and who divides up what power. But that is a narrow view of the concept of empowerment. Maeroff (1988) believes that empowered teachers have a sense of authority over what they do and are perceived as experts. "Empowerment can mean running the show, but many teachers say they do not want responsibility for all the decisions in their schools. What they desire is that their voices be heard and heeded. They yearn for dignity. They want their needs and opinions reflected in the policies of the school and of the district" (p. 475).

Empowerment comes from two sources: (1) structure, practices, and policies; and (2) personal choices professionals make in their own actions. In essence, empowerment is just as much a state of mind as it is authority for decision making. Empowered people feel that:

- Their survival is in their hands because they take responsibility for their situation and do not blame others.
- They have a sense of purpose and work means more than making money. They work for things that have meaning for them.
- They are committing themselves to achieving that purpose—they know what they want to do and get it done (Block, 1988, p. 65).

How organizations are run affects whether the environment will be an empowered or bureaucratic one. Leaders who want to develop an empowering environment must adopt tactics that foster it. Table 10–1 defines authentic behavior that is empowering.

Any dissonance in words and action of the leader will undermine credibility and will deter the creation of an empowered environment. According to the National Education Association study (1988) on the conditions of teaching, however, principals are not behaving in ways that empower. Only about 35 percent of the teachers in the study felt that their administrators asked them for their opinions or for information. Some 45 percent thought their administrators did not, and half indicated that they are seldom given information or suggestions. Knowledge in these circumstances is not shared.

Empowering leaders also confront. They confront people with reality, which is an act of compassion, not violence (Block, 1988). People are treated poorly when they do not receive communication and are kept in the dark; acts of withholding or omission are condescending and paternal. Bureaucracies do not want tension—smoothing the wa-

TABLE 10–1   Empowerment: Leader Behavior

Empowering Leaders:

Say No When They Mean No:
- let others know where they stand
- do not "fog" issues or study them to death

Share as Much Information as Possible:
- let people know plans, ideas, changes
- don't act as employees' parents—protecting them from information and facts

Express Themselves Clearly:
- don't use euphemisms
- get the message through

Avoid Repositioning for the Sake of Acceptance:
- don't pursue fads
- translate intentions into reality

Source: Peter Block, *The Empowered Manager* (San Francisco: Jossey-Bass, 1988), p. 90.

ters and "keeping the lid on" are virtues. Block asserts that tensions in organizations can only be postponed, not avoided. They are a sign of life and the beginning of a dialogue about issues. Growth of people or organizations does not exist without tension; fine lines can be drawn between anxiety and excitement.

Professional Empowerment

The roots of professional empowerment rest in knowledge and competence. Without mastery of skills, knowledge, and strategies, authority based on competence is a fleeting notion. Garrison (1988) states that knowledge and the ability to obtain it is power and "the legitimization of practitioner-knowledge would lead to the empowerment of teachers" (p. 501).

Teachers must polish, improve, and expand research, diagnostic, and teaching techniques. Instructors need a mastery of subject matter content and an understanding of the interdisciplinary nature of knowledge. The dynamics of curriculum structure, development, and evaluation must be conceptualized to be involved in those decisions with authority. Thoroughly understanding teaching and learning is the domain of professional empowerment for teachers.

For this empowerment to take place, several avenues must be open for teachers. Certainly inservice opportunities are available, but, as was stated in the previous chapter, the structure will have to change for it to be more effective. If inservice does not affect perception and thinking, then knowledge will not be translated into behavioral excellence. Staff training should not be aimed at conformity but at alternatives, and it should be solution-oriented, rather than simply product-centered (Perelman, 1987, p. 57).

TIP | TRANSFORMATION INTO PRACTICE

SPECIALISTS AND OVERSPECIALIZATION

The perception of specialists is different from that of generalists. Their view is based on concentrated knowledge and expertise in one facet of organizational life. Theodore Sizer, in *Horace's Compromise* (1984), stated, "The result of specialist training is to freeze high school organization into specialist molds. Teachers lose opportunities to help students when, because of the narrowness of their training, they shy away from these promising real views of the world" (p. 190).

Raelin (1986) indicates that organizational segmentation leads to overspecialization. He believes that as professionals specialize, they "know more and more about less and less. Feeling insecure and seeking comfort with associates in a similar predicament, professionals such as these concentrate more and more on what they know. Each skill group begins to think of itself as superior and independent of others. Coordination of these professional groups, by this point, becomes a management nightmare" (p. 101).

Schools have become more specialized. The general classroom teacher has been replaced by subject specialists, guidance and counseling specialists, gifted and talented specialists, administrative specialists, learning disabilities specialists, Chapter I specialists, emotional disturbance specialists, substance abuse specialists, evaluation specialists, sex education specialists, and others. Schools have become more segmented and fragmented, and the students and their problems have been categorized, grouped, and labeled. In some cases, responsibility for a student's achievement has been scattered among a group of specialists with no one person responsible for the overall program for the child. In other cases, when a student runs into difficulty, specialists review the situation and respond to it by recommending treatment or intervention by another specialist. Specialists develop different perceptions of problems and attack issues by applying their particular knowledge and methods. That is how they have been trained.

In the private sector, there is a move for people to work on entire projects, rather than just a small part of them. Collaboration and group problem solving is applied, matrix structures are instituted, and quality circles are used to improve quality and productivity and to expand perspective. Individuals receive training in the broad scope of projects and processes.

In other fields there is still a need for generalists. In medicine, there are general practitioners who practice family medicine. Law has an important niche for those in general practice, as well as for specialists in narrow legal areas. What about schools?

How does specialization affect service to students?
Do specialists promote bureaucractic practices in schools?
How should specialists be integrated into schools?
Should specialists receive higher status than general classroom teachers?
How specially or generally should teachers be trained and educated?
What impact do specialists have on how schools identify and think about problems?

Empowerment can also take place when teachers build networks, develop bonds to others, and collaborate to solve problems. They need to break out of their isolation and better understand how their roles tie into the greater mission of the school and district. Knowledge coupled with confidence can fire enthusiasm and influence. Personal competence is liberating and, in itself, authority inducing and influence producing.

A third avenue that must be open for empowerment to occur is the perception of teachers' organized bargaining units. First, "unless unions are willing to be flexible, there is not likely to be room for maneuvering that empowerment demands. The rigid enforcement of contract provisions is more suitable to the assembly line than to the classroom, where success often depends on improvision" (Maeroff, 1988, p. 477). Professionals in the classrooms and in the central offices must deal with the dichotomy of unions in professional organizations. Empowerment will not ever be implemented in its true form if it is a bargaining tool, instead of a common concept on which to build success.

Finally, the fourth and broadest avenue of empowerment is decision making. Knowledge and expertise must be applied to have effect. In schools, that means that intelligent decisions must be made. Schools cannot be successful if decisions are not effective in the classroom, in individual schools, or in the district collectively. In decentralized school systems, particularly, decision making needs knowledgeable people at all levels of the system who can interpret data and share information. If people are competent to make decisions and are involved in the process, their commitment and motivation increases. Decision making encourages reflective evaluation, change, and modification.

Research indicates teachers do not feel adequately involved in decisions. A National Education Association study (1988, p. 21) indicated that 63 percent of the teachers want more influence in hiring, testing, budget, spending, and faculty assignment and deployment decisions. Some 70 percent want more influence in staff development, and 63 percent desire greater influence in their own evaluation decisions. The study cautions, however, that "teachers can be involved in decision-making without becoming defacto administrators, and administrators can seek advice, suggestions and information from teachers without giving up their decision-making power or appearing weak" (p. 24).

Being empowered to make decisions requires competence and autonomy and brings with it responsibility and accountability. Teachers who are empowered cannot be dependent and hide behind the adage that "It's not my responsibility." Block (1988) states, "The payoff for dependency is that if we act on someone else's choice and it does not work out well, it is not our fault. Dependency is the wish not to be responsible and held accountable for our actions. It is the choice of innocence. Autonomy is the choice of guilt. When we act on our own choices, we define our own future" (p. 101).

Lack of responsibility and accountability can be the result of incompetence, complacency, or lack of interest in teaching. The small but significant number of teachers in this category cannot be ignored because empowerment will not work with them. Maeroff has strongly stated, "Meanwhile if they are serious about empowering teachers, unions must ultimately become partners with school systems in ridding schools of tenured teachers whose level of incompetence is such that empowering them would be like letting children drive cars" (1988, p. 477).

Transforming schools do end teacher "innocence" and incompetence. They require responsible and accountable decisions based on student needs. Providing the opportunity for personal and professional empowerment requires maturation on the part of teachers, their organizations, and the formal school structure. Teachers cannot be protected and treated as children.

Two kinds of autonomy have been discussed in the research—strategic and operational. Strategic autonomy concerns discretion over ends, whereas operational autonomy refers to means. Professionals need operational autonomy in schools (Elmore & McLaughlin, 1988, p. 106). Goodlad (1984) found that there are differences in perception of teachers' power and autonomy in schools they describe as "more" or "less" satisfying. Principals in the more satisfying schools felt they had more autonomy to work with the staff in the use of time and influence over decisions affecting their schools than those principals perceived by teachers to be less satisfying (p. 179). In classrooms, teachers perceive themselves to be quite autonomous. A large majority, 76 percent, indicated they had the right amount of autonomy in classroom decisions. But they felt progressively less control over setting goals and objectives, selecting content to be taught, grouping students for instruction, choosing instructional materials, and scheduling time (Goodlad, 1984, p. 188).

Empowerment and autonomy assume that teachers are going to be able to participate actively in the processes of planning, implementing, and evaluating. It also means that as a result of their participation, the structure of the school may differ, the perception of the professional's role is altered, and greater emphasis will be placed on accountability and responsibility. Transforming schools tap the knowledge of human resources to be successful, because serious progress cannot take place if talented people are isolated and cut off from participation.

Implications of Empowerment

Empowerment presumes there is a lack of power so that individuals must be given power or authority to act. A related term, *efficacy*, concerns the power to produce effects or intended results. Both empowerment and efficacy center around the linkage between power, control, and action.

Power and control concern structure. Structuring schools around a professional, rather than a bureaucratic, model alters roles, role relationships, the focus and locus of decisions, and expectations for teacher accountability. An empowering organizational structure implies that:

- Teachers have consistent input into the professional operation of the schools through their individual expertise, not simply via a negotiating and bargaining process.
- Ethical standards for accepted practice are stipulated and followed. Unacceptable professional behavior and malpractice would be defined with procedures established to deal with infractions.
- Accountability for student outcomes and instruction would rest with individual practitioners, instead of being buried in the bureaucracy. Teachers with autonomy and authority have the responsibility to meet accountability expectations.
- Teachers would have more time to reflect and think about educational practice (e.g., working a longer contract year for thoughtful input and evaluation).
- Teachers would have greater input into who teaches and practices in the district. They would have a role in setting professional standards, employment procedures, and evaluation processes. Decisions about colleagues' competence and development would be made on professional standards and not on the basis of a labor agreement.
- Teachers' ability-authority gap—that discrepancy between authority to act and the ability to take action—would be closed. In many schools, parents hear the refrain, "I don't have the authority to make those decisions." Teachers would have the authority and autonomy, with concomitant responsibility, for competent performance.
- Autonomy, a cherished commodity, would be tied with professional accountability, as in other professions.

Empowering teachers also has implications for leadership. In organizations with empowered professionals, the face of leadership changes. It focuses on values, mission, and purpose, rallying people to reach significant goals and objectives. Empowerment and leadership are not mutually exclusive concepts, implying laissez-faire or anarchistic management. The implications for transforming leaders in empowering organizations are:

- Authority for leadership comes from competence in motivating people, linking purpose and outcomes with practice and performance. The ability to define a vision of what the schools can be and fusing people's needs with organizational goals is essential.
- People are "pulled" by leadership more than they are "pushed." Purpose and mission motivates and attracts followers who become committed to them.
- Leaders have a strong ethical imperative and act on it to ensure that students' needs are being met and that ethical standards are followed. Leaders do not allow the core values of the organization to be violated.
- Decisions are shared with those closest to the issue who have the knowledge to solve problems and help the schools become more effective.
- Leadership comes from many areas, not just principals or positions with designated power. There is leadership density.

One other facet of school life that will be affected by empowerment is teacher organizations. Teacher organizations, as has been mentioned, wield a great deal of power and influence on the educational agenda and the structure of schools through negotiations and political pressure. They sanction the behavior of teachers positively or negatively. The implications of an empowered school for teacher organizations are:

- Teachers would be free to make choices in policy and practice without retribution, even if those choices do not agree with the political or policy decisions of the teacher organization, locally or nationally. Teachers must be free to practice outside union dogma or political needs.
- Teachers' organizations must empower their members to act as professionals with deference to clients' needs (the students) and not to colleagues or to the teacher organization itself. Student needs are primary.
- Seniority would not have a place in determining who works on what project, in what school, or in what position. Empowering schools are competence driven. Skill, knowledge, and perfor-

mance, not time, in a career are key ingredients in empowering schools.

* Because teacher roles are different, one universal contract clause cannot apply to all practitioners, whether they are teachers of kindergarten, physics, physical education, or home economics. Master contract clauses determine bureaucratic procedures, intensify rule-driven behavior, and limit teacher autonomy and choice.

The change needed in professional expectations and accountability, the redirection of educational leadership, and the alteration of the role and approach of teacher organizations are not easy issues. Power redistribution is threatening and laden with difficulty.

PROFESSIONAL PARTICIPATION

Gardner (1964) warned, "One of the clearest dangers in modern society is that men and women will lose the experience of participating in meaningful decisions concerning their own life and work, that they will become cogs in the machine because they feel like cogs in the machine" (p. 7). Participation is beneficial to individuals and productive for organizations.

Innovative organizations implement many changes through participation. Kanter (1984) indicates that masters of change also master using participation. Participation creates the excitement of being involved and having an impact, but it needs to be managed. Highly specialized and centralized organizations can make decisions faster and have a shorter "learning curve." Participatory organizations, while slower to get started, eventually respond faster.

Participation can enhance motivation, commitment to change, cooperation, and the quality of decisions. It also improves the flow of information because it must be shared in order for decisions to be made. A simple definition of *participation* is "joint decision making" (Baloff & Doherty, 1989, p. 52). For individuals, participation in decisions meets needs for personal control, and provides a sense of accomplishment and meaningfulness. In education, teacher participation is positively correlated to job satisfaction and morale, trust in school leaders, and reduced conflict in their jobs, according to Bacharach and Conley (Sergiovanni & Moore, 1989, p. 323). They indicate that a lack of participation is a factor in many teachers leaving the profession.

Participation: Dilemmas

Participation does have its dilemmas. It does not produce happy, contented employees automatically, and there is no no simple formula to make it meaningful and significant. Kanter (1984, pp. 241–275) identified, quite comprehensively, the dilemmas of and guidelines to effective participation. She defines several areas of dilemmas: beginning involvement, participation in what issues, the structure of participation, developing teamwork, and evaluation.

Many leaders want participation but do not know how to get it. Can participation be imposed on those who do not want it? Mandating involvement is a paradox that runs against the grain of people having some autonomy in their professional lives. On the other hand, if participation relies on volunteers, it may not be representative. If it is mandated, it might be perceived as coercive. From an organizational standpoint, problem-solving teams need the right skill and knowledge mix. Some leaders can fall into the paternalistic trap of granting participation—treating it as a gift—and then wonder why people are not grateful to them (pp. 244–246).

The second dilemma is defining the issues that need participation and involvement. Kanter indicates that employees would rather be involved in local issues—those that affect them and their jobs. Issues closest to jobs are ones that promote effective participation. But managers sometimes fall into the "Big Decision Trap," believing that people want to become involved in problems of greatest concern to the organization. In fact, Kanter asserts that people understand that some issues belong to management.

Another facet of the issue dilemma is the "Agenda Trap"—the need for visible results. "Too much talk and too little action" wilts enthusiasm for being involved. Spending time in participatory activities must produce something tangible and visible; otherwise, involvement is seen as a sham—a waste of valuable time. Involvement of people is not laissez-faire leadership. It requires structure and delegation because leadership must support the process and "mobilize others and set constraints" as "important ingredient(s) to making participation work" (p. 249). The key is to create a structure for participation that enables people to work creatively, autonomously, and responsibly within the boundaries that are established.

Third is the dilemma of creating effective teamwork. Experienced people leave and new ones come, so that maintaining continuity can be difficult. Newcomers often feel insecure and like outsiders, particularly if the team has a great deal of esprit. Not being involved previously in the problems can put new members at a participation disadvantage because of a lack of knowledge, information, and cultural expectations.

Even when teams remain constant, they still need renewal activities to avoid problems. For example, too much team spirit can be damaging, particularly if that feeling isolates team members from the rest of the staff. The committee may lose sight of the larger context and develop a narrow perception of the issues and possible solutions. Power problems can result when other people, who think they have a stake in the issue, feel segmented from the process.

Participation can also fall into bureaucratic traps. Committees can become rigid and operate with higher-status people dominating, if members fear challenging the notions of those with organizational titles. People who maneuver for status and play politics can disrupt committee effectiveness. Another political problem is the penchant for peer conformity or group-think. Peer conformity can oppress involvement just as easily as pressure from managers. Some committees deter discussion of differences because it seems disloyal to the concept of "team." Under this perception, people become hesitant to express differing opinions.

Finally, there is the dilemma of evaluation, specifically the "Great Expectations Gap." People can be disappointed in participation if too much is promised. Involvement is not a panacea that will solve all organizational problems, create perfect remedies, or stimulate high morale and good feeling. Productivity outcomes may be mixed, but there is usually an increase in the satisfaction of people if they realize that participation, as a process, can mobilize more resources in resolving issues.

Kanter (1984) indicates that leaders must maintain a shared vision in the organization around which participation revolves. The areas of participation need to be defined, as should the constraints of involvement. She defines the balance necessary for effective participatory systems as having:

- Clearly defined management structures
- Task assignment with clear boundaries
- Time frame for accountability and reporting relationships
- Mechanisms to involve others to avoid problems and resolve issues
- Processes to define and formulate groups and transfer knowledge and learning
- Means to recognize and reward groups and provide visibility (p. 275)

TABLE 10—2   Participation: When Inappropriate?

Participation is inappropriate when:
- One person has more expertise than others
- Those affected acknowledge that expertise
- People know the "right" answer because it is obvious
- No one really cares about the issue
- The subject is part of someone's responsibility and he or she did not formulate the committee
- No development or learning important to others will occur as a result of participation
- There's no time for discussion
- People work more productively and happily alone

Source: Rosabeth Moss Kanter, The Change Masters (New York: Simon and Schuster, 1984), p. 243.

Involvement is positive in the right situation, but participation is not universally appropriate. Table 10—2 specifies when participatory management may not be effective.

Participation: Negatives

Just as there are times when participation is inappropriate, people participating can feel negative consequences for doing so. Baloff and Doherty (1989, pp. 51—59) chronicle the negatives for participation which relate to peers, management, and their roles.

One obvious negative is the impact of peers. Negative peer pressure appears when participation is seen as collaboration with management against the interests of employees. In environments where there is tension between management and employees, peer pressure can be intense. This situation can result in sanctions against those who get involved. Sanctions range from mild (verbal cautions or reprimands and isolation from the group) to serious (acts of violence against property or persons).

A second negative arises from management if it attempts to coerce people during participation, to influence the outcome and retaliate if the results are contrary to management's wishes. Coercion can be a factor when management has a direct and critical stake in the outcomes, when it has little experience with participation, or when power differentials are high. In these circumstances, overt actions against an employee can occur, such as the assignment to undesirable duties or withholding desirable roles. The result is employee resentment toward management.

Baloff and Doherty (1989) indicate that participation, because of its positive characteristics of involvement and motivation, can create dissatisfaction with the individuals' previous roles. They may have difficulty adapting at the end of a highly motivating participative project, particularly if they must return to routine or rigidly structured activities. The duration and intensity of involvement are key factors, as well as the changed perceptions of the participants.

SUMMARY

Teachers desire to participate meaningfully in the life of schools. It is hard to argue against participation, since its intent is to increase morale and satisfaction, create greater commitment, and foster adaptation to change.

According to a study by Conley, Schmidle, and Shedd (1988, pp. 259–280), the case for teacher participation in school decisions will be weak if it is based on the premise that involvement is something "given" to teachers by school boards and administrators. Teachers must see participation as something received from rather than given by administrators and school boards. If the agenda is so circumscribed and tight, the resources so limited, the discretion so strangled, then benefits of participatory strategies will be doomed (p. 260).

The more teacher involvement in planning, implementing, and evaluating school district "policies, programs and resources, the more influence the school and district can be expected to have on the classroom" (Conley, Schmidle, & Shedd, 1988, p. 265). This involvement increases consensus on goals and priorities and breaks the narrow perception teachers may have when isolated. Seeing the broader picture and understanding their role in the greater scheme of things will influence classroom decisions.

Few teachers have "opportunities to engage in substantive dialogue and exchange of information, even though their pedagogical knowledge, skills, and information about students are arguably school systems' most valuable resource" (Conley, Schmidle, & Shedd, 1988, p. 266). The reason, they indicate, is the isolation of teachers because of the structure of their schedules, the layout of buildings, the solitary nature of their assignments, and the organizational norms that discourage giving advice or interfering.

Schools must cultivate organizational and professional knowledge. Otherwise, people may be working at cross-purposes or "reinventing the wheel." Teachers can help translate policies into assignments, design curriculum and programs, reconcile conflicting priorities, assist in developing human resources, distribute material resources, and monitor progress.

There are traditional means in schools today for participation. Department and faculty meetings have always been available, even though many times they are used to share information from the top down. Ad hoc committees and team-teaching designs are also used in some schools. Newer or nontraditional ways are quality circles, used in the private sector to share information, build commitment, and improve quality and productivity. Peer assistance, particularly in the staff-development process, is also a means to share information and proffer advice, as was discussed in the preceding chapter.

CONCEPTS

1. Uncertainty and ambiguity should not be considered negative forces in schools, because unpredictable situations require professional knowledge and innovative problem-solving strategies.

2. Teachers operate in constant uncertainty as they work with educating children who have complex and diverse needs and abilities.

3. *Personalized* power relates to domination, whereas *socialized* power is concerned with group goals and is at the heart of empowerment.

4. Empowerment means more than just participation in governance; it means involving people authentically in dealing with their professional lives—providing the climate and atmosphere for them to meet their potential.

5. Empowerment comes from structure, practices, policies, and personal choices professionals make. The roots of professional empowerment lie in knowledge and competence.

6. Transforming schools for professional empowerment requires a change in expectations and accountability, redirection of leadership, and alteration of the role and approaches of teacher organizations.

7. Empowerment and participation go hand in hand to create effective decision-making teams.

8. Participation has both positive and negative attributes.
9. Teachers should participate in decisions affecting curriculum, instruction, academic skills, and achievement; counseling, social and emotional needs of students; and the management of the physical and group environment.
10. Transforming schools must create new avenues for increasing teacher participation and empowering professionals to achieve success and productivity.

PART V SYNTHESIS

The transformation process is not fragmented or segmented. The emphasis is on an interdisciplinary and integrated view of broad-based organizational reform. The concepts and principles applying to organizational and human transformation and leadership cannot be applied effectively in isolation of each other. They must be fused into a coherent whole to have an impact on the schools' quality and success, the teachers' morale and motivation, and the leader's effectiveness and influence.

Part V synthesizes the concepts in these three areas and provides guidelines for transformational perception, thinking, and behavior to move schools beyond restructuring and into continuous adaptation and success.

11 Transformation: Schools, Leadership, and People

In the past, the United States was a competitive nation because its economic and political power were based on industrial prowess and the availability of natural resources. The invention of the microchip and other technological advances elevated knowledge as the major resource. Using knowledge and applying information require developed minds and reduce the reliance on strong backs or mechanized labor. A highly literate and educated populace is required, not only for economic reasons but also for a civil and cultured society. The quality of schools and how well our diverse society is educated forms the basis for the nation's integrity, competiveness, and stature. In this last decade of the twentieth century, public schools will either respond to the task of education or they will fail.

The major premise of this book is that without adapting to changing times and conditions, organizations will become ineffective and unsuccessful. Schools are no different. The past chapters have outlined the changed context of schools; presented the elements of successful schools, educational quality, and professional productivity; and discussed organizations, leadership, and human resources—the three major components of educational systems. An integrated perspective of organizations, leadership, and professionals is a prerequisite for understanding schools' operation and transforming them.

MAJOR PREMISES

The case for transforming schools rests on several premises, which concern the context, scope, and nature of bringing about change.

Proposition 1: Schools cannot remain the same when their context has changed dramatically. The demands on education are different because of the economic competition, which requires greater workforce skills and literacy. There has been a transformation in the world's economy over the past 20 years. U.S. military and economic power has been challenged—producing a monumental deficit, the loss of jobs to off-shore countries, the loss of basic industries like steel, and the development of new high-tech and service jobs. Knowledge will be the determining factor in nations' economies in the future, requiring higher levels of informed workers in the professions and in research and development.

The social context has also been altered. Most educators have observed and dealt with the impact on children—divorce, drugs, excessive poverty, and the like. These issues directly affect classrooms and the ability of students to learn. Only 41 percent of the students in school who reach the age of 18 come from a "nuclear family," the stereotype of earlier times. The rest come from different circumstances—12 percent are born out of wedlock, 40 percent will have their parents divorce before they are 18 years old, 5 percent are born to parents who separate, and 2 percent will have a parent die during their school years. There are more minorities, more boys and girls from impoverished households, more latchkey children, and more who have teenage parents.

Proposition 2: To be successful, schools must transform, not just restructure or renew. The major issue in schools is not governance (i.e., who makes what decision); it is greater than that. Transformation is a value-based, not structural-based, change. It requires that present perceptions be checked against the reality of the context of schools and outcomes they produce. If the perceptions are not valid, then thinking about programs, curriculum, instruction, and goals must change.

Restructuring does not target core values or question basic assumptions and perceptions; it focuses on structures and patterns of organization. Restructuring is a narrower concept and is a subset of transformation. The potential for long-lasting change is limited if organizational perception and thinking are not affected.

Proposition 3: Change must affect the entire organization, in a broad-based approach, and not in a small, piece-meal fashion. Any successful change initiative cannot be completed if the beginnings are so modest that no one knows an initiative is afoot. Small pilot projects may be good for developing prototypes, but transforming an organization requires that change affect all facets—personnel, program, staff development, structure, procedure, policy, and finances. Transformation is value-based, built around the precepts and standards the schools represent and wish to achieve. Without "getting the entire organization into the room" to participate in change, individuals will not understand the values behind it. Instead, they will build defenses, will not feel ownership in the process, and thus will not have to address priorities.

Proposition 4: People commit to values: Change, autonomy, and empowerment are derived from them. Values, not policy or structure, drive change. People do not commit to work because of practices or policies. The adults in schools need to grow to become competent professionals who are responsible for their decisions and who can be trusted with the power invested in them to act ethically in performing their roles. Professionals need standards around which to determine practice. Autonomy and empowerment are grounded in values and principles. Empowerment is not simply about decision making; it rests on a covenant of shared ideas, purpose, and values to which people commit, and a culture that allows them to be all they can be in their roles.

Proposition 5: Organizations, people, and leadership cannot be considered discretely in bringing about transformation; they are intimately integrated. Most textbooks on administration do not view organizations as a complex whole; they treat them as separate parts—structure, processes, decisions, leadership, people, and outcomes. Approaches for change need to view the interrelatedness of all components of the organization—leadership, structure and operations, and people with their personal and professional needs. A strategy focusing simply on leadership will not bring about change in the total organization, nor will changing structures necessarily alter attitudes, commitment, or performance. A holistic approach to transformation is needed; the synergy of taking a broad approach to organizations, leadership, and people produces a greater effect than intervening in one area.

Proposition 6: The people working in schools must be viewed as scarce resources, not as interchangeable parts. The transformation process must take into consideration the developmental levels and needs of the professionals and support staff. Awareness of and sensitivity to the fact that adults are operating at many different levels of growth and development is crucial to the success of transformation. The process must be designed to be responsive to new and veteran teachers and administrators, to build on their expertise, and to increase their confidence. People must acknowledge the circumstances and necessity for the changes, understand and participate in the process, and be transformed themselves into successful partners for the change. Transforming schools understand the diversity of people's gifts and talents and liberates them to reach their potential.

Proposition 7: Schools are not rational places that respond to scientific management or bureaucratic approaches to operation and change. Scientific management assumes that people and conditions respond to a logical and rational process. In people-dominated institutions, issues become emotional, conflict occurs when there is ambiguity, and feelings affect behavior and action. Schools are nonrational places that need consensus around values so people commit to ideals that are greater than themselves. If this was not the case, the traditional bureaucratic, rational model would have produced effective and responsive schools through rule-driven procedures.

Proposition 8: Fiscal support for schools is finite: The economic pie will remain proportional to the growth of the economy as a whole. A compelling argument for analyzing and appraising the basic perceptions, thought patterns, and behavior in schools is the issue of fiscal support. Financial resources must be spent on initiatives that are the most important and effective in producing desired outcomes. Ineffective and irrelevant programs take precious resources and divert them from the ones that work to reach the mission of the schools.

Resources must follow values, and programs that do not realize those principles should be eliminated. Schools have added many programs to address diverse and, sometimes, conflicting agendas. At times, these activities clash philosophically and are at odds with the school's values and sense of mission.

Proposition 9: Productivity, quality, and success are concepts that schools must address to gain and maintain credibility. The public is asking for demonstrated effectiveness through outcomes. The *process* outcomes of the past assumed that if a school had procedures and people assigned to functions, they were producing results. Those outcomes will be replaced by *performance* standards, which assume quality, productivity, and reaching goals and objectives at the highest levels —success. Defining these concepts may result in greater local autonomy than process expectations allow.

Teachers and administrators must make choices about what is important, what approaches to take, and what programs to offer. Performance standards expect the measurement and assessment of outcomes that exceed the limits of standardized tests and instruction. They require a constellation of performance measures that will determine complex and interdisciplinary outcomes successful schools desire to achieve.

Proposition 10: Successful schools reach more complex and interdisciplinary outcomes than do schools that aspire to the concept of effectiveness. Transforming schools are successful in the integration and scope of programs. The model in Chapter 3, Figure 3–3, identifies the components of a successful school that center around core values and sense of purpose.

These schools move beyond effectiveness and view education of children as more complex in desired outcomes and the measurement of them. Effective schools have focused on basic skills and assessment dominated by standardized tests. Successful schools aspire to higher and more comprehensive intellectual, academic, character, aesthetic, interpersonal, process, and affective goals. They operate under the assumption that all children have an equal opportunity to succeed in achieving these goals.

Proposition 11: A prerequisite for transforming schools is transformational leaders who define values and visions that attract people to important causes. In transforming schools, leaders must think and behave in new ways. They are creative risk takers, whose visions inspire and commit professionals to the mission of schools. They disperse power throughout the organization, which results in leadership density and shared purpose. They are culture builders, entrepreneurs, and social architects, instead of administrators of policies and procedures.

Transformation of schools rests on these propositions. Small changes do not cause schools to question the programs and outcomes they achieve against values and resources. The rest of this chapter will present a model of the components, process, and outcomes of the transforming school, and define a design for transformation concerning organization, people, and leadership.

TRANSFORMATION: AN INTEGRATED MODEL

Transforming schools require a comprehensive, integrated approach. Transformation involves checking perception and adjusting thinking to modify or sustain behavior. It requires an examination of the

FIGURE 11–1 Transformation: An Integrated Model

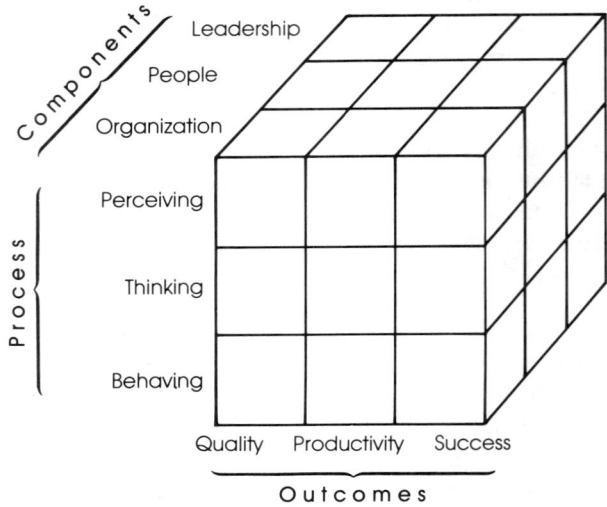

paradigm in use and adjustment if it is not congruent with the external and internal contexts. In Figure 11–1, perceiving, thinking, and behaving are the process components.

To reiterate transformation *process* definitions, *perception* involves grasping and developing comprehension of the internal and external context and performance of the school. *Thinking* concerns the cognitive structures—schemas, scripts, and symbols—that determine the paradigm for how organizations think collectively about the issues, problems, and success of schools. *Behaving*, which is guided by the paradigm, refers to the actions or outcomes that result from analytical or intuitive decision making.

The transformation *process* is applied to the major components of schools—organization, leadership, and people. *Organizational* components include context, structure, culture, and systems for sharing information and making decisions. *Leadership* relates to vision, mission, meaning, and action. The *people* component affects the role and participation of professionals, empowerment, and staff development.

The *outcome* elements include the concepts of quality, productivity, and success. Chapter 3 defines these concepts in detail. *Quality* is the degree of excellence or superiority in reaching schools' mission and goals. It concerns how reliably the schools perform for all students in reaching the definition of educational success. *Success*, for schools, means achieving favorable, quality outcomes in a productive way. The core of successful schools is values. They define the criteria for determining quality, productivity, leadership, and outcomes. *Productivity* involves students, time, cost, and outcomes.

A Design for Transforming Schools: Process and Components

Transformation requires that schools are looked at anew, almost as if from an aerial view, to determine how they operate within their context in meeting their mission. They must be perceived from their very fundamentals, to rethink the way the entire enterprise works and what it achieves. The basis for this design is the process of examining the perception and thinking patterns that are the foundation for behavior.

There are several questions to be answered. What is important to perceive and how do people perceive it? How does the organization think—its way of defining and dealing with problems, issues, priorities, strategies, and solutions? What behavior is effective and how is it measured? Figure 11–2 illustrates a design for transformation and its major components.

Values—standards, precepts, and principles—start the process. They screen the events, activities, conditions, and circumstances that affect schools. What we perceive as being important is based on personal and professional values. Our perception of reality comes from the values we carry; they help us make judgments about what issues to respond to and assist us in evaluating "what is" against "what should be." Values filter or screen the external and internal worlds and are at the core of professional thinking and behavior.

What is important? Professionals have to examine their perception of the entire system—organization, leadership, and people. People include both the human resources of the organization and the clients it serves. Perception of these three components, which are at the core of school life, is the key to change. Is the organization successful? Are programs relevant? What kind of leadership is needed? How can people be motivated and continue to grow? How should organizations be structured so that leadership can be developed and people can be valued? Are the school organization, leadership, and professionals effective in the internal and external contexts in which they operate?

Our perceptions of the schools and their context leads to thinking. Are the schools successful in reaching outcomes that are characterized by quality and productivity? Thinking about schools and their outcomes requires information that is used in making decisions about behavior—strategies, procedures, and practices. Thought in organizations is both intuitive and analytical, as discussed in Chapter 2. Behavior derived

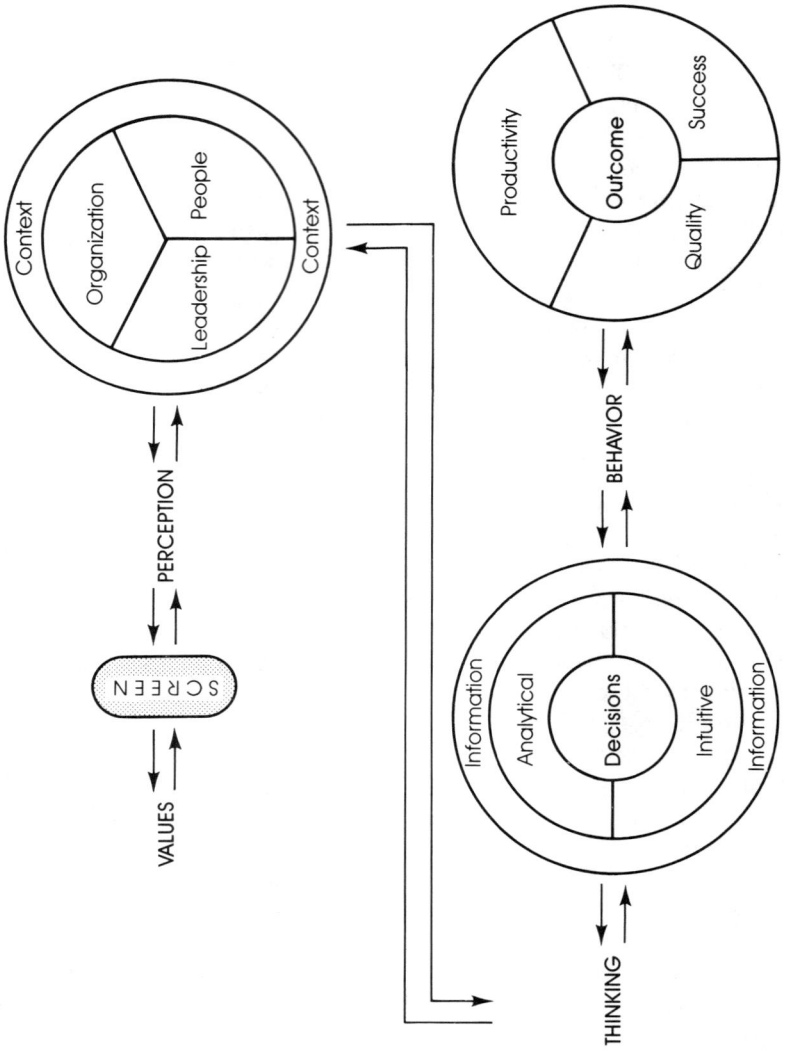

FIGURE 11-2 A Design for School Transformation

from our decision-making process must be geared to reaching important, desired outcomes of the school. Reaching these outcomes achieves quality, productivity, and success. Behavior, even in organizations, is not judgment-free.

It Begins with Values

Values are at the heart of organizations. If people believe in values, they will be attracted to the mission and goals like iron filings to a magnet. People work not simply to pay the mortagage but to become engaged in something bigger than their own self-interest. Teachers, who generally have a sense of service, want a system that has strong, important values. That is what motivates people and develops commitment through a bond or covenant of meaning and purpose.

Schools that have a covenant of purpose know what they are about—what is important, where they collectively take a stand, and around what basis decisions are made. The values underlying that covenant drive the organization, leaders, and people because there is an understanding of the core purpose of the school. A covenant is an agreement between the people in the organization to live those values and not practice in any way that would violate them. From this covenant comes a sense of community that can unite a school system composed of decentralized sites, grades, and departments.

Values provide the base for professional autonomy. If there is a covenant around the core values, then individuals have the freedom to meet them in diverse ways. Autonomy and empowerment are the offspring of values. Just as practice in medicine is based on the Hippocratic oath, practice in classrooms is based on values and ethics, which releases the teachers to find many ways to meet the needs of their students. The result is diversity, not practice based on recipes or behavioral guidelines.

Teachers become empowered because the covenant is the guidepost for their decision making. Strong understanding of the school's values provides a framework for autonomous behavior and action, without individuals having to ask permission. In addition, if practice is congruent with values, the school has integrity and credibility.

Before schools can be transformed, the system's value structure must be identified, core values defined, and strategies specified to maintain the covenant around those principles. Philosophies and mission statements indicate the values the organization believes are important. The structure of the organization and the procedures it formally defines unveil some operational values. The data organizations keep demonstrate what is important in decision making and document the action taken. They also give an indication of what is monitored, assessed, and measured, which attests to priorities.

The language used in organizations—both its content and intent—mirrors values. Verbal and written communication express what is perceived as important to people and to the organization. The content illustrates the priorities and the intent reflects the attitudes toward those priorities.

Another value indicator is resources. Where do they go? Trailing the fiscal and human resources will lead to what the organization values. Allocation decisions are difficult because resources are finite. In these circumstances, values will determine how the resources are deployed. Budgets, staffing patterns, equipment and materials, time, and functions need to be assessed to see the values of the organization applied to difficult choices.

A final value indicator is the behavior of people—open or closed, friendly or aloof, formal or informal, concerned or ambivalent. How are people treated in person, on the phone, or in various circumstances throughout the organization? How are decisions made, through consensus or unilaterally? Observing behavior is a powerful indicator of values in action.

Defining Values and Strategies

After identifying the values-in-use, the next step is to define the desired core values. Leaders gain people's commitment through a vision or an expression of the desired values and consequent outcomes. There is no magic to this process, but leadership is the key.

People like to dream and become a part of noble causes. They have a value system that guides them in their classrooms or administrative roles. Transforming schools define what students, parents, teachers, school board members, administrators, and others value in terms of organizational operation, interpersonal interaction, program performance, and client service. That process can be completed in surveys, focus-group interviews, discussions, or nominal group processes.

Once the desired values are defined, comparisons between groups can be made and a common core of values specified. The strands of similar values and principles form the basis for a common vision. Visions are mental images of what the schools can become, a uniting force that attracts and motivates teachers, parents, and administrators. A value-based vision also provides the anchors for setting priorities and can assist school boards in making decisions on resource deployment and allocation, assessment of programs, and monitoring progress. As times and context change, once successful programs may not continue to be in line with the values of the organization and may need to be replaced and have resources reallocated to other places. Defined values may be the constants around which change is designed.

The school organization and its leadership must *live* those values, not use them when they are advantageous and ignore them when they are inconvenient. The basis of the covenant is that all people adhere to and do not violate the values. Several strategies can be used to bring about values-based transformation.

> *Value-based missions:* Visions steeped in values should lead to a concrete mission statement for the organization and program. Mission statements are practical expressions of values.
>
> *Model values:* Everyone—administrators and teachers—must model their values through behavior. Modeling, particularly from top leaders, is a potent reinforcement.
>
> *Reinforce values:* Continue to refer to values and reinforce the people who demonstrate them in their professional practice. Reinforcement can be as simple as a comment or note, or a more formal recognition like more responsibility or involvement.
>
> *Professional codes:* Most other professions have codes of practice that define ethical standards and principles. Teachers and their unions or associations, in cooperation with administrators and others, can specify expectations based on high standards and strong professional values. Professional codes can also be termed "compacts" between the organization and the professionals that work in it. Sanctions must be applied by fellow professionals to those who violate the code or compact.
>
> *Resources follow values:* Human, time, and fiscal resources must follow the expressed values. If they do not, they never become part of the values-in-practice in the district, which will result in people becoming cynical. Values are powerful tools, but people will believe in them only if the organization adheres to them in decision making.
>
> *Value-based assessment:* Measuring the effectiveness of programs must be based on the espoused values. If programs are not meeting values, then they should be redesigned or eliminated.

Table 11–1 summarizes the strategies for identifying and defining organizational values.

Transforming schools begins with values. Once they are defined and consensus around a value-based mission is obtained, then change is

TABLE 11–1   Values: Identification and Definition Strategies

Task	Source	Indicator
Identification	Philosophy	Stated values
	Documents/Forms	Data/Monitoring of important information
	Resources	Priorities
	Language	Values-in-use
	Behavior/Practice	Values-in-use
Definition	Vision	Core values
	Mission	Values implementation
	Professional code/Compact	Desired values-in-practice
	Sanction system	Reinforce values
	Resource allocation	Priorities
	Assessment	Value monitoring

tied to those values and principles. They act as a rudder, guiding decisions, practice, procedure, and policy. Behavior follows values, not procedure or policy.

TRANSFORMING ORGANIZATIONS

What are the perceptions, thinking, and behavior that will transform schools? This section defines the perceptions and thinking that will influence and direct the behavior of people working in school organizations.

Context

We have established the *perception* that schools exist in an economic, political, and cultural context. They are open, not closed, systems, under the influence of multiple pressures, some of which are conflicting. These pressures create demands, requiring decisions for which there are no clear, simple answers. Decisions can become political when there are no obvious solutions. These circumstances require consensus and call for high degrees of credibility.

In this context, schools must *think* in broad, multidisciplinary ways, incorporating information from economic, social, political, and cultural areas. Schools' effectiveness in a global context must be assessed, and they need to establish their philosophy, values, and priorities with this perspective.

Transforming schools *behave* as open systems that require a written philosophy and a process to define core values. They balance academic, personal, citizenship, and employment goals. Processes are defined to identify goals, resolve differences, and respond to the environment.

These schools have a formal procedure to scan the external environment to obtain input for the system. Contextual information must be scanned and monitored to determine pressures and demands. In addition, the schools invite feedback on programs and functions from experts, leaders, parents, and other constituents.

Organizational Culture

Organizational culture is an important influence in the operation of schools. Our *perception* is that culture can be created—the values, symbols, and myths that affect how people interact and relate. One characteristic of transforming cultures is the habit of breaking habits. Culture should not be the bulwark that resists change; it should create an environment where change is embraced and innovation is valued.

Analysis, synthesis, and evaluation are the main *thought* processes used to keep the culture adaptive. New ideas can be synthesized and programs can evolve rather than remain static or tied to tradition. Thinking about culture in transforming schools helps focus on how culture can embrace the change process, not impede it.

In such a culture, the *behavior* of the organization is change oriented to provide successful service to clients, with the focus on achievement and quality. These organizations live the culture they want by having actions follow words and by reinforcing people for behaving in accord with it. New values, rituals, celebrations, and stories are established to promote change and adaptation.

This culture encourages people to be proactive, not reactive, anticipating needs and finding solutions. The organization also looks forward, defines trends, and finds ways to incorporate new ideas and technology into its operations. Innovation is encouraged and rewarded, and districts make procedural and fiscal resources available to do it.

Organizational Structure

The structure should be *perceived* as supporting and realizing the basic mission and objectives of the organization. Since teaching and learning are the primary outcomes of schools, the structure must be designed to reinforce those purposes and make teaching and learning easier, not more difficult.

Professionals must have the authority to make decisions affecting instruction and student achievement as well as in determining where, how, and when education happens. Achieving results is the focal point of organizational *thinking*. Questioning to find better ways, striving for excellence, and restlessness and dissatisfaction with what is are characteristics of the faculty and staff.

Divergent ideas are accepted, and thinking differently about present programs and achieving outcomes is encouraged. Creativity by professional staff is supported by all in the school. There is no "sandbagging" other teachers who want to try new ideas: The climate is stimulating and encouraging. Teachers evaluate, analyze, and synthesize ideas and methods.

Transforming schools are structured to promote client-focused decisions, so *behavior* may look quite different. In that regard, the walls of the school must be broken down and the learning environment expanded. Schools must be open longer hours and all year-round to accommodate working parents and student learning needs, and to offer the opportunity for more learning to occur each day and year. Learning takes place at different rates and times, and students need to do more than grasp the basics; they must move beyond rote learning and literacy and become fully educated. This requires different schedules, learning outside the school, new methods, incorporating technology, and other active and cooperative means.

Technology, customized learning, and variation in year and hours can make local schools centers for community education. Adults could use the schools during the day, in the evenings, or through technological programs. Special courses for parents, hobbyists, senior citizens, and others could be implemented evenings and summers, creating a greater stake in the schools and improving the productivity of the district's capital investment in buildings and equipment. In addition, special programs for parents to support the education of their children could be designed around basic skills, study tips, support groups, and other areas. Teachers and staff could help plan and support these ventures.

Teachers need decision-making authority with accompanying responsibility for producing outcomes. Measuring student performance must be based on "value-added" outcomes because students come to the learning process at different places and with varying capabilities. The role of the school is to increase each student's achievement and to have each student move closer to his or her potential.

Transforming schools review structural performance through:

Reality checks: Is the program meeting the needs in today's context and environment for all students?

Gap analysis or matching the real with the ideal: Are we doing what we say?

Barrier analysis: What structures, processes, or programs are standing in the way of achievement? Is group-think a barrier to risk taking?

Innovation audits to assess readiness for change: What attitudes, skills, and resources are needed to get innovations operational?

Planning review: Is planning balanced with action or is it an excuse for not taking action?

Imaging: Is dreaming encouraged to see how schools would look if innovations were implemented?

Authority

The fact that change is inevitable and places demands and stress on organizations is an established *perception*. Schools are perceived of as wholes, not parts or fragments. Integration, not segmentation, is the way schools adapt to altering times and issues. Schools are not *thought* of as totally rational places; they face ambiguity and uncertainty. Although not rational, they are not irrational. They face issues that are not always clearly defined—information is not always complete.

Transforming schools recognize the tyranny of absolutes. Understanding that being cemented to one approach or pattern of organization can be the start of decline. Uncertainty and lack of information are expected and accepted as facts of life that do not debilitate the problem-solving process. Conflict is a part of organizations because many decisions are political, open to alternative solutions.

Schools, as organic structures, *behave* in free-flowing and information-sharing ways. Organic organizations are characterized by collaboration, low centralization, horizontal and vertical communication, and networks between and among people. Cooperation, not competition, is encouraged. Schools are flat organizations with authority for decision making close to the client, with high degrees of accountability and responsibility.

Responsive structures adapt to local needs. Site-based management has the potential for promoting quality decisions, innovation, and professionalism. In this structure, principals and teachers have the autonomy to make decisions about what is best for the school and its students. Under site-based management, the locus of control and the accountability unit is the individual school for decisions on:

- Fiscal priorities and expenditures
- Instructional strategies

- Staff-development activities
- Program implementation (schedules, time allotments, materials)

Accountability for results must be demonstrated in achievement, productivity, and mission implementation. The accountability process must satisfy district requirements and values.

These schools have systems in place to gather the best data possible, data are turned into information, and then shared through a horizontal and vertical network. Decisions are made at the point of impact, and risk is recognized as a part of life with advantages and disadvantages. Teachers are free and secure to try ideas, measure results, and compare outcomes in gathering data about what works and what does not.

Human Resource Costs

People must be *perceived* as valuable resources. In organizations, there are direct and indirect human resources as labor costs. Direct labor costs are those associated with providing service to the client group. In the case of schools, teachers are direct labor costs. Indirect labor costs are those incurred for supporting the basic service, such as curriculum specialists or staff developers.

Money for schools is finite and even though educational reform is discussed, there is little likelihood that more money will be available. When resources are finite, priorities must be assessed to ensure that they are spent on services of greatest impact to achieving the school's mission. Leaders must *think* about the costs for direct and indirect labor because not all staff services are of equal importance. In decentralized structures, more control is placed in the hands of direct labor, therefore requiring less indirect labor investment. Specialists who are not directly involved in providing professional service may not be as necessary for quality as generalists who are directly involved.

Transforming organizations *behave* responsibly by:

- Reviewing requests for indirect labor costs to determine if those resources will starve basic, vital services
- Examining other interventions like reducing class size, adding greater direct labor costs at the expense of indirect labor specialists
- Questioning creeping specialization that can remove resources from basic services
- Using technology to increase the productivity and the impact of direct labor

A summary of the organizational components of transformation are identified in Table 11–2.

TABLE 11–2   Transforming Organizations

Perception	Thinking	Behavior
Context: Open systems	Multidisciplinary	Core-value directed Written philosophy Scan and monitor context
Culture: Embraces change	Analyze, synthesize, evaluate	Proactive Innovative Collaborative Communication— Vertical/horizontal
Structure: Support basic mission	From governance to teaching/learning	Client-focused decisions Open longer Teacher decision making Community education
Promote Innovation	Focus: Achieving outcomes Questioning Divergent approaches	Support for colleagues Reality checks Barrier analysis Innovation audits Planning and action Imaging
Authority: Information required Change inevitable Holistic, not fragmented	Schools: Nonrational organizations	Organic structures Collaboration Low centralization Networks Site-based management
	Recognize tyranny of absolutes	Information systems
Resource Allocation: Finite resources	Analysis Priority	Technology Decentralization

TRANSFORMING LEADERSHIP

Without leadership, transformation cannot occur because it affects vision, people, and action. It requires credibility to cause people to review perceptions, rethink issues, and try new ways of doing things.

Transforming leaders take the risks necessary to eliminate inertia and organizational defensiveness.

Our perception is that leaders are not the same as managers. Leaders ask different questions and are concerned with effectiveness, whereas managers consider efficiency. Leaders have an entrepreneurial mindset: They encourage independent thinking and can accept and adapt to ambiguity and uncertainty. They can conceptualize issues and mobilize alternatives for actions and are long-range thinkers who do not adopt a "quick-fix" approach to problems or organizational development. Intuitive thinking is balanced with rational and practical approaches, and leaders are comfortable with change and taking action.

It is easy to notice the behavior of transforming leaders—they find and define problems, make decisions in uncertain situations, and are good interpreters of the organizational context and environment. They have ideas and can translate them, and encourage contrary opinions because they know they do not know everything. Although they desire efficiency, leaders push for accountability for results and provide people with autonomy to operate within ethical and value-based standards. They focus on effectiveness and push for *breakthrough*, not incremental, results.

Such leadership stresses commitment—it inspires and pulls people through ideas and values. Leaders create a climate for growth and nurture people by breaking isolation and providing for collaboration and input into decisions. They push responsibility downward and find ways to empower people by including them in decisions. Transformational leaders know that leadership is a gift from those they lead; therefore, they build genuine relationships with people to get them involved meaningfully. They realize people want to be involved, feel needed, and contribute. Transforming leaders help people become their best, and understand that in organizations people are interdependent.

Credibility

Leaders must be *perceived* as having credibility and as being believable and reliable. Credibility gaps—the fissure between what people say and do—are fatal. Credible leaders *think* about the values and purpose of the organization and how to maintain program integrity. Their motives are clear and congruent with values. Solutions are defined that are consistent with the espoused values and the culture of the organization.

Transforming leaders *behave* in the following ways to establish credibility:

- Define and model ethical standards and behavior.
- Be visible and accessible to promote trust.
- Allocate resources based on values.
- Ensure that words and behavior are congruent.
- Trust people by delegating responsibility and giving autonomy.
- Demonstrate reliable behavior consistent with values; they cannot be barometric or inconsistent.
- Be knowledgeable and confident. Others must perceive them as so, they must demonstrate their expertise, and they must have a strong sense of self.
- Behave in open, not closed, ways, so that motives and intent are clear. There is no manipulation or secrecy.

Leaders have diverse traits; they do not all behave the same. Each leader must find the best way to express his or her ideas and values.

Leaders and People

Leaders *perceive* people as resources and assets, and recognize the importance of their development in the transformation process. Being optimistic about people is a characteristic of transforming leaders. They *think* of the growth and maintenence needs of people to promote and develop potential. They find divergent ways to help people develop commitment and grow personally and professionally.

Transformational leadership *behavior* includes:

- Taking a developmental, not evaluative, attitude toward people
- Furnishing safety and security for people to try ideas, pursue goals, and attend growth activities
- Providing teachers with autonomy and responsibility
- Ensuring that staff development and inservice programs are available and valued
- Acting as "champions" for ideas and experiences that staff members want to pursue
- Allocating the resources—technology and finances—to become more productive and acquire more and better information

Leaders and Vision

Leaders *perceive* their role to create and communicate a vision of what the organization can become through collective action. Vision is required to see new directions and develop potential for successful schools. To develop a vision, leaders need to be conceptual *thinkers—*

individuals who can understand interrelationships of school to the greater context, analyze trends, and recognize when fundamental changes in paradigms or conditions exist. Leaders do not think in terms of fixed solutions or recipes. They dream and imagine what can be and are not deterred by what is or what has been tried in the past. They see possibilities, not problems.

Leaders who create visions *behave* by breaking addiction to the past. They scan the environment for ideas, have connections to leaders outside their fields, and listen to suggestions and alternatives regardless of their past application. Leaders use metaphors and other symbols to communicate and translate their vision. They behave by living their vision and are consistent in pursuing action that will bring it to life.

Credible leaders understand their schools and have a strong respect for the potential of the people, resources, and structure of the organization. They also realize the outcomes their schools must attain to achieve success and even greatness. Transformational leaders recognize the signals of organizational entropy that can cause deterioration:

- Fearing complexity and ambiguity
- Spending time on superficial matters
- Controlling, not liberating, people
- Getting buried in day-to-day activities and eliminating discussion of vision
- Emphasizing procedural manuals, quantifying data, and relying on structure, not people

Leaders and Action

Leaders know that visions and plans are benign without action. They *perceive* their role as initiators of action—with followers and with the context in which schools exist.

The primary focus of *thinking* is goal attainment—bringing the vision into reality. Creative and flexible approaches to problems are tried, and ambiguity is seen as a given, which requires the application of professional knowledge and skills. Power is thought of as a tool. It is not seen as a means of domination but is used as fuel to be dispersed to people needing it to bring ideas into reality.

The *behavior* of leaders is geared to releasing people to act in the interest of the school. Transforming leaders share power with people closest to the decision. Teachers and others are provided with the responsibility and autonomy to place plans and ideas into action, as long as those initiatives do not violate the school's standards and values. High levels of accountability are required. People can take action and take risks. There are errors, but not failures.

Transforming leaders provide people with the opportunity to assume responsibility and apply their expertise. The operation does not rely on one person because there is leadership density in the school—leadership comes from many people when and where it is needed based on competence and knowledge.

A summary of the perception, thinking, and behavior of leaders in transforming schools is summarized in Table 11–3.

TABLE 11–3   Transformational Leadership

Perception	Thinking	Behavior
Leadership: Different from management	Intuitive/Rational Entrepreneurial Long range	Effectiveness Comfort with ambiguity Accountability for results Breakthrough results
People: Assets	Optimistic Need centered Divergent/Convergent	Developmental Autonomy/Responsibility Model values Growth programs
Credibility: Action and words	Values/Purpose Congruent Program integrity	Ethical standards Resource allocation Promote trust Delegate Reliable/Consistent Knowledge/Confident
Vision: Create/ communicate	Define values Conceptual Imaging/Dreaming	Stated vision Model values Proactive Take risks Break addiction with past
Action: Role to initiate	Power is tool Focus on goals Flexibility/Creativity	Power dispersed Delegate authority Allow autonomy Accountability Take risks Leadership density

TRANSFORMING PEOPLE

Teachers are key people in making schools transform. They consider themselves professionals and want to be respected as knowledge workers who provide service to their clients—students.

People

It is important to establish the *perception* that all people in school deserve and need respect. Without respect, there cannot be commitment or trust because it is the antecedent for developing the climate for personal and professional growth and a mutually supportive working relationship. In addition, children and parents are shown respect as clients or customers. They must be perceived as the focal point for professional service.

In transforming schools, teachers are *thought* of as assets, who need affective and cognitive support to have their professional and personal needs fulfilled. Students and parents are thought of as clients, not subordinates or outsiders. Transforming schools are devoted to building a professional community in which teachers and parents are bonded in developing quality programs.

The *behavior* of everyone in the school revolves around respect. Language used in the schools shows respect—people are not dehumanized by stereotypes, categorizing, slang, or other uncomplimentary terms. Participation in the organization is welcomed from professionals, parents, and community members, and parents are given the feeling that they are a part of the learning community.

Communication in transforming schools is two-way. Dissent and divergence are valued and not to be scorned. Dialog and professional discussion are key ingredients because good communication builds a "stake" in the organization, where people feel important, where information is shared, and where everyone is included in organizational rituals and ceremonies.

Client Service

Schools are *perceived* as client-focused service organizations. They do not produce products but provide a professional service that is geared to the needs of children. *Thinking* focuses on meeting the needs of learners, which is the prime purpose of schools at all levels. Teaching and learning are conceptualized in relation to outcomes, and there is an understanding of child development, achievement, and methods and strategies that can enhance the instructional process.

There are several *behavioral* characteristics of client-focused schools:

- Equity of opportunity exists for all students.
- Equity of outcome for all students is a desired and stated goal. Social factors are not excuses for poor achievement.
- Choice is provided for students. Options are available for learning because there is no one best way to teach children.
- Education is geared to promoting individual potential.
- Practice follows ethical guidelines and organizational values.
- Learning goals and priorities are clear, expressed, and followed.
- Goals incorporate personal, citizenship, and employment objectives.
- Higher-order thinking skills are integrated in all content areas.

Teachers as Knowledge Workers

Teachers are *perceived* as knowledge workers who need information and sophisticated skills to meet the needs of their students. They cannot be *thought* of as technicians who follow directions or recipes in completing their role; instead, divergent thinking is used to address varying needs. As a group, teachers review their mindscapes that frame how they define and approach issues and problems. Not only are rational processes used but there is an appreciation for intuition and serendipity. Hypothesizing and theorizing are common.

Teachers' *behavior* as knowledge workers requires the following:

- Integration—they do not practice in isolation.
- Networks are there for sharing, with communication flowing vertically and horizontally.
- Information about performance is also shared with students.
- Technology is available to turn data into information. The technology also allows teachers to increase their productivity.
- Results are assessed on information drawn from the data.
- Measurement of outcomes is complex and multidimensional in both the affective and cognitive domains.
- Steps are taken through summer schools, clinics, or other interventions to create "hot-houses" for new ideas and experiences for teachers and students.

Teachers as Professionals

As stated above, teachers as knowledge workers are *perceived* as professionals who are accountable for results. As professionals, they *think* about ethics, focusing primarily on student needs. Outcomes and achievement are emphasized and measured to determine professional effectiveness. There is deference to professional practice, not to bureaucratic standardization. Higher-order thinking skills are applied to issues, problems, and strategies.

These *behavioral* characteristics of transforming schools consider teachers as professionals:

- Written codes of ethical standards for professional practice are stated.
- Teachers practice self-management in making classroom decisions in accord with those codes. They participate in classroom, school, and districtwide decisions.
- Decisions are made on client needs.
- Accountability structures for teachers are specified and in place based around value-added outcomes.
- Time is available for reflective practice, either through released time, changed calendars, or extended contract years.
- Diversified programs are available for teachers to polish and hone their skills. There are mentors, networks, and experiment-research centers.
- Peer evaluation and supervision are accepted practices.

Finally, the organization's hiring procedures are geared to recruiting and retaining qualified, smart talent. There is care in its selection, training, development, and evaluation programs.

Self-Actualization

Professionals want to work toward fulfilling their potential. Their *perception* is that they reach self-actualization as they move through progressive developmental stages. *Thinking* about development is long range and considers cognitive and affective components.

Transforming schools exhibit *behavior* patterns that help people meet their potential and self-actualize.

- They focus on the intrinsic rewards in teaching, as well extrinsic ones.

- There is an openness to individuality, new ideas, and change.
- There are skill sessions to update and upgrade teacher abilities.
- The status of teachers is based on knowledge and expertise.
- Teachers have an opportunity to try different roles—there is variation in assignments that can promote growth.
- The staff is results-oriented—obtaining and measuring them. The mission is most important.
- Leadership is assumed based on knowledge and abilities, and inspiration and motivation flow from challenges.

Table 11–4 summarizes the perception, thinking, and behavior of people in transforming schools.

SUMMARY

Transforming schools have the subtle differences that make for great changes in outcomes. They perceive and think in ways that make anything seem possible and are not constrained by obstacles. This mindset helps people grow and reach beyond normal performance because they believe in what they are doing and they believe that it can get done.

In summary, transforming schools:

Build a covenant around purpose: The values and belief system drive the organization, not structures or procedures. Leaders do not worship scientific management because they realize that schools exist in a context that is not always controllable and rational.

Have integrity: They are true to their purpose in allocating resources, developing people, and living their values.

Respond to change: They are not isolated or divorced from their surroundings. They are vital, dynamic organizations that have a sense of awareness of their role in the community and the nation at large. They respond to changes in their context and are aware of and use research to find better ways.

Listen and know they don't know everything: A dialogue of ideas, aspirations, and wishes takes place within the organization on how to reach goals and respond to changes. Leaders and professionals are open to ideas and innovations because they are humble enough to realize they do not have all the answers or know all the questions.

TABLE 11–4   Transforming People

Perception	Thinking	Behavior
People deserve respect	Affective Need centered Nonjudgmental	Communication: Safe, two-way, dissent Participation People accepted Language shows respect All people feel stake Parents have active roles
Schools are client centered	Outcome/ Achievement focus Conceptualize teaching and learning	Equity of opportunity Equity of outcome Choice Ethical practice
Teachers as knowledge workers	Divergent Review paradigms Intuitive Theorizing/ Hypothesizing	Turn data into information Technology for productivity Networking No isolation Communication: Vertical horizontal Share information
Teachers are professional	Outcome/ Achievement Ethical standards Deference to profession Client needs	Reflective practice Codes of professional conduct Self-management Accountability: Results Networks Staff development Participate in decisions
Professionals desire self-actualization	Cognitive Affective Future-oriented	Openness to ideas Status based on knowledge Orientation to results Intrinsic rewards

End isolation and promote networking: People are involved and can share. They understand the organization's mission and see how their efforts contribute to the success of the school. People count more than structure, and there is an intimate relationship between people and their work.

Continue to learn as a community: Reaching and growing are key components. Complacency and stagnation are resisted, and value is placed on learning by everyone in the school. Ample time and diverse approaches are used to elicit growth.

Have momentum: They remove obstacles so people can try new ways to achieve results. Action follows mission—planning is not used as an excuse for not implementing ideas. Teachers and others feel movement and progress toward goals because activities are purposeful.

Exude leadership: Leaders, with ideas, liberate people's potential to reach the covenent of purpose. Leadership is not unidimensional—it does not rely on one person for progress. There is leadership density that is characterized by people assuming responsibility and leadership when knowledge and expertise are needed. Leaders believe in the potential of people.

Are holistic, not fragmented or segmented organizations: They are synergistic—the whole is greater than the sum of the parts. Through unified action around their missions, these schools do not disintegrate into isolated, segmented efforts at implementing programs. All efforts are geared to the achievement of the values and mission of the schools; there is a sense of wholeness and identity that directs each department or program. Leadership, structure, and people are not seen as isolated organizational components.

Think about how they think: They continually assess their paradigms and mindscapes to ensure that they are effective and are not barriers to progress. Everyone in the schools checks to eliminate "formula" thinking and approaches to problems. Diverse and ceative thought—in issue identification and resolution—is solicited.

Have a sense of wonder: Having a sense of wonder about how things work and how people learn is not lost. Curiosity is applauded and continuous searching are a part of a professional's restless spirit to find better ways. Childlike wonderment and excitement are cherished and nourished.

12 Transforming Schools: Quality and Productivity Outcomes

Transformation results in successful schools that continue to adapt to changing needs and contexts and achieve their goals. The seriousness of the reform movement is best expressed by John Sculley of Apple Computers, who told the president of the United States at the education summit in 1989, "The single most important thing you can do as President is to reform public education." The destiny of the country rests more on the quality of its schools than at any other time in its history because the currency of prosperity and culture for the future is knowledge and information.

Chapter 11 identified the process and components of transformation. This chapter deals with outcomes—the results and characteristics of successful schools that are both productive and quality oriented.

Successful schools, as stated in Chapter 3, have certain characteristics:

Values: They are "loose-tight" organizations: tight around core values but loose around the the means to reach them. There is a pervasive sense of purpose or mission that binds the organization and attracts teachers and others. The meaning of work is clear to teachers and students.

Comprehensive outcomes: Programs are not just aimed at effectiveness or basic skills but include intellectual, academic, character, citizenship, interpersonal, social, physical, and cultural goals. Educated people need more than basic and employment skills.

Quality and productivity: Successful schools embrace account-ability and measure outcomes. Measurement is complex and diverse, not tied to norm-referenced tests or other simplistic measures. Accomplishments are recognized, and multiple goals are set.

Culture and climate: Cooperation is evident between students and teachers. The culture is strong, emphasizing openness, auton-omy, empowerment, and accountability. Teaching is viewed as a decision-making process, and love of learning is dominant.

Leadership: Leaders are competent, credible professionals, who set clear visions and model values of the school. They are genu-ine in their dealings, establish trust, and share their authority throughout the organization.

With limited fiscal resources, productivity and quality are the new cornerstones of public schools. Without them, the credibility of schools is lost and support disintegrates. Schools must define and achieve qual-ity in a cost-effective, productive manner.

Quality, as defined earlier, is the degree of excellence in an act, product, service, or organization. Quality schools have integrity in that there is honesty of purpose. Values, effort, and performance are linked and congruent. Quality schools stress high achievement in academics, ethical and responsible behavior, and a structure that promotes caring and equity and commitment. They are innovative and flexible. Quality programs produce equity in student achievement and exemplify that all students can learn, and they assess outcomes through specific, data-based measures, goal achievement, and affective behavior.

School productivity means achieving more effective educational results while using and applying resources more efficiently. Meeting client needs with the resources at the organization's disposal is a factor in productivity, which includes the utilization of people and resources.

Creating a structure in which people get information that enables them to make better decisions, that allows them to share and network, and that provides continued opportunity for training and development contributes to productivity. Schools in which isolation, bureaucratic, rule-driven behavior predominates do not utilize the talents of people well.

Productivity also considers cost-effectiveness. The cost-benefit of education is obvious, because ignorance or illiteracy are not options. To measure productivity then, cost-effectiveness is appropriate. It mea-sures the cost of achieving outcomes through specific approaches or methods.

TIP | TRANSFORMATION INTO PRACTICE

WHY SCHOOLS DON'T WORK: WHAT THE REPORTS DON'T SAY

School reform has been discussed and rehashed from faculty lounges to the Oval Office. Problems have been identified, solutions proposed, hopes raised, and outcomes targeted. Despite the evaluation of the condition of schools, few reports address some pertinent issues to improved school performance.

Issue: Teachers can do a professional job in a 10-month work year
A schedule based on an agrarian work year reminiscent of the the early part of this century cannot provide the time for reflection, sharing, and evaluating needed in schools. Teachers must work an extended year to meet their responsibility.

- Time between each quarter for evaluating lessons and planning new ones
- Time for curriculum planning and evaluation that is unfettered and thoughtful
- Time for learning new approaches and skills
- Flexible schedules to give more individual attention to students and to extend learning beyond the classroom

Issue: Teachers should be rewarded on the basis of time and credits, not performance and skill
Present salary schedules reward teachers by longevity and college credits. Talent, performance, or skill are assumed to be a product of time—seniority—or college courses.

Teaching, a profession that is supposed to nurture talent, does not recognize talent among its own practitioners. The premise is that there are not adequate measures for what teachers do and that there are too many variables that affect learning that are beyond the control of classroom teachers. As a result, the argument goes that salary should not be based on performance.

Concepts like skill-based pay—paying teachers if they demonstrate advanced knowledge and application of skills in teaching, curriculum, and motivation—go unexplored as union-management negotiations continue to focus on seniority and credits. Talent—reward for skill and performance—is reduced to master teacher plans (do more–get more) or totally objective participation on committees or assignments.

Issue: Teachers are interchangeable parts—they can be assigned without regard to qualifications
Schools are one of the few organizations that take talent from universities

and colleges or other districts and do not orient it to the culture and values of the workplace. It is assumed that teachers are interchangeable parts—that there are few differences in philosophy and approach between them.

In addition, all teachers are treated uniformly and consistently—as per master contract—despite levels of performance, experience, or commitment. Rule-driven treatment, devoid of reward for performance and commitment, is discouraging and dehumanizing.

Issue: Objectivity is the only criterion that matters in teacher evaluation
Schools have tunnel vision in measuring teacher performance, relying only on objective criteria. As a result, evaluation systems measure the measureable—those things easily quantifiable but not always most important to high-level performance. Although lessons and lesson plans can be assessed for the proper number of steps or sequence, they do not guarantee inspired, committed performance.

Students indicate that inspiration, caring, and commitment are factors that cause them to work and perform in class. How does one objectively measure caring and commitment? All of us remember those special, talented teachers who had the ability to inspire us. Sterile and totally objective evaluation systems do injustice to the creative and inspirational personality that makes learning come alive. There is a difference between being technically proficient and being able to inspire students. Rational evaluation methods do not account for the emotional and affective connections exceptional teachers produce.

Issue: Reforming schools means change in structure and governance but not tools and technology
In the private sector, organizational reform affects not only structure but tools and methods. Teachers as information or knowledge workers require better and more information to make instructional decisions, eliminate overlap in curriculum, and teach in an interdisciplinary manner, emphasizing concepts and ideas, not bits and pieces of information or facts.

Technology—computers, interactive video, and other tools—can expand learning beyond traditional boundaries, bring participative teaching into classrooms, help customize instruction, and monitor student progress. Schools need to be retooled in the transformation process.

OUTCOMES FOR SUCCESSFUL SCHOOLS: QUALITY AND PRODUCTIVITY

Obviously, the application of the transformation process—perceiving, thinking, behaving—to the organizational components discussed in Chapter 11 has an effect on outcomes. This chapter is meant to be complementary to the prior one, but with quality and productivity as the emphases. A more complete picture of the transforming school is achieved by reviewing both chapters together.

Quality in transforming schools must be discussed in terms of the clients they are to serve—the students. If student outcomes are not improved significantly, then change and reform are exercises in structural manipulation. There must be significant outcomes in performance, not simply in process, which has been the focus of most mandates geared to school improvement. Process reform may create a situation where "the operation is a technical success but the patient dies." The second facet of quality is how the mission of the school reflects commitment to quality, and how the structure of the school supports it.

Quality and Students

If schools do not believe that all students can learn, then some students will not achieve. The *perception* of some students as "damaged goods" (because of family background, socioeconomic status, or other extraneous variables) compromises student potential and talent. Perceiving students as being capable of learning all that the schools have to offer affects how we think about the outcomes they can achieve.

One outcome is that students are not *thought* of as stereotypes or labels: Thinking is open-minded and client-centered. Professionals do not give excuses for student nonachievement, but think in terms of alternatives to help them reach their goals. Students are thought of as workers, not products. Accepting students as workers presupposes that growth and development are continuous processes and that they are active in them. If teachers perceive and think of students in these ways, they will accept all students as equal, deserving of their best efforts in cognitive and affective areas. Equity of opportunity, expectations (within the confines of ability), and results are expected.

The *behavior* of staff who deliver quality service to students can be illustrated by the following outcomes:

- Behavior and learning expectations are clearly defined and communicated to staff and students.
- The school has a variety of instructional techniques available for students to master academics and other aspects of the program. Diversity of strategy includes differing modes of learning and varied pacing and step size of instruction and depth of content for all students.
- Tracking or grouping students is limited and based on multiple criteria, but labeling is nonexistent because students live up or

down to expectations. Teaching students requires a moral commitment to not separating them based on uncertain criteria and standards, which may set limitations on what is expected of them.

- Students are given the opportunity to assume responsibility for their learning and they are held accountable for their attitudes, behavior, and performance.
- Performance results of students and schools are analyzed and evaluated by grade, socioeconomic status, and race to ensure that all students are learning.
- Technology is applied to the learning process to make learning more active and customized. Students use computer technology, not as rewards, but as tools for word processing, data bases, and spreadsheets. Games are not emphasized, but multistimulus approaches to instruction are used.
- Students and parents receive regular and consistent feedback, beyond grade reports, about achievement and behavior. Information about performance and behavior is obtained, assessed, and shared.

Quality and the School's Mission

As a value, quality requires that schools invest resources, skill, and effort to achieve the finest results possible based on standards. It is reflected in the multifaceted goals and academic orientation of the curriculum. Quality means that the curriculum works consistently over time for all students from all kinds of backgrounds. Achieving quality outcomes is the *perceived* mission.

Philosophy is *thought* about seriously and is used as the basis for program development. Program values undergird the philosophy and are defined. The concept of the educated person is thought of beyond the bounds of employment to incorporate the broad goals of cultural, affective, academic, psychomotor, and citizenship education.

Transforming schools direct *behavior* at these ends:

1. Standards are explicit and rigorous in the stated mission, with success, not simply effectiveness, as the goal. There is a distinct, definable philosophy for the schools: They know their role and mission and do not try to be all things to all people.

2. Resources follow the values and the essentials that support them. There is a process for renewal of pertinent programs based on systematic analysis and evaluation. Reality checks are built into the program to assess purpose versus outcomes, and outcomes versus the demands of the external context. The curriculum is pruned as ineffective courses and experiences are weeded out because they starve resources from the valued ones.

3. Teachers demonstrate commitment by giving feedback to parents and students, tutoring students who need assistance, and communicating between home and school. Teachers reach out and call parents and do not wait for parents to contact them. They have a service-to-the-customer orientation and work actively to garner the support of the entire community for school programs.

4. The world is brought into the schools—the curriculum is not isolated from reality. Connections are made to economic, political, historical, technological, scientific, and ethical facets of life. Controversial issues are debated, seminars are held, and role models (people who brought ambition and aspiration into reality) are provided for students. These role models do not deal in diversion, but they are from the business, political, cultural, and social worlds.

Quality and Structure

Structure should be *perceived* as serving the purpose and mission of the organization; it should portray the values of the school. Centralized as well as decentralized systems convey a certain value pattern. If decisions need to be made at the point of impact, then the structure should reflect decentralization. Mission, and the values underlying it, drives structure, not vice versa. Quality control is perceived as a function of organizational culture.

Structure is *thought* of as a means to an end, not an end in itself. As a result, organizational structure is "not cast in stone"; it is subject to modification and redesign. Such flexible configurations meet changes in mission, program, and need. Clients' needs require structures that are adaptive, not static, in providing proactive service. Adaptive organizations are innovative. They mesh form and function like good architecture and design.

Defining what a quality structure is *not* is easy because of the concerns usually expressed by people working in them. The outcomes of an organizational structure should not:

- Obfuscate roles and lines of authority.
- Overspecialize roles and work, denying teachers and others the

opportunity to assume responsibility and examine issues from a broad perceptual base.
* Create red tape and unnecessary forms and procedures.
* Develop a bureaucratic mentality.

Instead, successful school structures emphasize *behavior* that is personalized and individualized based on the needs of students, parents, and the community. People are the key to quality control. Educational service is the goal of everyone in the organization—from professional to support staffs. Parents and children are given some choice in programs based on the needs of students, and some input into the design and emphasis of the curricular and instructional undertaking.

Because the values of the school are defined and communicated, the structure is designed to promote them. Although tight around these values, the structure allows for teachers and others to have the autonomy to achieve the mission of the school.

Professional structures are liberating to teacher behavior. They release potential, not constrain it; they stimulate creativity, not stifle it; and they allow people to assume responsibility, not restrict individuals to technical solutions. Quality schools allow for:

* Continued, year-round professional growth opportunities.
* Communication between teachers.
* Innovation, where teachers can try ideas, and discuss and share with colleagues and administrators. Funds are available for new approaches and projects as seed money, and young teachers can find advocates and mentors to champion ideas.
* School structures are responsive—they get feedback from customers (the community, parents, and students) and use it for information to find answers to better ways of serving and teaching.

Quality and Assessment

Outcomes are affected by assessment, which is a prerequisite for determining productivity. Assessment and productivity are intertwined, because evaluation of outcomes forms the basis for determining how productive a strategy or program is.

Transforming schools believe that they can measure and assess performance outcomes, even complex ones. To deny measurement and assessment is to deny the relationship between professional service and outcomes. Is performance in school solely a result of factors beyond the control of teachers and principals? Transforming schools perceive assessment and evaluation as the key to checking program and student performance against achievement. Perceptions of program performance must be validated by data and information.

Analyzing and evaluating are the two thought processes used in assessment. Analysis requires that a program, strategy, or act be separated into its components to discover their interrelationships. Evaluation involves making judgments about the effectiveness or values of a program, act, or strategy. Evaluation is the product of analysis and appraisal. These processes are the critical components to any assessment plan.

Transforming schools think of assessment in terms of value added. What value is added after a student completes a unit, an instructional strategy, or a course? We know that all students do not come to the instructional process with the same background or knowledge. The issue at hand is the value that was added after the process was complete in terms of increased skills, understanding concepts, deeper knowledge, or positive attitudes.

Assessment and evaluation are multifaceted and comprehensive, formulated around the goals of successful schools. They measure cognitive, affective, and psychomotor outcomes, and are based on performance and behavior measures. The assessment program is grounded in the values and mission of the organization. The pertinent question is: Is the organization living its values and achieving its mission and purpose? Data from internal and external sources are gathered to provide the information to determine the match between purpose and performance.

The behavior in transforming schools produces the following assessment outcomes:

- Curricular assessment is based on key questions that are measurable. These questions are geared to the values and mission statement.
- Processes are in place to gather pertinent data. Appraisals are not made on the basis of impressions or conventional wisdom.
- Evaluation is used to sustain or change programs. There is a direct link between evaluation and the decision-making process. The results of evaluation are applied to the decisions and are not isolated or forgotten.

Students do not live in a multiple-choice world. Adults' performance is seldom assessed by multiple-choice tests. Why, then, do schools rely so heavily on them? In transforming schools, student learning outcomes are measured by performance: Can the student show competence by speaking, writing, performing, demonstrating, defending, or constructing? Student performance portfolios will replace the multiple-choice tests if students are to become more sophisticated learners and move beyond rote activities or memorization.

Transforming teaching can be done by curriculum changes and by outcome assessment. Figure 12–1 contains a schematic showing the influences on curriculum and divergent and comprehensive approaches to outcome assessment. The combination of revised curriculum programs and different and more comprehensive ways to assess student performance can have a dynamic impact on transforming teaching and learning.

Teaching can be transformed by the two "drive shafts" of curriculum and outcome assessment. Many schools have revised curriculum, but teaching remains much the same in approach and style. The assessment "drive shaft" has the potential to have a significant impact on how students are taught.

Assessment measures requiring students to perform complex learning tasks will cause teachers to instruct so that pupils can do those things. If problem solving is important, then the assessment process must have students defining strategies to problems under circumstances when information is incomplete. If writing a literate essay with two ideas is significant, then pupils must create one. With an emphasis on the application of learning and learning skills, teachers will teach in these more active and participative ways.

Transforming schools also report on the progress of the entire system. They define vital signs that compose information on the critical fiscal, performance, demographic, and behavioral components of the school system and share them with the public regularly and systematically. Like vital signs in medicine, these idicators provide a profile of the health of the school system as a whole. The results of assessment are open and communicated.

Productivity in Schools

Productivity in schools is a controversial concept. As indicated in Chapter 3, productivity is the outcome of student and teacher work, contrary to the private sector where client output is not always a factor. It is a difficult concept, but transforming schools do not deny its relevance, particularly in times of conflicting demands and limited resources.

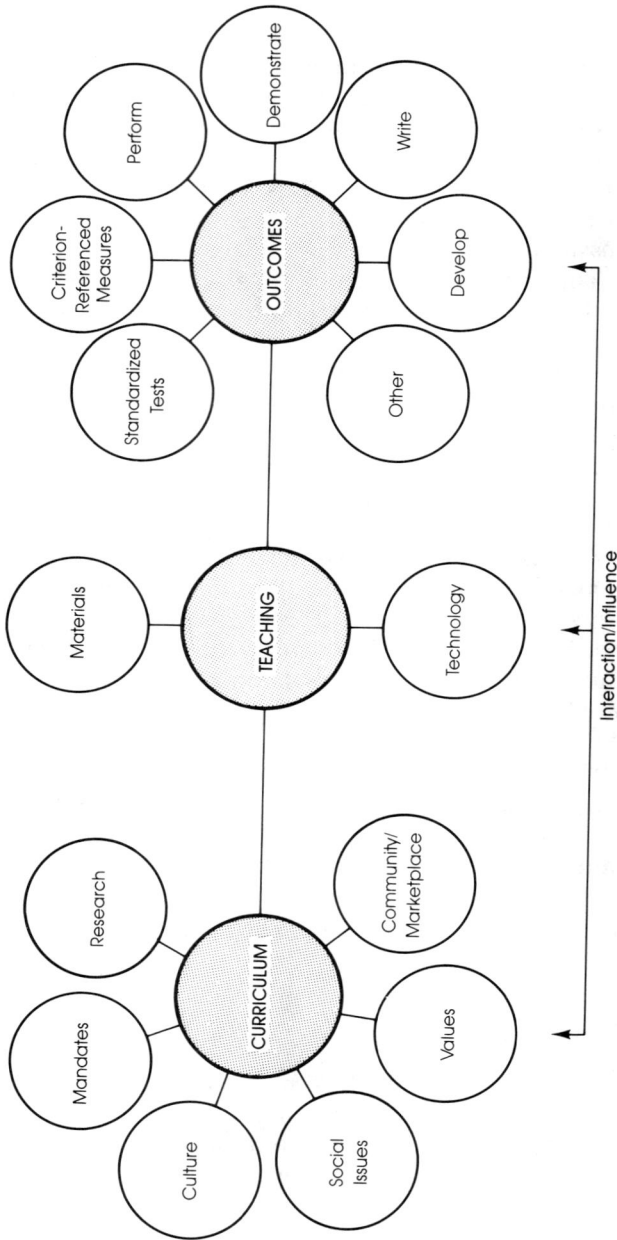

FIGURE 12–1 Transforming Teaching: Curriculum Teaching—Outcomes

To maintain credibility, schools need to address the productivity issue. Some strategies and programs are more effective than others. Transforming schools *perceive* productivity positively, and approach it to better invest the scarce resources of time and money. These two resources are the framework around which human resources and talent are applied. Transforming schools have a different *mindset* about productivity. They have moved away from the assembly-line viewpoint. Parts of that mindset include students as workers who contribute to productivity. It defines teachers' professional productivity in terms of use of time, number of students, amount of learning, and cost.

Two concepts are vital in *thinking* about productivity—effectiveness and efficiency. Effectiveness + Efficiency = Productivity. Efficiency relates to how time and resources are applied to students and their learning. Effectiveness concerns the amount of content, skills, and concepts students have learned and can demonstrate through performance.

Transformation implies that total programs are assessed and that decisions are made about their nature and scope. Schools that assess productivity exhibit these *behaviors*. They:

- Have clear, stated expectations that are used to measure outcomes—cognitive, psychomotor, or affective.
- Remove redundancies in expectations across curriculum areas. Time is not squandered by students being exposed or expected to learn the same content or concept repeatedly.
- Measure performance against role objectives.
- Use short-term measures as well as longitudinal data.
- Monitor the quality of work life to determine which factors stymie teacher productivity and which ones stimulate it. False incentives—those that are presented and then altered or removed —are eliminated.
- Assess individual student status and measure the value added in terms of cognitive and affective learning and performance. They do not see all students as the same and measure growth from the baseline established by the initial status of students.
- Assess school productivity in terms of the number of students learning, the time it takes for learning to occur, and the amount learned.

To measure efficiency, effectiveness, and productivity, intelligent baseline information needs to be gathered. It should not be reduced to mindless test data, but must include complex measurements defined in the assessment section. Technology can assist in the process.

The technology system in productivity-oriented schools must have two features. First, it must be a network so that teachers and students have access to it. Second, it must be integrated across functions so that different data bases can be integrated to assess productivity. Too frequently, teachers do not have access to computers, nor do students use them for instruction, beyond electronic worksheets or rote, drill programs.

Integrated data bases include fiscal, administrative, or management and instructional components. The fiscal data base includes budget and expense information, as well as inventory and other management measures. The administrative data base includes scheduling, grading, and student and personnel records. The instructional data base includes curriculum objectives and outcomes, student productivity tools for learning, and learning packages. Teachers' gradebooks and other classroom management and instructional programs can also be kept electronically.

Integrated data bases allow teachers and school leaders the opportunity to assess learning outcomes of student(s) by cost. Unless these data bases can be integrated, performance data and cost-effectiveness cannot be determined. Technology can lay the foundation for cost-effectiveness studies and determinations because data can be assessed over time, large amounts of information can be analyzed, and complex factors can be correlated and evaluated. Although productivity is a complex concept, the technology is available for teachers and principals to begin defining and using it.

Some day, through technology, students will have access to learning programs 24 hours a day. Technology will blow the doors of the schoolhouse off, giving access to learning for the entire community throughout the day, week, and year. Technology will allow students to learn at their own pace and depth; rate of learning will not be a significant factor. Customized education will be possible, and students will not be segregated or tracked. Technology will help them by appealing to a number of senses, by being inherently patient, and by monitoring progress without being judgmental. Table 12–1 reviews what perception, thinking, and behavior are needed to transform schools in respect to quality and productivity outcomes.

SUMMARY

Transforming schools demonstrate their success by defining quality and developing the means to assess it. They do not ignore issues of

TABLE 12–1   Summary: Quality and Productivity

Perception	Thinking	Behavior
Students: All students can learn	No stereotyping Open minded Client centered Students as workers	Learning expectations defined Variety of teaching methods Students accountable Technology applied
School's mission	Philosophical Analytical	Standards explicit Resources follow values Schools reach out World brought into school
Structure	Means to an end	Flexible Personalized Liberates teacher behavior Promotes innovation
Assessment	Analytical Evaluative	Multifaceted, comprehensive Value-added Grounded in values Data gathering Curriculum-assessment drives teaching
Productivity	Students as workers Teacher effectiveness/ Efficiency	Cost-effectiveness Clear expectations Remove redundancies Measure performance vs. purpose Short term and longitudinal Monitor work life Technology: Networked and integrated Value-added

productivity but work to develop ways to measure it that incorporates teacher and student behavior.

In summary, transforming schools:

Have an obsession with quality service: They evaluate which services meet the needs of students, are convenient, and are effective.

Embrace accountability for performance: Understanding that credibility is critical to continued support, transforming schools measure productivity and performance, moving beyond defining if processes are in place. Performance, not processes, are emphasized, allowing for diversity in techniques and approach.

Adapt structure to ends: Structure is perceived as a means to an end, not an end in itself. Structures are accountable to produce results, and if they do not, they are changed.

Assess performance in multidimensional, complex ways: They move beyond standardized tests to methods that assess complex learning skills, demonstrating competence by applying learning and solving problems. Transforming schools do not live in a multiple-choice, fill-in-the-blank world. They assess student performance in an organization over time and with diverse, multiple options.

Stress productivity: These schools want to discover the methods and approaches that are most productive. They do not live with the perception that all techniques are equally cost-effective. They explore the complex issues of teacher and student productivity because they know credibility rests on results that are achieved efficiently.

Epilogue

Whether schools transform or do not respond to changing times is not dependent on one particular program, style, or approach. Recipes and "quick fixes" will not create school organizations that are productive and successful over time. The foundation for transformation is in their approaches to perceiving and thinking that directs their behavior— therein lies the answer to the elements of their success or demise.

In the private sector marketplace, organizations learn very quickly if they are out of step—through the loss of profit or demand for their service or product. Publicly supported institutions, like schools, have no such barometer but must float on the tides of public opinion and credibility. All organizations, private or public, must understand the contextual forces and demands placed on them, even though there is greater ambiguity and fluidity in events and context.

Leaders must be aggressive in understanding and evaluating the life of their schools in the greater environment. They must have methods and tools to scan trends and issues and evaluate their impact on the educational program. This requires multi- and interdisciplinary thinking—not isolated to educational perspectives, strategies, or experts. Issues of economic, political, cultural, and social trends must be integrated into the construction and implementation of school programs and approaches. Even within the world of education, there are changes and dynamics through research, technology, and assessment that should cause schools to rethink their approaches to instruction and curriculum.

One of the major tenets of this book is that scientific management does not work very well in a nonrational world or organization. Logical and linear structures and processes do not produce results—people with commitment and motivation do. And people need nurturing, consideration, and respect to help guide organizations in their decision making in ambiguous and uncertain situations.

School leaders undergo too much training in rational management, task analysis, and systems approaches, and do not receive enough emphasis on the values and principles of public service that drives and attracts talent. Talent withers and dies under the weight of manuals, formulas, regulations, and procedures that deny the autonomy and motivation people gain from noble pursuits and causes.

School systems are not tidy flowcharts with clear and distinct roles, lines of authority, and power that can be manipulated with cause-and-effect precision. They are messy conglomerates of people, groups, aspirations, causes, and ideas—more akin to a rope with its strands interwoven and tied together.

Organizations with these characteristics need strong leadership, not leadership grounded in transactions that are arranged to meet needs in exchange for performance. People must react to unclear circumstances, gain consensus, and make decisions in accord with the values and principles that are the heart of the organization. Decisions need input and have to be made closest to the point of impact, carrying accountability for results. Transforming leaders gain commitment and help people realize their aspirations and live their values. They need credibility and the stamina to build consensus among divergent demands and groups.

We must operate with the perception that the people who work in schools are professionals. Transformation can make that a reality. Although teachers and principals may come to the schools with different agendas, motivations, and levels of development, the educational environment and culture will establish norms and values for people to move toward self-actualization. Transforming schools enable all people in them—children and adults—to become their best, through high expectations, high standards of quality, equal access to growth opportunities, and shared values. Such schools are committed to hiring, training, and developing talented professionals, who are then respected in their field, satisfied in their jobs, and productive in meeting educational outcomes for success.

Finally, public institutions are not forever. They can be phased out of existence if they do not garner and maintain support. Alternatives will be found, particularly if economic, cultural, and political welfare depend on them. Although the public demands stability in its public organizations, it also requires productivity and effectiveness. Change is necessary to do both—transformation of how the organization perceives, thinks, and behaves.

References

Albert, Steven S. In J. Kimberly and Robert Quinn, eds., *Managing Organizational Transitions*. San Francisco: Jossey-Bass, 1984.

Allen, Steve. "Humor Me." *Creative Living* (Autumn, 1988): 2–5.

American Association of School Administrators. "Challenges for School Leaders." 1988.

Argyris, Chris. *Personality and Organization*. New York: Harper and Row, 1957.

Argyris, Chris. *Integrating the Individual and the Organization*. New York: Wiley and Sons, 1964.

Argyris, Chris. *Strategy, Change, and Defensive Routines*. Boston: Pitman, 1985.

Argyris, Chris, and Schon, Donald A. *Theory and Practice: Increasing Professional Effectiveness*. San Francisco: Jossey-Bass, 1977.

Association for Supervision and Curriculum Development. "Leadership: Examining the Elusive." 1987.

Baloff, Nicholas, and Doherty, Elizabeth M. "Potential Pitfalls in Employee Participation." *Organizational Dynamics* (Winter 1989): 51–62.

Barnard, Chester I. *The Functions of the Executive*. Cambridge, MA: Harvard University Press, 1938.

Bass, Bernard M. *Leadership and Performance Beyond Expectations*. New York: Free Press, 1985.

Bennis, Warren. "Leadership: A Beleaguered Species?" *Organizational Dynamics*, 5 (Summer 1976): 2–16.

Bennis, Warren. *Why Leaders Can't Lead*. San Francisco: Jossey-Bass, 1989.

Bennis, Warren, and Nanus, Bert. *Leaders: Strategies for Taking Charge*. New York: Harper and Row, 1985.

Blake, Robert, and Mouton, Jane. *The Managerial Grid*. Houston: Gulf, 1964.

Blau, Peter M., and Scott, W. Richard. *Formal Organization*. San Francisco: Chandler, 1962.

Block, Peter. *The Empowered Manager*. San Francisco: Jossey-Bass, 1988.

289

Blumberg, Arthur. *School Administration as Craft: Foundations for Practice.* Boston: Allyn and Bacon, 1989.

Boyer, Ernest L. *High School.* New York: Harper and Row, 1983.

Boyer, Ernest L. "Leadership: A Clear and Vital Mission." *The College Board,* 150 (Winter 1989): 6–9.

Brandt, Ronald (interviewer). "On Assessment of Teaching: A Conversation with Lee Schulman." *Educational Leadership* 46 (November 1988): 42–46.

Brandt, Ronald. "On Teacher Empowerment: A Conversation with Ann Lieberman." *Educational Leadership,* 46 (May 1989): 23–26.

Brimfiels, Reneé M. B. "Imagination, Rigor, and Caring: One Framework for Educational Reform." *Journal of Curriculum and Supervision, 3, 3* (Spring 1988): 253–262.

Burns, James McGregor. *Leadership.* New York: Harper and Row, 1978.

Carver, Fred, and Sergiovanni, Thomas. *Organizations and Human Behavior: Focus on Schools.* New York: McGraw-Hill, 1969.

Chase, Aurora, and Wolfe, Pat. "Off to a Good Start in Peer Coaching." *Educational Leadership,* 46 (May 1989): 37.

Chew, W. Bruce. "No-nonsense Guide to Measuring Productivity." *Harvard Business Review* (January–February 1988): 110–118.

Chrisco, Ingrid M. "Peer Assistance Works." *Educational Leadership* 46 (May 1989): 31–34.

Chubb, John E. "To Revive Schools, Dump Bureaucrats." *New York Times* (December 9, 1988): 31.

Combs, Arthur W. "New Assumptions for Educational Reform." *Educational Leadership* (February 1988): 38–40.

Conley, Sharon C.; Bacharach, Samuel B.; and Bauer, Scott. "The School Work Environment and Teacher Career Dissatisfaction." *Educational Administration Quarterly, 25,* 1 (February 1989): 58–81.

Conley, Sharon C.; Schmidle, Timothy; and Shedd, Jospeh B. "Teacher Participation in the Management of School Systems." *College Record, 90,* 2 (Winter 1988): 259–280.

Corwin, Ronald G. "Professional Persons in Public Organizations." In Fred D. Carver and Thomas Sergiovanni, eds., *Organizations and Human Behavior.* New York: McGraw-Hill, 1969.

Costa, Arthur L. *Developing Minds.* Association for Supervision and Curriculum Development, 1985.

Cuban, Larry. "The District Superintendent and the Restructuring of Schools: A Realistic Appraisal." In Thomas Sergiovanni and John H. Moore, eds., *Schooling for Tomorrow.* Boston: Allyn and Bacon, 1989, pp. 251–271.

Daft, Richard L. *Organizational Theory and Design.* St. Paul: West, 1989.

Danner, Mark D. "How Not to Fix the Schools." *Harpers* (February 1986): 39–51.

Davis, Stanley M. "Transforming Organizations: The Key to Strategy Is Context." *Organizational Dynamics* (Winter 1982): 64–80.

Deal, Terrence E., and Kennedy, Allan A. *Corporate Cultures*. Reading, MA: Addison-Wesley, 1982.

Dempsey, John R. "A President's Perspective on Leadership." *The College Board Review 150* (Winter 1989): 16–19.

Deutsch, Claudia H. "U.S. Industry's Unfinished Struggle." *New York Times* (February 21, 1988): 1.

Dowling, William. *Effective Management and the Behavioral Sciences*. American Management Association, 1978.

Drucker, Peter F. *The Frontiers of Management*. New York: Harper and Row, 1986.

Drucker, Peter F. "The Coming of the New Organization." *Harvard Business Review*, 88, 1 (January–February 1988): 45–53.

Duncan, W. Jack, and Feisal, J. Philip. "No Laughing Matter: Patterns of Humor in the Workplace." *Organizational Dynamics*, 17 (Spring 1989): 18–30.

Dunham, Randall B. *Organizational Behavior: People and Process in Management*. Homewood, IL: Richard D. Irwin, 1984.

Ellson, Douglas. "Improving Productivity in Teaching." *Phi Delta Kappan*, 68, 2 (October 1986): 111–124.

Elmore, Richard F., and McLaughlin, Milbrey Wallin. *Steady Work*. The Rand Corporation, 1988.

Etzioni, Amatai. *A Comparative Analysis of Complex Organizations*. New York: The Free Press, 1973.

Etzioni, Amatai. "Humble Decision Making." *Harvard Business Review*, 67, 4 (July–August, 1989): 122–126.

Feldman, Steven P. "How Organizational Culture Can Affect Innovation." *Organizational Dynamics* (Summer 1988): 57–68.

Fiedler, Fred E. *A Theory of Leadership Effectiveness*. New York: McGraw-Hill, 1967.

Fielding, Glen D., and Schalock, Del H. *Promoting the Professional Development of Teachers and Administrators*. University of Oregon: Center for Educational Policy and Management, 1985.

Floder, Robert E., and Clark, Christopher M. "Preparing Teachers for Uncertainty." *Teachers College Record*, 89, 4 (Summer 1988): 505–524.

Galbraith, Jay R. "Designing Innovative Organizations." *Organizational Dynamics* (Winter 1982): 5–25.

Galloway, Charles M., ed. *Theory and Practice*, 19, 4 (1980). Ohio State University.

Gardner, John W. *Self-Renewal*. New York: Harper and Row, 1964.

Gardner, John W. *Morale*. New York: W. W. Norton, 1978.

Gardner, John W. *Self-Renewal* (revised edition). New York: W. W. Norton, 1981.

Gardner, John W. *Excellence*. New York: W. W. Norton, 1984.

Gardner, John W. "The Task of Leadership: Part 1: Getting Things Moving." *Personnel* (October 1986).

Garfield, Charles. "Peak Performers, The New Heroes of American Business." *McMillian Executive Summary*, 2 (Winter 1986).

Garrison, James W. "Democracy, Scientific Knowledge and Teacher Empowerment." *Teachers College Record, 89,* 4 (Summer 1988).

Garvin, David A. "Competing Dimensions of Quality." *Harvard Business Review, 65,* 6 (November–December. 1987): 101–109.

Georgiades, William; Fuentes, Ernestina; and Snyder, Karolyn. *A Meta-Analysis of Productive School Cultures.* Pedamorphosis, Inc. (No date given)

Glasser, William. *The Quality School.* New York, Harper & Row, 1990.

Glickman, Carl D. "Unlocking School Reform: Uncertainty as a Condition of Professionalism." *Phi Delta Kappan, 69,* 2 (October 1987): 120–122.

Goens, George A. "Myths About Evaluation." *Phi Delta Kappan, 63* (February 1982): 411.

Goens, George A. "Zen and the Art of School Administration." *Forward, 10* (Fall 1984): 56–59.

Goens, George A. "Culture and the School Superintendent." *Wisconsin School News* (August 1985).

Goens, George A. "Program Evaluation: Process or Product?" Texas Elementary Principals and Supervisors Association *TEPSA Journal,* (Winter 1987).

Goens, George A., and Clover, Sharon I. R. *Getting the Most from Public Schools.* Englewood, FL: Pineapple Press, 1987.

Goens, George A., and Koehn, John J. "The Talent We Nourish: A Word for Supervisors." *Educational Leadership, 34* (May 1977).

Goens, George A., and Kuciezyck, Janet. "Supervision: Stress Inducer or Stress Reducer?" *National Association of Secondary School Principals Bulletin, 65* (December 1981).

Goens, George A., and Lange, Ronald W. "Supervision as Self-Management." *National Association for Secondary School Principals Bulletin, 59* (December 1975): 1–6.

Goens, George A., and Lange, Ronald W. "Supervision as Instructional Analysis." *National Association of Secondary School Principals Bulletin, 60* (September 1976).

Goens, George A., and Lange, Ronald W. "Creative Supervision: Antidote to Burnout." *The Iowa Curriculum Bulletin* (Spring 1980): 34–38.

Goens, George A., and Lange, Ronald W. "A Design for Staff Management and Development." *The Developer* (Spring 1983).

Goens, George A., and Schulze, Gary. "School Organization: Building Walls or Bridges?" *Association of Wisconsin School Administrators Bulletin* (April 1980).

Goens, George A., and Vyskocil, Janet R. "Collective Bargaining and Supervision: A Matter of Climate." *Educational Leadership, 37* (November 1980): 175–177.

Golembiewski, Robert T. *Behavior and Organization.* Chicago: Rand McNally, 1962.

Goodlad, John I. *A Place Called School.* New York: McGraw-Hill, 1984.

Goodman, Jesse. "The Disenfranchisement of Elementary Teachers and Strategies for Resistance." *Journal of Curriculum and Supervision, 3,* 3 (Spring 1988): 201–220.

Graham, Patricia Alberg. "Schools: Cacaphony About Practice, Silence About Purpose." *DAEDALUS, 113,* 4 (Fall 1984): 49.

Griffiths, Daniel; Clark, David L.; Wynn, D. Richard; and Iannacone, Laurence. *Organizing Schools for Effective Education.* Danville, IL: Interstate Publishers, 1962.

Gryskiewicz, Stanley; Shields, James; and Sensabaugh, Sharon. *Creativity Week VI, 1983—Blueprint for Innovation.* Greensboro, NC: (April 1984).

Guild, Pat Burke. "How Leaders' Minds Work." *Leadership: Examining the Elusive.* ASCD Yearbook, 1987.

Guthries, James W. "Campaign '88 and Education: A Primer for Presidential Candidates." *Phi Delta Kappan* (March 1988): 514–519.

Halpin, Andrew. *Theory and Research in Administration.* New York: Mac-Millan, 1966.

Hanson E, Mark. *Educational Administration and Organizational Behavior.* Boston: Allyn and Bacon, 1985.

Harmon, Frederick G., and Jacobs, Garry. *The Vital Difference.* New York: American Management Association, 1985.

Harris, Ben. *Inservice Education for Staff Development.* Boston: Allyn and Bacon, 1989.

Harvey, Jerry B. "The Abilene Paradox: The Management of Agreement." *Organizational Dynamics* (Summer 1988): 17–43.

Heirs, Ben. *The Professional Decision-Thinker.* New York: Dodd, Mead, and Company, 1987.

Hemphill, John, and Coons, Alvin. *Leader Behavior Description.* Ohio State University: Columbus Personnel Research Board, 1950.

Heneman, Herbert G. III; Schwab, Donald P.; Fossum, John A.; and Dyer, Lee D. *Personnel/Human Resource Management.* Homewood, IL: Richard D. Irwin, 1980.

Hersey, Paul, and Blanchard, Kenneth H. *Management of Organizational Behavior: Utilizing Human Resources.* Englewood Cliffs, NJ: Prentice-Hall, 1977.

Hirsch, F. D. *Cultural Literacy: What Every American Needs to Know.* Boston: Houghton-Mifflin, 1987.

Hodgkinson, Harold L. *All One System.* Washington, DC: Institute for Educational Leadership, 1985.

Hoy, Wayne, and Clover, Sharon I. R. "Elementary School Climate: A Revision of the OCDQ." *Education Administration Quarterly, 22* (Winter 1986): 93–110.

Hoy, Wayne K., and Miskel, Cecil G. *Educational Administration: Theory, Research and Practice.* New York: Random House, 1978.

Hyman, Ronald, T. "Peer Coaching: Premises, Problems, and Potential." *N.J.A.S.C.D. Focus on Education,* 1989, pp. 64–73.

Iannaccone, Laurence. "An Approach to the Informal Organization of the School." *Sixty-Third Yearbook of the National Society for the Study of Education.* Chicago: University of Chicago Press, 1964.

Jung, Carl, G. *Psychological Types* (H. G. Baynes, trans.; revised by R.F.C. Hull). Princeton, NJ: Princeton University Press, 1971.

Kanter, Rosabeth Moss. *The Change Masters*. New York: Simon and Schuster, 1984.

Kast, Fremont E., and Rosenzweig, James E. *Organization and Management: A Systems Approach*. New York: McGraw-Hill, 1970.

Kegan, Robert. *The Evolving Self: Problems and Process in Human Development*. Cambridge, MA: Harvard University Press, 1982.

Kilmann, Ralph H.; Covin, Teresa Joyce; and Associates, eds. *Corporate Transformation*. San Francisco: Jossey-Bass, 1988.

Korn, Lester B. "How the Next CEO Will Be Different." *Fortune* (May 22, 1989): 157–161.

Kuhn, Thomas S. *The Structure of Scientific Revolutions*. Chicago: University of Chicago Press, 1962.

Lambert, Linda. "The End of an Era of Staff Development." *Educational Leadership*, 47 (September 1989): 78–81.

Lawler, Edward E. "Substitutes for Hierarchy." *Organizational Dynamics* (Summer 1988): 4–15.

Levin, Henry, M. "Cost-Effectiveness and Educational Policy." *Educational Evaluation and Policy Analysis*, 10, (Spring 1988): 51–69.

Levine, Sarah L. *Promoting Adult Growth in Schools*. Boston: Allyn and Bacon, 1989.

Levitt, Ted. "The Innovating Organization." *Harvard Business Review*, 1 (January–February 1988): 7.

Lewis, Anne C. "Read the Writing on the Wall." *Phi Delta Kappan* (March 1988): 469.

Lewis, James, Jr. *Re-Creating Our Schools for the 21st Century*. Westbury, NY: J. L. Wilkerson, 1987.

Lieberman, Ann, and Miller, Lynne. *Teachers, Their World and Their Work: Implications for School Improvement*. Association for Supervision and Curriculum Development, 1984.

Loevinger, Jane. *Ego Development: Conceptions and Theories*. San Francisco: Jossey-Bass, 1976.

Lombardo, Michael. "Looking at Leadership: Some Neglected Issues." *Center for Creative Leadership* (January 1978).

Lortie, Dan C. *School Teacher: A Sociological Study*. Chicago: University of Chicago Press, 1975.

Mackay, D. A. "Using Professional Talent in a School Organization." In Fred D. Carver and Thomas Sergiovanni, eds., *Organizations and Human Behavior*. New York: McGraw-Hill, 1969.

Maeroff, Gene I. "A Blueprint for Empowering Teachers." *Phi Delta Kappan*, 69, 7 (March 1988): 472–477.

Main, Jeremy. "The Battle for Quality Begins." *Fortune* (December 29, 1980): 28–33.

Main, Jeremy. "The Curmudgeon Who Talks Tough on Quality." *Fortune*, 109, 13 (June 25, 1984): 118–122.

Maslow, Abraham. *Toward a Psychology of Being*. Princeton, NJ: Van Nostrand, 1962.

Massing, Michael. "Detroit's Strange Bedfellows." *New York Times Magazine* (February 7, 1988): 20–52.

McCall, Morgan W., Jr., and Lombardo, Michael M., eds. *Leadership: Where Else Can We Go?* Durham, NC: Duke University Press, 1978.

McKenzie, Jamieson A. *Making Change in Education—Preparing Your Schools for the Future.* Westbury, NY: J. L. Wilkerson, 1987.

McKibben, Michael, and Joyce, Bruce. "Psychological States and Staff Development." *Theory into Practice* (Autumn 1980): 248–255.

Melohn, Thomas H. "How to Build Employee Trust and Productivity." *Harvard Business Review* (January–February 1983): 56–59.

Miller, Donald B. "How to Improve the Performance and Productivity of the Knowledge Worker." *Organizational Dynamics* (Winter 1977): 62–79.

Mintzberg, Henry. *The Nature of Managerial Work.* New York: Harper & Row, 1973.

Mintzberg, Henry. *The Structuring of Organizations.* Englewood Cliffs, NJ: Prentice-Hall, 1979.

Miskel, Cecil; McDonald, Davis; and Bloom, Susan. "Structural and Expectancy Linkages Within Schools and Organizational Effectiveness." *Educational Administration Quarterly*, 19, 1 (Winter 1983).

Morgan, Gareth. *Images of Organizations,* Beverly Hills: Sage, 1986.

Myers, Isabel Briggs, and McCaulley, Mary H. *Manual: A Guide to the Development and Use of the Myers-Briggs Type Indicator.* Palo Alto, CA: Consulting Psychologists Press, 1985.

National Education Association. *Conditions and Resources of Teaching.* NEA, 1988.

Netzer, Lanore; Eye, Glen; Dimock, Marshall E.; Dumont, Mathew P.; Homme, Lloyd; Kast, Fremont E.; and Knezevich, Stephen J. *Education, Administration, and Change.* New York: Harper and Row, 1970.

Nutt, Paul C. *Making Tough Decisions.* San Francisco: Jossey-Bass, 1989.

Odiorne, George S. *The Human Side of Management.* Lexington, MA: Lexington Books, 1987.

Olson, Lynn. "The 'Restructuring' Puzzle." *Education Week, 8,* 9 (November 2, 1988): 7–11.

Page, R. "The Position Description Questionnaire." Unpublished paper. Minneapolis: Control Data Business Advisors, 1985.

Passow, A. Harry. "Present and Future Directions in School Reform." In Thomas Sergiovanni and John H. Moore, eds., *Schooling for Tomorrow.* Boston: Allyn and Bacon, 1989, pp. 13–37.

Patten, Thomas H. "The Productivity of Human Resources in Government: Making Human Effort and Energy Count for More." *Human Resource Management, 19,* 1 (Spring 1980): 2–10.

Patterson, Jerry L.; Purkey, Stewart C.; and Parker, Jackson V. *Productive School Systems for a Non-Rational World.* Association for Supervision and Curriculum Development, 1986.

Perelman, Lewis J. *Technology and Transformation of Schools.* National School Boards Association, 1987.

Perrow, Charles. *Complex Organizations*. Glenview, IL: Scott, Foresman, 1972.

Peters, Thomas J., and Waterman, Robert H., Jr. *In Search of Excellence*. New York: Harper and Row, 1982.

Petty, Richard E. and Cacioppo, John T. *Attitudes and Persuasion: Classic and Contemporary Approaches*. Dubuque, IA: William C. Brown, Publishers, 1981.

Pfeffer, Jeffrey. "The Ambiguity of Leadership." In Morgan W. McCall, Jr., and Michael M. Lombardo, eds., *Leadership: Where Else Can We Go?* Durham, NC: Duke University Press, 1978, pp. 13–34.

Pondy, Louis R. "Leadership is a Language Game." In Morgan W. McCall, Jr., and Michael M. Lombardo, eds., *Leadership: Where Else Can We Go?* Durham, NC: Duke University Press, 1978, pp. 87–99.

Public School Forum of North Carolina. *The Condition of Being an Educator.* Raleigh, NC: Public School Forum of North Carolina.

Raelin, Joseph A. *The Clash of Cultures.* Boston: Harvard Business School Press, 1986.

Raney, Patricia, and Robbins, Pam. "Professional Growth and Support Through Peer Coaching." *Educational Leadership*, 46 (May 1989): 35–38.

Ravitch, Diane. *The Troubled Crusade.* New York: Basic Books, 1983.

Reeves, Elton T. *The Dynamics of Group Behavior.* American Management Association, 1970.

Reitz, H. Joseph. *Behavior in Organizations.* Homewood, IL: Richard D. Irwin, 1981.

Rokeach, Milton. *International Encyclopedia of Social Sciences.* New York: MacMillan and Free Press, 1968.

Rosenthal, Robert, and Jacobson, Lenore. *Pygmalion in the Classroom.* New York: Holt, Rinehart & Winston, 1968.

Sanders, Donald, and Schwab, Marion. "A School Context for Teacher Development." *Theory into Practice* (1980): 271–277.

Schein, Edgar H. *Organizational Culture and Leadership.* San Francisco: Jossey-Bass, 1985.

Schon, Donald. "Leadership as Reflection-in-Action." In Thomas Sergiovanni and John Corbally, eds., *Leadership and Organizational Culture: New Perspectives on Administrative Theory and Practice.* Urbana, IL: University of Illinois Press, 1984, pp. 36–63.

Sculley, John. *Odyssey.* New York: Harper and Row, 1987.

Sculley, John. "The Relationship Between Business and Higher Education." *EDUCOM Conference* (October 1987).

Sergiovanni, Thomas. "Leadership for Quality Schooling: New Understandings and Practices." Paper, 1987a.

Sergiovanni, Thomas J. *The Principalship: A Reflective Practice Perspective.* Boston: Allyn and Bacon, 1987b.

Sergiovanni, Thomas J. "Will We Ever Have a True Profession?" *Educational Leadership*, 444, 8 (May 1987c): 44–49.

Sergiovanni, Thomas J. "The Theoretical Basis for Cultural Leadership." *Leadership: Examining the Elusive.* ASCD Yearbook, 1985d, pp. 116–129.

Sergiovanni, Thomas J., and Corbally, John E., eds. *Leadership and Organizational Culture*. Urbana, IL: University of Illinois Press, 1984.

Sergiovanni, Thomas, and Moore, John H., eds. *Schooling for Tomorrow*. Boston: Allyn and Bacon, 1989.

Sergiovanni, Thomas J., and Starratt, Robert J. *Supervision: Human Perspectives*. New York: McGraw-Hill, 1983.

Shanker, Albert. "An Open Letter to Secretary Bennett." *New York Times* (April 27, 1988).

Shanker, Albert. Speech presented at ASCD conference, San Antonio, TX, March 1990.

Sherif, Muzafer, and Sherif, Carolyn W. *Reference Groups*. New York: Harper and Row, 1964.

Simon, Herbert A. "Making Management Decisions: The Role of Intuition and Emotion." *The Academy of Management Executive* (February 1987): 57–64.

Sims, Henry P., Jr.; Gioia, Dennis A.; and Associates. *The Thinking Organization*. San Francisco: Jossey-Bass, 1986.

Sizer, Theodore. *Horace's Compromise*. Boston: Houghton-Mifflin, 1984.

Skibbens, Gerald. *Organizational Evolution*. New York: American Management Association, 1974.

Smith, Wilma, and Andrews, Richard L. *Instructional Leadership: How Principals Make a Difference*. Association for Supervision and Curriculum Development, 1989.

Spring, Joel. *American Education*. New York: Longman, 1989.

Sprinthall, Norman A., and Sprinthall-Theis, Lois. "Educating for Teacher Growth: A Cognitive Developmental Perspective." *Theory into Practice*. Ohio State University, 1980.

Srivastva, Suresh, and Associates. *Executive Integrity*. San Francisco: Jossey-Bass, 1988.

Tannenbaum, Arnold S. *Social Psychology of the Work Organization*. Belmont, CA: Wadsworth, 1966.

Taylor, James C., and Asadorian, Robert A. "The Implications of Excellence: STS Management." *Industrial Management* (July–August 1985): 545.

Tice, Louis. *New Age Thinking*. Seattle, WA: The Pacific Institute, 1980.

Tichy, Noel M., and Devanna, Mary Anne. *The Transformational Leader*. New York: John Wiley, 1986.

Tuchman, Barbara W. "The Decline of Quality." *The New York Times Magazine* (November 2, 1980): 38–41.

Wagner, Harvey M. *Principles of Operations: Research Applications to Managerial Decisions*. Englewood Cliffs, NJ: Prentice-Hall, 1969.

Walberg, Herbert. "Improving the Productivity of America's Schools." *Educational Leadership* (May 1984): 19–27.

Waterman, Robert H. *The Renewal Factor*. New York: Bantam Books, 1987.

Weber, Max. *The Theory of Social and Economic Organizations* (T. Parsons, trans.). New York: Free Press, 1947.

Weisbard, Marvin R. *Productive Workplaces*. San Francisco: Jossey-Bass, 1987.

Wiggins, Grant. "The Quality of Trying to Teach Everything of Importance." *Educational Leadership, 47* (November 1989): 44–48.

Wirth, Arthur G. "Socio-Technical Theory: An Alternative Paradigm for Schools as 'Good Work' Places." *Teachers College Record, 82,* 1 (1981): 1–13.

Wirth, Arthur G. "Violations of People at Work." *Teachers College Record, 90,* 4 (Summer 1989): 535–549.

Yankelovich, Daniel. *New Rules.* New York: Bantam Books, 1982.

Yukl, Gary A. *Leadership in Organizations.* Englewood Cliffs, NJ: Prentice-Hall, 1989.

Zaleznik, Abraham. "Managers and Leaders: Are They Different?" *Harvard Business Review, 64* (1986).

Zuboff, Shoshana. *In the Age of the Smart Machine.* New York: Basic Books, 1988.

Zuboff, Shoshana. "How to Help America's Schools." *Fortune, 120,* 14 (December 4, 1989a): 137–160.

Zuboff, Shoshana. "Redefining Supervision." *Educational Leadership, 46* (May 1989b).

Index